Get the eBook FREE!

(PDF, ePub, Kindle, and liveBook all included)

We believe that once you buy a book from us, you should be able to read it in any format we have available. To get electronic versions of this book at no additional cost to you, purchase and then register this book at the Manning website.

Go to https://www.manning.com/freebook and follow the instructions to complete your pBook registration.

That's it!
Thanks from Manning!

Data Analysis with LLMs

Text, tables, images and sound

IMMANUEL TRUMMER

MANNING

SHELTER ISLAND

Manning Publications Co. 20 Baldwin Road PO Box 761 Shelter Island, NY 11964	Development editor: Dustin Archibald Technical editor: Timothy Andrew Roberts Review editor: Kishor Rit Production editor: Keri Hales Copy editor: Tiffany Taylor Proofreader: Melody Dolab Technical proofreader: Karsten Strøbaek Typesetter: Ammar Taha Mohamedy Cover designer: Marija Tudor

ISBN 9781633437647
Printed in the United States of America

To my beloved family

brief contents

contents

preface

Using a large language model for the first time is an almost magical experience. I still remember my first chat with GPT-3 (nowadays an outdated model). For the first time, it seemed to me that my computer actually understood me and could react appropriately to a wide range of complex inputs. What's more, I gave it various tasks, ranging from text analysis to coding, and the model was able to solve them based on my instructions alone! I was used to a world in which neural networks had to be trained for highly specialized tasks using large amounts of task-specific training data that had to be labeled tediously by hand, so this was an absolute game-changer that opened a world of new and exciting possibilities.

I was hooked, and since then I have dedicated a large portion of my professional career to exploiting the amazing capabilities of language models. Coming from a data-analysis background, it was natural for me to look at language models from a data-analysis perspective. How can we use language models to make the most of our data sets? Since I started using language models, a big change has been the types of data to which language models can be applied. Starting with text analysis, modern models have expanded their scope to multimodal inputs including images, audio, video, and text. This makes them an invaluable tool for any kind of data science, allowing users to build complex analysis pipelines with just a few lines of Python code along with instructions for the model in natural language describing the task to solve.

In my work, I regularly meet data scientists and data workers who could benefit tremendously from the possibilities offered by language models. However, getting into this new area can be challenging.

I had to rely on blog posts and online tutorials to piece together the information I needed to use language models for various data-analysis tasks. This is the book I wish I'd had when I started my journey. I hope you will find the book useful and enjoyable!

acknowledgments

Thanks to the editorial staff at Manning, as well as to the behind-the-scenes production staff who helped shepherd this book into its final format. In addition, thanks to Timothy Andrew Roberts, the technical editor for this book.

Also, thanks to all the reviewers: Al Pezewski, Amitabh Premraj Cheekoth, Anindita Nath, Anto Aravinth, Brendan O'Hara, Clemens Baader, Darrin Bishop, Dotan Cohen, Eli Mayost, George E. Carter, Giri Swaminathan, Harcharan Kabbay, Ikechukwu Okonkwo, Jaume Valls Altadil, Jeremy Chen, John Guthrie, John V. McCarthy, John Williams, Krzysztof Jędrzejewski, Lex Drennan, Marcio Francisco Nogueira, Marjorie Roswell, Marvin Schwarze, Paul Silisteanu, Rahul Jain, Robert Rozploch, Sumit Bhattacharyya, Swapna Yeleswarapu, Thiago Britto Borges, Todd Cook, Tony Holdroyd, Vatsal Desai, Vinoth Nageshwaran, and Walter Alexander Mata López. Your suggestions helped make this a better book.

about this book

This book was written to help developers build applications for multimodal data analysis using state-of-the-art language models. It introduces language models and the most important libraries for using them in Python. Via a series of mini projects, it showcases how to use language models to analyze text, tabular data, graph data, images, videos, and audio files. By discussing topics such as prompt engineering, fine-tuning, and advanced software frameworks, the book will enable you to quickly build complex data-analysis applications with language models that are effective and cost-efficient.

Who should read this book?

Whether you are a software developer, data scientist, or hobbyist interested in data analysis, this book is for you if you want to exploit the powerful abilities of large language models to perform various types of data analysis. Prior experience with language models is unnecessary, as the book covers all the basics. However, experience with Python is helpful, at least at a beginner's level, as this book uses Python to interact with language models.

How this book is organized: A road map

This book has 10 chapters in three parts. Part 1 introduces language models and gives a first impression of their benefits for data analysis:

- Chapter 1 introduces language models and explains how they can be used for data analysis.
- Chapter 2 guides you through a chat with ChatGPT, illustrating the analysis of text and tabular data in the ChatGPT web interface.

Part 2 introduces OpenAI's Python library and shows how to analyze various types of data using language models directly from Python:

- Chapter 3 introduces OpenAI's Python library, enabling users to send requests to language models and configure their behavior in various ways.
- Chapter 4 shows how to use language models to process text data: for example, to classify text documents or extract specific information.
- Chapter 5 demonstrates how to build natural language query interfaces using language models, translating questions in natural language to formal queries referring to data tables or graphs.
- Chapter 6 describes how to use multimodal language models to process images or video data for tasks such as object detection, question-answering, and captioning.
- Chapter 7 illustrates multiple use cases for language models in analyzing audio data: for instance, transcribing audio recordings, realizing voice query interfaces, or translating spoken input to other languages.

Part 3 covers advanced topics, enabling you to optimize your choice of models, configurations, and frameworks:

- Chapter 8 discusses different providers of large language models and gives a short overview of the models they offer and the corresponding Python libraries.
- Chapter 9 demonstrates methods that can be used to minimize processing fees and maximize output quality when working with language models, including optimizing model choices and parameter settings and fine-tuning.
- Chapter 10 discusses several software frameworks, particularly LangChain and LlamaIndex, that can be used to build complex applications on top of large language models with lower implementation overheads.

It is recommended that you start by reading chapter 1, which introduces important terms and concepts. You can skip chapter 2 if you have already used language models via web interfaces. Most of the remaining chapters are based on OpenAI's Python library. It is therefore a good idea to read chapter 3 before diving into any later chapters. Chapters 4 to 7 focus on different data types and can be read in any order. Similarly, chapters 8 to 10 are independent, and you can study them in any order.

About the code

This book contains various code samples in numbered and unnumbered listings. All code in numbered listings is available for download from the book's companion website at www.dataanalysiswithllms.com. Code, as well as suitable test data, is categorized by book chapter. Code files are named using the number of the corresponding listing in the book. The entire code and data repository can also be downloaded from the publisher's website at www.manning.com/books/data-analysis-with-llms.

The source code is formatted in a `fixed-width font like this` to separate it from ordinary text. In many cases, the original source code has been reformatted;

we've added line breaks and reworked indentation to accommodate the available page space in the book. Additionally, comments in the source code have often been removed from the listings when the code is described in the text. Code annotations accompany many of the listings, highlighting important concepts.

liveBook discussion forum

Purchase of *Data Analysis with LLMs* includes free access to liveBook, Manning's online reading platform. Using liveBook's exclusive discussion features, you can attach comments to the book globally or to specific sections or paragraphs. It's a snap to make notes for yourself, ask and answer technical questions, and receive help from the author and other users. To access the forum, go to https://livebook.manning.com/book/data-analysis-with-llms/discussion. You can also learn more about Manning's forums and the rules of conduct at https://livebook.manning.com/discussion.

Manning's commitment to our readers is to provide a venue where a meaningful dialogue between individual readers and between readers and the author can take place. It is not a commitment to any specific amount of participation on the part of the author, whose contribution to the forum remains voluntary (and unpaid). We suggest you try asking the author some challenging questions lest his interest stray! The forum and the archives of previous discussions will be accessible from the publisher's website as long as the book is in print.

about the author

IMMANUEL TRUMMER is an associate professor of computer science at Cornell University. His research focuses on topics at the intersection of data analysis and machine learning. In particular, he studies applications of large language models to data-analysis problems, resulting in various award-winning publications and industry collaborations. His video tutorials have obtained over a million views on YouTube. Besides working with language models, Immanuel enjoys playing the violin, exploring the beautiful outdoors in upstate New York, and spending as much time as possible with his family.

about the cover illustration

The figure on the cover of *Data Analysis with LLMs*, titled "Le Spéculateur," or "The Speculator," is taken from a book by Louis Curmer published in 1841. Each illustration is finely drawn and colored by hand.

In those days, it was easy to identify where people lived and what their trade or station in life was just by their dress. Manning celebrates the inventiveness and initiative of the computer business with book covers based on the rich diversity of regional culture centuries ago, brought back to life by pictures from collections such as this one.

Part 1

Introducing language models

So what are language models, exactly? And how can we use them for data analysis? This part of the book answers both those questions.

In chapter 1, we discuss the principles underlying language models and what makes them special. We also discuss all the different ways in which language models can be used for data analysis, covering options to use them directly on data as well as the possibility of using them as interfaces to more specialized data-analysis tools.

In chapter 2, we have a "chat" with ChatGPT: that is, we interact with a popular language model by OpenAI. We witness the flexibility of ChatGPT when performing a variety of tasks on text, ranging from text classification to extracting specific pieces of information from text based on a concise task description. We also see that ChatGPT does well when translating questions about data, formulated in natural language, to formal query languages such as SQL.

After reading this part, you should have a good understanding of what language models are and how you can use them for data analysis.

Analyzing data with large language models

Language models are powerful neural networks that can be used for various data-processing tasks. This chapter introduces language models and shows how and why to use them for data analysis.

1.1 What can language models do?

We will start this section with a little poem and an associated picture (figure 1.1) connecting the two main topics of this book, data analysis and large language models:

In the silent hum of the server's light,
Data flows through the veins of night.
Rows and columns, a structured sea,
With stories hidden, waiting to be free.

Each number sings of pasts untold,
Trends and truths in patterns bold.
And here arrives a curious friend,
A language model, eager to comprehend.

It listens close, with circuits keen,
To turn raw facts into insight unseen.
From scatter plots to sentences clear,
Data's language is all it can hear.

The figures dance, the texts reply,
As code meets meaning under AI's eye.
They merge their worlds, a seamless blend,
Where logic and language have no end.

For in this bond, both deep and wide,
Data's essence finds a guide.
And in the neural net's embrace,
Data analysis gains a poetic grace.

Figure 1.1 Illustration by GPT-4o, connecting the topics "data analysis" and "large language models"

The poem and the picture were generated by GPT-4o ("o" for "omni"), a language model by OpenAI that processes multimodal data, based solely on the instructions "Write a poem connecting data analysis and large language models!" followed by "Now draw a corresponding picture!" Both the picture and the poem seem to relate to the requested topics. Although the poem may not win any literature awards, its text is coherent, it is structured as we would expect from a poem, and it rhymes! Perhaps most importantly, all it took to generate the poem and the picture were short instructions expressed in natural language. Whereas prior machine learning methods relied on large amounts of task-specific training data, this requirement is now obsolete. And, of course, the task is specific enough to convince us that the language model is not copying existing solutions from the web and generates original content instead.

Writing poems and generating pictures are only two of many possible use cases (albeit possibly the most entertaining ones). Models like GPT-4o can solve various tasks, such as summarizing text documents, writing program code, and answering questions about pictures. In this book, you will learn how to use language models to accomplish a plethora of data-analysis tasks ranging from extracting information from large collections of text documents to writing code for data analysis. After reading this book, you will be able to quickly build data-analysis pipelines that are based on language models and extract useful insights from a variety of data formats.

What does GPT stand for?

GPT stands for *Generative Pretrained Transformer*.

Generative: GPT is a large neural network that generates content (e.g., text or code) in response to input text. This fact distinguishes it from other neural networks that, for example, can only classify input text into a fixed set of predefined categories.

Pretrained: GPT is pretrained on large amounts of data, solving generic tasks such as predicting the next word in text. Typically, the pretraining task is different from the tasks it is primarily used for. However, pretraining helps it learn more specialized tasks faster.

The *Transformer* is a new neural network architecture that is particularly useful for learning tasks that involve variable-length input or output (such as text documents). It is currently the dominant architecture for generative AI approaches.

1.2   *What you will learn*

This book is about using language models for data analysis. We can categorize data-analysis tasks by the type of data we're analyzing and by the type of analysis. This book covers a wide range of data types and analysis tasks.

We focus on *multimodal* data analysis: that is, we use language models to analyze various types of data. More precisely, we cover the following data types in this book:

- *Text*—Think of emails, newspaper articles, and comments on a web forum. Text data is ubiquitous and contains valuable information. In this book, we will see how to use language models to automatically classify text documents based on their content, how to extract specific pieces of information from text, and how to group text documents about related topics.

- *Images*—A picture is worth a thousand words, as they say. Images help us to understand complex concepts, capture fond memories of our last holiday, and illustrate current events. Language models can easily extract information from pictures. For instance, we will use language models to answer arbitrary questions about images or identify people who appear in pictures based on a database of profiles.

- *Videos*—A large percentage of the data on the web is video data. Even on your smartphone, video data is probably taking up a significant part of your phone's total storage capacity. In this book, we will see that language models can be applied to analyze videos as well: for instance, to generate suitable video titles based on the video content.

- *Audio*—To many people, speech is the most natural form of communication. Audio recordings capture speeches and conversations and complement videos. In this book, we will see how to transcribe audio recordings, how to translate spoken language into other languages, and how to build a query interface that answers spoken questions about data.

- *Tables*—Imagine a data set containing information about customers. It is natural to represent that data as a table, featuring columns for the customer's address, phone number, and credit card information, while different rows store information about different customers. In this book, we will see how to use language models to write code that performs complex operations on such tabular data.

- *Graphs*—From social networks to metro networks, many data sets are conveniently represented as graphs, modeling entities (such as people or metro stations) and their connections (representing friendships or metro connections). We will see how we can use language models to generate code that analyzes large graphs in various ways.

Structured vs. unstructured data

Data types are often categorized into two groups: *structured* and *unstructured data*. Structured data has a structure that facilitates efficient data processing via specialized tools. Examples of structured data include tables and graph data. For such data, we typically use the language model as an interface to specialized data-processing tools. Unstructured data, including text, images, videos, and audio files, does not have a structure that can be easily exploited for efficient processing. So, for unstructured data, we typically need to use the language model directly on the data.

For most of this book, we will use OpenAI models via OpenAI's Python library. Toward the end of the book, we will also discuss language models from other providers. As libraries from different providers tend to offer similar functionality, getting used to other models shouldn't take long.

Typically, using language models incurs monetary fees proportional to the amount of data being processed. The fees depend on the language model used, the model configuration, and the way in which the input to the language model is formulated. In this book, not only will you learn to solve various data-analysis tasks via language models, but we will discuss how to do so with minimal costs.

1.3   How to use language models

State-of-the-art language models are used via a method called *prompting*. We discuss prompting next, followed by the interfaces we can use for prompting.

1.3.1   Prompting

Until a few years ago, machine learning models were trained for one specific task. For instance, we might have a model trained to classify the text of a review as either "positive" (i.e., the review author is satisfied) or "negative" (i.e., the author is dissatisfied). To use that model, we only need the review text as input. There's no need to describe the task (classifying the review) as part of the input because the model has been specialized to do that task and that task only.

This has changed in recent years with the emergence of large language models such as GPT. Such models are no longer trained for specific tasks. Instead, they are intended to serve as universal task solvers that can, in principle, solve any task the user desires. When using such a model, it is up to the user to describe to the model in precise terms what the model should do.

The prompt is the input to the language model. The prompt can contain multimodal data: for example, text and images. At a minimum, to get the language model to solve a specific task, the prompt should contain a text instructing the model on what to do. Beyond those instructions, the prompt should contain all relevant context. For instance, if the instructions ask the model to determine whether a car is visible in a picture, the prompt must also contain the picture. The instructions in the prompt should be specific and clarify, for instance, the expected output format. For example, if we want the model to output "1" if a car is present and "0" otherwise, enabling us to easily add the numbers generated by the model to count cars, we need to explicitly clarify that in the prompt (otherwise, the model might answer "Yes, there is a car in the picture," which makes it harder to count in the post-processing stage). Besides instructions and context, the prompt may contain examples to help the language model understand the task.

Few-shot vs. zero-shot learning

We can help the language model better understand a task by providing examples as part of the prompt. Those examples are similar to the task we want the model to solve and specify the input and desired output. This approach is sometimes called *few-shot learning*, as the model learns the task based on a few samples. On the other hand, we can use *zero-shot learning*, meaning the model learns the task without any (zero) samples based only on the task description.

1.3.2 Example prompt

Let's illustrate prompts with an example. A classical use case for language models is analyzing product reviews to determine the sentiment underlying the review: whether the review is positive (i.e., the customer recommends the product) or negative (i.e., the customer is unhappy with the product). Assume that we have a review to classify as positive or negative. If we have a specialized model trained for review classification for the specific product category we're interested in, all it takes is to send our review to that model. As the model is specialized to the target problem, it already "knows" what to do with the input and the required output format. However, because we use large language models, we have to provide a bit more context along with the review.

Our prompt should contain all relevant information for the model, describing the task to solve and all context. In the example scenario, we probably want to include the following pieces of information:

- *Review text*—The text of the review we want to classify.
- *Task description*—A description of the task to solve.
- *Output formats*—What is the required output format?
- *Relevant context*—For example, are we reviewing laptops or lawn mowers?

Optionally, we can include a few example reviews with their associated correct classification. This may help the model classify reviews more accurately.

The following prompt includes all the relevant pieces of information for an example review.

Listing 1.1 Prompt for classifying a laptop review

```
We are considering product reviews for laptops.      ❶ Context
For each review, output "satisfied" or "dissatisfied",
depending on whether the customer is satisfied
with the product or not.              ❷ Task description and output format
Examples:
This is a great laptop! I recommend everyone to buy it!
satisfied                             ❸ First example
This laptop did not work. I had to return it.
dissatisfied                          ❹ Second example
The screen is too small and it takes too long to start.   ❺ Review
```

This prompt starts with a description of relevant context (❶). Customers are reviewing laptops, so, for example, if they label items as "heavy," that's probably a bad sign (unlike analyzing reviews for, let's say, steamrollers). The task description (❷) tells the model what to do with the reviews and specifies the desired output format (output "satisfied" or "dissatisfied") as well. Next, we have a list of examples. Strictly speaking, adding examples in the prompt may not be necessary for this simple task. However, adding examples in the prompt can sometimes increase the accuracy of the output. Here, we add two example reviews (❸ and ❹), together with the desired output for those reviews. Finally, we add the review (❺) that we want the model to classify. Given the preceding prompt, state-of-the-art language models are likely to output "dissatisfied" when sent this prompt as input. That, of course, is indeed the desired output.

1.3.3 Interfaces

So how can we send prompts to a language model? Providers such as OpenAI typically offer web interfaces, enabling users to send single prompts to their language models. In chapter 2, we will use OpenAI's web interface to send prompts instructing the model to analyze text or to write code for data processing.

The web interface works well as long as we send only a few prompts. However, analyzing a large collection of text documents would require sending many prompts (one per text document). Clearly, we don't want to enter thousands of prompts by hand. This is where OpenAI's Python library comes in handy. Using this library enables us to send prompts to OpenAI's models directly from Python and to process the model's answer in Python. This enables us to automate data loading, prompt generation, and any kind of post-processing we need to do on the model's answers. It also allows us to integrate language models with other useful tools: for example, to use the language model to write code for data processing and immediately execute that code using other tools.

We will review OpenAI's Python library in chapter 3. We will use this library throughout most of this book. Other providers of language models, including Google, Anthropic, and Cohere, offer similar Python libraries to send prompts to their language models. We will discuss those libraries in more detail in chapter 8.

1.4 Using language models for data analysis

So how do we use language models specifically for data analysis? This book considers two possibilities. First, we can use the language model *directly* on the data. This means the language model receives the data we want to analyze as part of the prompt (along with instructions on which analysis to perform). Second, we can use the language model *indirectly* to analyze data. Here, the language model does not directly "see" the data: that is, we do not include the data in its entirety in the prompt. Instead, we use the language model to write code for data processing, executed in specialized data-processing tools. Which approach to use depends on the data properties and the task. Let's have a closer look at both methods.

1.4.1 Using language models directly on data

The most natural approach to analyzing data with language models is to put the data directly into the prompt. This is what we did in section 1.3.2: to analyze a review, we include the review text in the prompt, along with instructions on what to do with the text. We can use the same approach for other types of data besides text. For example, when using multimodal models such as GPT-4o, we can simply include the pictures to analyze, together with analysis instructions, in the prompt.

Typically, we do not want to analyze a single picture or review but a whole collection of them. For instance, assume that we want to classify an entire collection of reviews, determining for each of them whether the review is positive or negative. In such cases, we generally take the following approach, implemented in Python using OpenAI's Python library (or an equivalent library allowing users to send prompts to other providers' models). We load the reviews to classify and generate one prompt for each review. Then, we send those prompts to the language model, extract the classification result from the answer generated by the model for each review, and save the results in a file on disk.

In this scenario, we want to solve the same task (review classification) for multiple text documents (i.e., reviews). As you can imagine, the prompts for different reviews should therefore bear some similarity. Although the text of the review to classify changes each time, the task description and other parts of the prompt remain the same.

To generate prompts in Python, we use a *prompt template*. A prompt template specifies a prompt associated with a specific task to solve. In our example, we would use a prompt template to classify reviews as positive or negative. A prompt template contains placeholders to represent parts of the prompt that change depending on the input data. Considering our prompt template for review classification, we should probably include a placeholder for the review text. Then, when generating prompts in Python, we replace that placeholder with the text of the current review to classify.

For instance, we can use the following prompt template to classify reviews.

Listing 1.2 Prompt template for classifying laptop reviews

```
We are considering product reviews for laptops.        ❶ Context
For each review, output "satisfied" or "dissatisfied",
depending on whether the customer is satisfied
with the product or not.                               ❷ Task description and output format
Examples:
This is a great laptop! I recommend everyone to buy it!
satisfied                                              ❸ First example
This laptop did not work. I had to return it.
dissatisfied                                           ❹ Second example
[ReviewText]                                           ❺ Placeholder for review text
```

This prompt template generalizes the prompt we saw for classifying one specific review (have a look at listing 1.1 in section 1.3.2). Again, we provide context (the fact that we're classifying laptop reviews) (❶) and instructions describing the task to solve, as well as the output format (❷). We also provide a few example reviews with associated classification results (❸ and ❹). Although the review to classify changes, depending on the input, we do not need to change the example reviews. Those reviews merely illustrate what task the language model needs to solve. Finally (❺), we have a placeholder for the review text. When iterating over different reviews, we generate a prompt for each of them by substituting the review text for this placeholder.

The example prompt template has only a single placeholder. In general, several parts of the prompt may change depending on the input data. If so, we introduce placeholders for each of those parts and substitute all of them to generate prompts.

Figure 1.2 summarizes how we use prompt templates when analyzing data directly with language models. For each data item (e.g., a review to classify), we substitute for placeholders in the prompt template to generate a prompt (we can also say that we *instantiate* a prompt). We then send this prompt to the language model to solve the data-analysis task we're interested in.

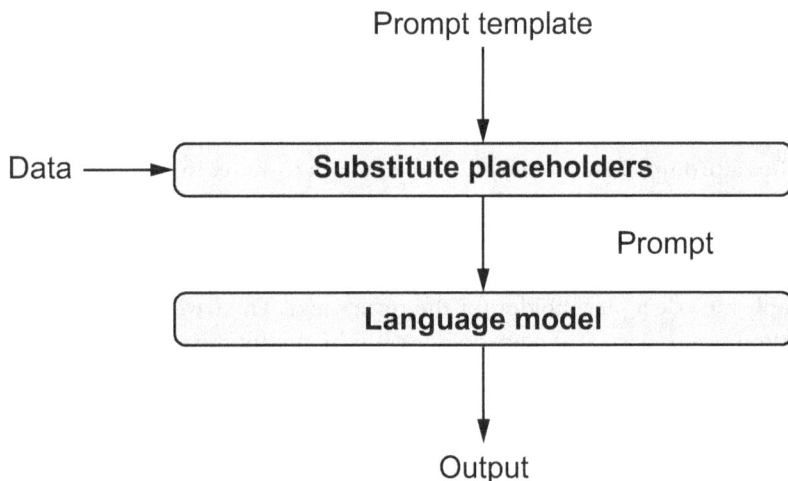

Figure 1.2 Using language models directly for data analysis. A prompt template describes the analysis task. It contains placeholders that are replaced with data to analyze. After substituting for the placeholders, the resulting prompt is submitted to the language model to produce output.

1.4.2 *Data analysis via external tools*

Putting data directly into the prompt is not always the most efficient approach. For some types of data, specialized tools are available that process certain operations on that data very efficiently. In those cases, it is often more efficient to use the language model to write code for data processing (rather than analyzing the data directly). The code generated by the language model can then be executed by the specialized tool.

We will apply this approach to structured data. For structured data such as data tables and graphs, specialized data-processing tools are available that support a wide range of analysis operations. Those operations, such as filtering and aggregating data, can be performed very efficiently on structured data. Even if it was possible to perform the same operations reliably with language models (which is not the case), we would not want to do it because the fees we pay to providers like OpenAI are proportional to the size of the input data. Processing large structured data sets (such as tables with millions of rows) using language models is prohibitively expensive. In the following chapters, we discuss the following types of tools for structured data processing:

- *Relational database management system*—Stores and processes relational data: that is, collections of data tables. Most relational database management systems support *SQL*, the Structured Query Language. We will use language models to translate questions about data to queries in SQL.
- *Graph data management system*—Handles graph data representing entities and the relationships between them. Different graph data management systems support different query languages. In chapter 5, we see how to use language models to translate questions about data into queries in the *Cypher* language, supported by the Neo4j graph data management system.

For instance, let's assume we want to enable lay users to analyze a relational database: that is, a collection of data tables. Perhaps a table contains the results of a survey, and we want to let users aggregate answers from different groups of respondents. The survey results are stored in a relational database management system (the most suitable type of tool for this data type). Using language models, we can enable users to ask questions about the data in natural language (that is, in plain English). The language model takes care of translating those questions into formal queries. More precisely, given that the data is stored in a relational database management system, we want to translate those questions into SQL queries.

Again, we introduce a prompt template for the task we're interested in. Here, we're interested in text-to-SQL translation, meaning we want to use the language model to translate questions in natural language to SQL queries. Although the task (text-to-SQL translation) and the data (the database containing survey results) remain fixed, the user's questions will change over time. Therefore, we introduce a placeholder for the user question in our prompt template. In principle, the following prompt template should enable us to translate questions on our survey data into SQL queries.

Listing 1.3 Prompt template for translating questions to SQL

```
Database:                                    ❶ Description of database
The database contains the results of a survey, stored
in a table called "SurveyResults" with the following
columns: ...
Question:    ❷  Question to translate
```

```
[Question]
Translate the question to SQL!    ❸  Task description
```

First the prompt describes the structure of our data (❶). This is required to enable the system to write correct queries (e.g., queries that refer to the correct names of tables and columns in those tables). The description in the example template is abbreviated. We will see how to accurately describe the structure of a relational database in later chapters. Next, the prompt template contains the question to translate (❷). This is a placeholder to enable users to ask different questions using the same prompt template. Finally, the prompt template contains a (concise) task description (❸): we want to translate questions to SQL queries!

Figure 1.3 summarizes the process for text-to-SQL translation. Given a corresponding prompt template, we substitute the user question for the placeholder, translate the question to an SQL query via the language model, and finally execute the query in a relational database management system. The query result is shown to the user.

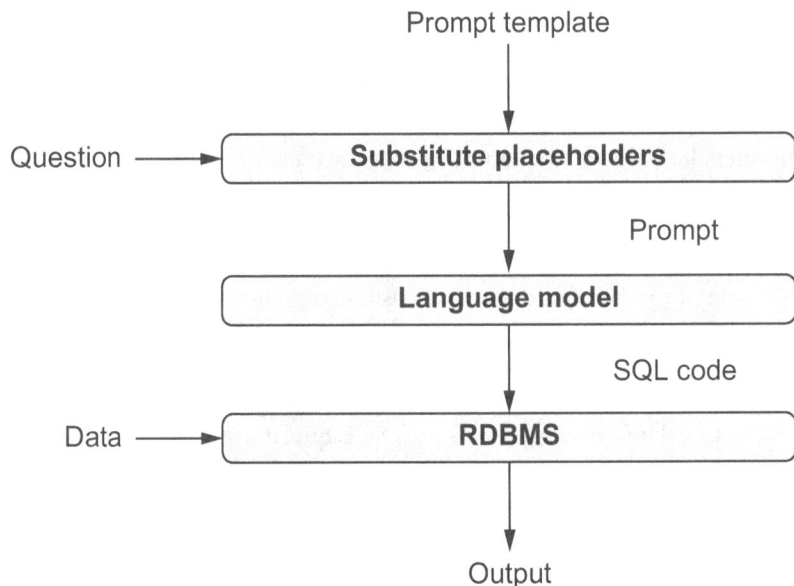

Figure 1.3 Using language models indirectly to build a natural language interface for tabular data. The prompt template contains placeholders for questions about data. After substituting for placeholders, the resulting prompt is used as input for the language model. The model translates the question into an SQL query that is executed via a relational database management system.

1.5   *Minimizing costs*

When processing data with language models, we typically pay fees to a model provider. The larger the amount of data we process, the higher the fees. Before analyzing large amounts of data, we want to make sure we're not overpaying. For instance, using larger language models (the neural network implementing the language model has more "neurons," so to speak) is often more expensive, but for complex tasks, it may pay off with higher-quality results. But if the large model is not needed to solve our current task well, we should save the money and use a smaller model. Fortunately, there are quite a few ways in which we can optimize the tradeoff between processing costs and result quality. We discuss the different options next. All of them are covered in more detail in later book chapters.

1.5.1 Picking the best model

OpenAI offers many different versions of the GPT model, ranging from relatively small models to giant models like GPT-4. At the time of writing, using GPT-4 is over 100 times more expensive, per input token, than using the cheapest version.

> **What are tokens?**
>
> The processing fees for language models like GPT-4 are proportional to the number of tokens read and generated by the model. A *token* is the atomic unit at which the language model represents text internally. Typically, one token corresponds to approximately four characters.

Given those price differences, it is clearly a good idea to think hard about which specific model satisfies our needs. For instance, for a simple task like review classification, we probably don't need to use OpenAI's most expensive model. But if we want to use the model to write complex code for data processing, using the most expensive version may be worth it.

Of course, we don't need to restrict ourselves to models offered by OpenAI. Language models are offered by many providers, including Google, Anthropic, and Cohere. In principle, we might even choose to host our own model, using models that are publicly available: for example, on the Hugging Face platform. Some of those models are generic (similar to OpenAI's GPT models), whereas others are trained for more specific tasks. If we happen to be interested in tasks for which specialized models exist, we may want to use one of them. We discuss models from other providers in more detail in chapter 8.

Picking the right model for your needs is not an easy task. As a first step, you might want to look at benchmarks such as Stanford's Holistic Evaluation of Language Models (HELM, https://crfm.stanford.edu/helm/; see figure 1.4). This benchmark compares the quality of results produced by different language models on different types of tasks. Ultimately, you may have to try a few models on your task and a data sample to ensure that you choose the optimal one. In chapter 9, we will see how to benchmark different models systematically for an example task.

A holistic framework for evaluating foundation models.

Model	Mean win rate
GPT-4o (2024-05-13) 13	**0.945**
GPT-4o (2024-08-06)	0.937
Claude 3.5 Sonnet (20240620)	0.896
GPT-4 (0613)	0.881
GPT-4 Turbo (2024-04-09)	0.879
Llama 3.1 Instruct Turbo (405B)	0.868
Gemini 1.5 Pro (002)	0.853

Figure 1.4   Holistic Evaluation of Language Models (HELM): comparing language models offered by different providers according to various metrics

1.5.2 *Optimally configuring models*

The OpenAI Python library offers a variety of tuning parameters to influence model behavior. For instance, we can influence the probability that certain words appear in the output of a model. This can be useful, for instance, when classifying reviews. If the output of the model should be one of only a few possible choices (such as "positive" and "negative"), it makes sense to restrict possible outputs to those choices. That way, we avoid cases in which the model generates output that does not correspond to any of the class names. To take another example, we can fine-tune the criteria used to decide when the model stops generating output. For instance, if we know that the output should consist of a single token (e.g., the name of a class when classifying reviews), we can explicitly limit the output length to a single token. This prevents the model from generating more output than necessary (saving us money in the process, as costs depend on the amount of output generated).

We will discuss those and many other tuning parameters in more detail in chapter 3. In chapter 9, we will see how to use those tuning parameters to get better performance from our language models.

Another option to configure models is to fine-tune them. This means, essentially, that we're creating our own variant of an existing model. By training the model with a small amount of task-specific training data, we get a model that potentially performs better at our task than the vanilla version. For instance, if we want to classify reviews, we might train the model with a few hundred example reviews and associated classification results. This may enable us to use a much smaller and cheaper model, fine-tuned for our specific task, that performs as well on this task as a much larger model that has not been fine-tuned.

Of course, fine-tuning also costs money, and it may not be immediately clear whether it is worth it for a specific task. We discuss fine-tuning and the associated tradeoffs in more detail in chapter 9.

1.5.3 Prompt engineering

The prompt template can significantly affect the quality of the results produced by the language model. A good prompt template clearly specifies the task to solve and provides all relevant context. We will see how to map various tasks to suitable prompt templates throughout the following chapters, covering a variety of data types. After working through those examples, you should be able to design your own prompt templates for novel tasks, following the same principles.

Similar to the model choice, it can be hard to pick the best prompt template for a given task without doing any testing. In chapter 9, we will test prompt templates in an example scenario and illustrate how different prompt templates lead to different outcomes. In some cases, investing a little time in finding the best prompt template may enable you to get satisfactory performance with fairly cheap models (whereas working with the unoptimized prompt template may make a more expensive model necessary).

> **Where to get prompt templates**
>
> Finding a good prompt template for a new task may take some time. If you do not want to spend that time, have somebody else do it for you! More precisely, you can find platforms on the web that enable users to buy and sell prompt templates. One of them is PromptBase (https://promptbase.com). Say you want to translate English questions into SQL queries. By entering corresponding keywords, you will find not one but multiple alternative prompt templates on that platform. If the prompt template seems like a good match based on the associated description, you can buy it and use it for your data-analysis needs.

1.6 Advanced software frameworks and agents

Throughout most of this book, we will use OpenAI's Python library and similar libraries from other providers. For instance, these libraries enable you to send prompts to language models and receive the models' answers. Although they are entirely sufficient for many use cases, you may want to consider more advanced software frameworks when developing complex applications that are based on language models.

In this book, we discuss two advanced software frameworks for working with language models: LangChain (https://langchain.com) and LlamaIndex (www.llamaindex.ai). Both make it easier to develop Python applications for data analysis with language models.

Besides many other features, these frameworks make it easy to create agents that use language models. This approach is useful for complex data-analysis tasks requiring, for instance, combining data from multiple sources. For most of this book, we solve data-analysis tasks with a single invocation of the language model, whether it is analyzing a text document or translating a question about data to a formal query. If the task requires multiple steps, such as performing preprocessing before calling the language model or post-processing on the model's answer, we must hard-code the corresponding processing logic.

This approach works as long as we can reliably predict the sequence of steps required for data processing. However, in some cases, it can be difficult to predict which steps are required. For instance, we may get questions from users that refer either to a text document or to a relational database. So, depending on the question, we need to either write an SQL query or extract information from text documents. Or perhaps we might need information from both the text and the relational database, extracting information related to the question from the text and then using the information we obtain to formulate an SQL query.

In such cases, it is not possible to hard-code all possible sequences of steps in advance. Instead, we want to design an approach that is flexible enough to decide independently what step is required next. This can be done using agents and language models. With this approach, the language model is used to decompose complex analysis tasks into subproblems. Furthermore, the language model may choose to invoke *tools*: arbitrary functions whose interfaces are described in natural language. Such tools can, for instance, encapsulate the invocation of an SQL query on a relational database. After invoking a corresponding tool, the language model is given access to the invocation result (e.g., the query result) and can use that result to plan the next steps. We will see how to use agents to solve complex data-analysis tasks where it is unclear, a priori, which data sources and processing methods are required to solve them.

Summary

- Language models can solve novel tasks without specialized training.
- The prompt is the input to the language model.
- Prompts may combine text with other types of data, such as images.
- A prompt contains a task description, context, and (optionally) examples.
- Language models can analyze certain types of data directly.
- When analyzing data directly, the data must appear in the prompt.
- Prompt templates contain placeholders: for example, to represent data items.
- By substituting for placeholders in a prompt template, we obtain a prompt.
- Language models can also help to analyze data via external tools.
- Language models can instruct other tools on how to process data.
- Models are available in many different sizes with significant cost differences.
- Models can be configured using various configuration parameters.
- LangChain and LlamaIndex help to develop complex applications.
- Agents use language models to solve complex problems.

Chatting with ChatGPT

This chapter covers

- Accessing the ChatGPT web interface
- Using ChatGPT directly for data processing
- Using ChatGPT indirectly for data processing

Time to meet ChatGPT! In this chapter, we will have a chat with ChatGPT and start using it for data analysis. If you have never used ChatGPT, this chapter will teach you how to access it and give you a first impression of its capabilities (as well as its limitations). If you have used ChatGPT but have not yet done so for data analysis, this chapter will show you some of the many ways you can exploit ChatGPT in this context.

   We will first discuss a web interface that will give you access to OpenAI's ChatGPT. We will go over the OpenAI registration process, discuss the main functions offered by the interface, and use it to have a first dialogue with ChatGPT. After that, we will start using ChatGPT to analyze data in a few example scenarios. We will see two different ways to exploit ChatGPT for data analysis: directly and indirectly. When using ChatGPT directly, we have it do the actual data processing given data and a task description as input. This works for data types that ChatGPT processes natively (such as text data).

On the other hand, we can also use ChatGPT to analyze data indirectly. Here, ChatGPT merely serves as a translator, translating descriptions of analysis tasks into formal languages that are understood by external data-processing tools. The actual data processing is then handled by those external tools. In this chapter, you will see that ChatGPT is useful in both scenarios.

2.1   Accessing the web interface

Open your web browser, and type https://chat.openai.com/ into the address bar. You will create an OpenAI account that enables you to use ChatGPT. If you already have an account, you can skip the following steps, log in to your account, and proceed with the next section.

To create an account, click the Signup button. This brings you to the screen shown in figure 2.1.

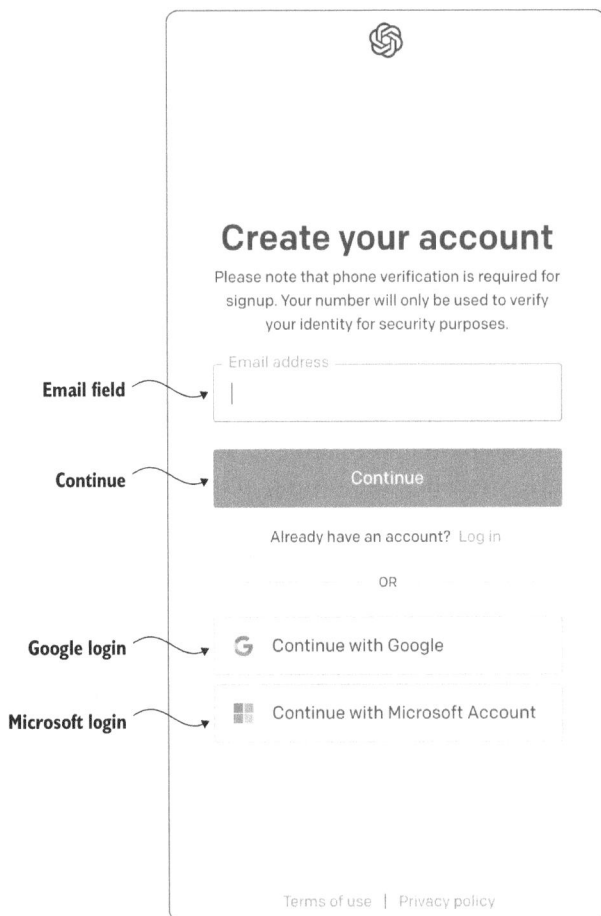

Figure 2.1   Signup page for an OpenAI account. Enter your email address, and click the Continue button, or sign up using a Google account or a Microsoft account.

You have several options when signing up for an OpenAI account:

- Sign up using a Google account (by clicking Continue with Google).
- Sign up using a Microsoft account (by clicking Continue with Microsoft Account).
- Sign up with an arbitrary email address by entering that address into the Email Address field and then clicking Continue. After that, follow the instructions given on the screen.

After creating your account using any of these options, log in to your newly created account, and continue with the steps outlined in the next section.

OpenAI subscriptions

OpenAI offers different types of accounts; some are free, and others come with a monthly fee. For the following examples, a free account is sufficient. You may still choose to sign up for the paid subscription to gain access to more models and get faster answers from ChatGPT. Depending on which subscription you choose, your screens may look slightly different from the screenshots in this chapter.

2.2 Making introductions

After logging in to your OpenAI account, you should see the interface shown in figure 2.2.

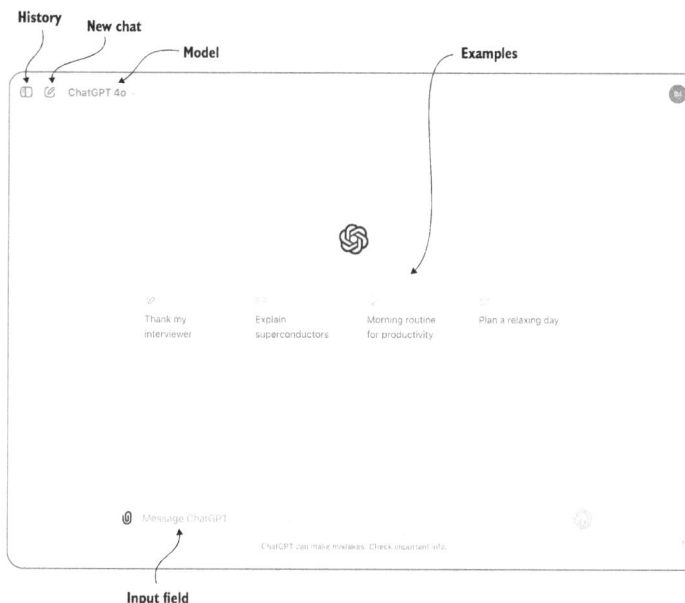

Figure 2.2 ChatGPT web interface. Interact with ChatGPT by clicking predefined example inputs or entering arbitrary text into the input field. Click the New Chat button to reset the conversation.

This interface enables you to have a dialogue with ChatGPT by submitting text input and receiving answers. Let's take a moment to understand the most important interface components in figure 2.2. First, you have a couple of predefined input examples. You can simply click any of those examples to get the conversation started. Besides predefined examples, you have the option to enter arbitrary text into a text field. We will refer to this interface element as the *input field* in the rest of this chapter. Finally, you can start a new conversation at any point via the New Chat button. Doing so erases ChatGPT's memory of all prior dialogue steps.

Which model should I choose?

Clicking the button labeled Model in figure 2.2 enables you to choose between different language models. ChatGPT supports several models from OpenAI's GPT model series. The examples discussed next should, in principle, work with any of the available models. You might try a few different models to see how the output differs. Depending on your subscription, the number of requests you can send to specific models may be limited.

Time to say hello! Click the input field, and say hello to ChatGPT. You can type anything. ChatGPT has been trained to conduct dialogues with human users and should be able to answer most inputs in a reasonable manner. For instance, tell ChatGPT a little about yourself! Ask for opinions or help with upcoming tasks! Or, perhaps, ask it to write a poem about a topic of your choice! You may want to spend a few minutes chatting with ChatGPT to get a better sense of its capabilities as well as its limitations.

Note that ChatGPT can refer back to prior inputs. For instance, if you are not satisfied with a prior reply, you may ask ChatGPT to correct it or to change it. No need to repeat the original request. Also, if you are not satisfied with an answer but do not want to provide further clarifications, try the button labeled Regenerate in figure 2.3.

Regenerate

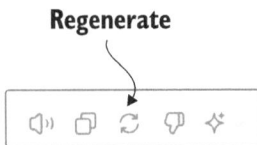

Figure 2.3   After ChatGPT generates an answer, the Regenerate button appears below the generated response. Click this button to receive an alternative answer to your last input.

Clicking that button will cause ChatGPT to regenerate its last answer. As ChatGPT uses a certain degree of randomization while generating output, chances are good that the second output will be different (and possibly better) than the first version.

Typically, all text you enter is part of the same conversation. If at any time you want to start a new chat (essentially erasing ChatGPT's "memory" of the prior conversation), simply click the button labeled New Chat in figure 2.2. Note that prior conversations are not lost, even when you start a new one. Instead, OpenAI stores past conversations and enables users to go back and study them (or continue the conversation from where it ended last time). You can access a history of prior conversations by clicking the button labeled History in figure 2.2. Each conversation is assigned a short title, generated automatically based on the conversation content.

Using ChatGPT for the first time is often an impressive experience. ChatGPT generates polished and reasonable answers for a variety of topics. This may mislead users into putting too much faith in the information it provides. It's important to avoid losing sight of the various limitations that apply to the current generation of language models. In general, always verify the output of the language model before relying on it.

What are hallucinations?

The term *hallucination* in language models refers to situations in which a language model invents new content in the absence of information and integrates it into answers. Often the result sounds convincing, and it can be hard to recognize instances of hallucination. Ongoing research [1] explores methods to reduce the chances of hallucinations. However, at the time of writing, no reliable strategies to avoid hallucinations are known. So don't blindly trust information from language models, and always use alternative sources for corroboration.

2.3 Processing text with ChatGPT

Let's start using ChatGPT for data processing! In this section, we will use ChatGPT to analyze text, a common type of unstructured data. At the same time, text is ChatGPT's native input and output format. This means we can use ChatGPT directly to analyze our (text) data without involving external analysis tools. That helps keep things simple, and that's what we want for our first steps toward ChatGPT-supported data analysis.

Imagine the following situation: you're an employee of Banana, a producer of various consumer electronics, including laptops and smartphones. The Banana website enables users to post free-form text comments. It turns out that many users comment on their satisfaction or dissatisfaction with specific Banana products. Users often point out specific aspects of these products that stand out or need improvement. In aggregate, all those reviews should be very helpful to inform the design of future Banana products! But to make that possible, you first need to analyze all of them and extract common points. Your boss asks you to do just that: prepare statistics that summarize reviews for different products and product categories. Also, while you're reading through reviews, your boss encourages you to write a few nice replies to the product reviews. Ideally, you want to avoid spending the next weeks reading and aggregating reviews. Can't you automate that? Perhaps ChatGPT can help.

Next, we'll use the ChatGPT web interface to analyze an example review. If that works well, it may be possible to scale up the process to automatically analyze all of them! If you have started a dialogue previously, first click the button labeled New

Chat in figure 2.2 to start a new conversation. This will make sure that the topics you discussed with ChatGPT previously won't interfere with the analysis examples we try next.

Let's start by telling ChatGPT about the review that we want to analyze. Click the input field, enter the text after the User marker in the following dialogue, and then press Enter.

User: Have a look at the following product review:

"I bought the BananaBook a year ago and I'm super happy with this product! The screen is awesome and allows me to easily read content, even in bright sunshine. It's fast enough for everything I want to do with it, e.g., coding, office work. The only drawback is its weight, I wish it were a little lighter as I have to carry it around quite a bit. But, for that price, it's a great offer."

GPT: Based on the review, the BananaBook is a product that the reviewer purchased a year ago and is still satisfied with. The screen of the BananaBook is impressive, allowing the user to read content easily, even in bright sunshine. The device is also fast enough for the user's needs, including coding and office work. However, the reviewer did mention that the BananaBook is a bit heavy, which can be an inconvenience when carrying it around. Overall, the reviewer seems to think that the BananaBook is a great value for its price.

The text after the GPT marker is the answer generated by ChatGPT during a sample session. In this case, ChatGPT simply repeats the review, albeit with slightly different wording, demonstrating that it has accepted and "understood" your input.

Why am I getting different output?

ChatGPT uses a certain degree of randomization when generating output. This means you generally won't see the same output, even when you submit exactly the same input twice. For that reason, the chances of you seeing the precise output shown here are small. However, you are likely to get output of similar quality.

Let's start our text analysis with a simple classification, mapping the review to a category. Specifically, we will try to classify the review into one of three product categories: mobile phones, personal computers, and game consoles.

WARNING   Do *not* click the New Chat button before entering the next text! The purpose of the New Chat button is to erase ChatGPT's memory of prior conversation steps. But that's not what we want here at all. All of the following analyses refer to the same review that we entered initially. This works only if ChatGPT remembers that review.

User: Which product category does the review refer to (mobile phones, personal computers, game consoles):

GPT: Based on the information provided in the review, it is not clear which product category the BananaBook belongs to. The reviewer did not specify whether it is a mobile phone, personal computer, or game console. However, based on the fact that the reviewer mentioned using the device for coding and office work, it is more likely that the BananaBook is a personal computer or a laptop rather than a mobile phone or a game console.

Not bad! ChatGPT has clearly understood the task and provides a detailed reply. The BananaBook is a fictitious device, and it's not immediately clear what type of product we're talking about. However, as ChatGPT rightfully points out, coding and office work are most typically associated with personal computers (more so than with mobile phones or game consoles). Despite the uncertainty, ChatGPT can come up with a reasonable answer and justify it thoroughly. In this instance, the answer from ChatGPT is even more fine-grained than required: although ChatGPT links the review to one of the three provided categories, it additionally hypothesizes that the review refers to a laptop (a subcategory of personal computers). This assumption seems reasonable in this context, given that the user carries the computer regularly (typically associated with laptops rather than desktop machines).

The previous answer is reasonable but maybe a bit lengthy. In fact, its length is similar to the original review. No point in using ChatGPT for text analysis if the resulting answer is as long as the source text. Let's ask ChatGPT to be a little more concise. There's no need to provide a detailed justification; rather, we want to get only the name of the most likely category for the review.

User: Answer concisely, only write the name of the most likely product category (mobile phones, personal computers, game consoles):

GPT: Personal computers.

That's much better! Clearly, ChatGPT was able to understand our instructions and adapt its prior answer accordingly. Besides being faster to read, the concise output has another advantage. If, ultimately, we want to analyze many reviews as opposed to a single one, it is important to have homogeneous output across reviews. For instance, having homogeneous output makes it easier to count the number of reviews in each of the three categories.

Let's classify the review according to different categories. This time, we will directly hint at the desired output format (note that our specification "answer concisely" refers back to the previous instructions).

User: Which product category out of food, cosmetics, electronics does the review refer to? Answer concisely:

GPT: Electronics.

Perfect! That is the right category, and the output format is as expected. So far, we have seen that ChatGPT is able to classify reviews according to different criteria. This seems useful, for instance, for creating statistics by counting the number of reviews in each category. But ideally, we also want to analyze the content of those reviews. Which products or product categories need improvement most urgently? To determine that, we need to know whether reviews are positive or negative: that is, whether the user is satisfied or dissatisfied with the product. This is yet another way to categorize the review text. However, this time, our classification refers not to the product being reviewed but to the review content.

User: Is the customer satisfied or dissatisfied with the product? Answer with "satisfied" or "dissatisfied":

GPT: Satisfied.

Yes, that's correct! Using the combination of the capabilities seen so far, we could already use ChatGPT to count the number of positive and negative reviews for different product categories. This gives us some information about which product categories urgently need improvements, but that may not be specific enough. For instance, it may be interesting to find out what aspects of a product users are most happy or unhappy with. Let's try using ChatGPT to extract this information as well.

User: Which positive aspects of the product does the review mention? Answer with a numbered list, each aspect is described by maximally three words:

GPT: 1. Impressive screen
2. Fast performance
3. Suitable for coding
4. Great value

Correct again! ChatGPT extracts the most salient product advantages mentioned in the review. Note that the output format complies again with the corresponding instructions: it's a numbered list, and each entry has at most three words. How about the drawbacks mentioned in the review?

User: Which negative aspects of the product does the review mention? Answer with a numbered list, each aspect is described by maximally three words:

GPT: 1. Heavy weight

Indeed, the only drawback of the BananaBook is the weight, according to the user. Note that ChatGPT sticks to the requested output format (a numbered list) even though the result contains only a single entry.

Classifying reviews and extracting specific strengths and weaknesses works great if we want to aggregate reviews into statistics. However, doing so may discard information: for example, a more detailed justification for why users do or do not like specific aspects of a product. Sometimes we may just want to read a review sample. But to avoid spending time reading overly long reviews, it would be great to summarize those reviews first. Let's use ChatGPT to do so.

User: Summarize the review in three sentences:

GPT: The reviewer purchased the BananaBook electronics product a year ago and remains satisfied with it. The BananaBook has an impressive screen that allows for easy reading in bright sunlight and is fast enough for coding and office work. The only drawback is its heavy weight, but for the price, the BananaBook is a great value.

The result is a reasonable summary that uses precisely the number of sentences requested in the instructions. Can we get it even more concisely?

User: Summarize the review in one sentence:

GPT: The reviewer is happy with the BananaBook electronics product due to its impressive screen, fast performance, and great value, despite it being a bit heavy.

Yes, that works as well! Indeed, after initial testing, it seems that ChatGPT may help automate various analysis tasks. Finally, let's see whether we can exploit it for tasks beyond mere analysis. Maintaining good customer relationships is a priority for Banana! Hence the question from your boss, asking you to write friendly answers to the user comments wherever possible. But doing that takes time as well. Can't we use ChatGPT to automate that step too? Let's see ...

User: Write a friendly reply to the review from the company producing Banana-Book!

GPT: Sure, here's a friendly reply to the review:

Dear valued customer,

We are thrilled to hear that you are still happy with your BananaBook electronics product a year after your purchase! We designed the BananaBook to offer an impressive screen and fast performance for our users, and we are glad to see that these features meet your needs for coding and office work. We appreciate your feedback on the weight of the device and will take it into consideration for future improvements. Thank you for choosing BananaBook, and we hope to continue exceeding your expectations!
Best regards,
[Company Name]

Pretty good! ChatGPT answers with a friendly message to the customer, referencing specific points in the review in the appropriate manner (confirming positive points mentioned by the customer and promising improvements with regard to the weaknesses). Note that ChatGPT leaves a placeholder for the name of the corresponding company (marked by square brackets). So far, we haven't told ChatGPT the name of our company (Banana) yet. Let's fix that.

User: The name of the company is Banana - replace the corresponding placeholder in your answer.

GPT: I apologize for the mistake in my previous response. Here's an updated reply with the correct company name:

Dear valued customer,

We are thrilled to hear that you are still happy with your BananaBook electronics product a year after your purchase! We designed the Banana-Book to offer an impressive screen and fast performance for our users, and we are glad to see that these features meet your needs for coding and office work. We appreciate your feedback on the weight of the device and will take it into consideration for future improvements. Thank you for choosing Banana, and we hope to continue exceeding your expectations!

Best regards,
The Banana Team

Okay, that works! Based on the additional information, ChatGPT was able to substitute the name of the company for the placeholder in the previous answer.

> **WARNING**   Language models like ChatGPT may occasionally generate harmful content, even though recent models have significantly decreased the chance of such occurrences. It is recommended to check the text generated by Chat-GPT before posting it on public forums. Hence, automatically writing answers to customer reviews is not a good use case without some degree of human oversight.

We have seen that we can use ChatGPT for various tasks in text processing. We have used ChatGPT for categorizing text based on different criteria and using custom categories (classification according to review target and according to review content). We have also used it to extract specific pieces of information from a text and to summarize documents (i.e., reviews). Finally, we have used ChatGPT to generate text answering a customer review. In all cases, ChatGPT was able to follow instructions about the task and the desired output format. If you want, try writing a different review, and make sure ChatGPT can still solve all of these tasks.

Until recently, each of the different text-processing tasks we discussed in this section would have required a specialized language model. The latest generation of language models is flexible enough to solve a variety of tasks based on a description of the task in plain English (as well as other natural languages).

Note that we have processed only one short review so far. Here, using ChatGPT does not really provide a benefit. We could have classified or summarized the review manually and done it much more quickly than with the help of ChatGPT. Of course, the goal of automation is to scale processing up to a large number of (possibly longer) reviews. If we're talking about hundreds, perhaps thousands, of reviews, manual analysis will take much longer than setting up ChatGPT to do the task. But a crucial component is still missing: How do we inform ChatGPT about all the review text? Can we simply copy and paste the whole collection of reviews into the ChatGPT web interface?

That approach won't work. Language models generally come with restrictions regarding the amount of information they can process at once. Hence, we need a mechanism that automatically "feeds" single reviews (or small collections of reviews) to ChatGPT for processing. We will discuss corresponding approaches in the following chapters. For now, we just want to verify that ChatGPT can be used, in principle, to perform a diverse range of analysis tasks on text documents.

2.4 Processing tables with ChatGPT

In the last section, we used ChatGPT directly for data processing, providing ChatGPT with data as well as a task description as input. This approach is reasonable as long as we're processing text, the "native" input and output format of ChatGPT. For other types of data, it is much more efficient to use specialized, data type–specific tools for data processing. You may be wondering: If we process data with external tools, how can ChatGPT still be helpful in this context?

There are many tools for processing data, specialized for different types of data, processing, and hardware or software platforms. To use such tools, users often need to express the desired analysis operations in tool-specific formal languages. Writing code to analyze data can be tedious for experts and even more so for users with a limited IT background. Here, language models like ChatGPT can help because they understand natural language as well as the formal languages used by data-analysis tools. This means we can use ChatGPT as a sort of "translator," translating our questions about the data, formulated in plain English, into code in various languages to be executed via external tools. This is what we will do next.

You're back at Banana and have successfully used ChatGPT to analyze all the various reviews submitted by users. It is natural to represent this information as a data table. Each row corresponds to one review, and the columns represent the different types of information extracted from the review. Table 2.1 shows the first few rows.

Table 2.1 Example table with three columns representing the review ID, a flag indicating whether the reviewer is satisfied with a product, and the product category

ReviewID	Satisfied	Category
1	1	Laptops
2	0	Phones
2	1	Gaming
...	...	...

To keep the example simple, we use a table with a few columns corresponding to a subset of the analyses described in the previous section. The first table column contains the review ID. The second column contains a flag indicating whether the reviewer is satisfied with the product (1) or dissatisfied with the product (0). The final column contains the category. For this example, we consider only three categories: laptops, phones, and gaming.

This table is already a much more concise representation of the original reviews. But the full table has many rows (because we started with many reviews), and reading the raw table data doesn't provide very much insight. Ideally, we want to aggregate data in interesting ways and present only the high-level trends to our boss. Which tools can we use to do that?

2.4.1 Processing tables in the web interface

The first option is using the OpenAI web interface directly to analyze tabular data. First, let's download an example table with the review analysis results. Search for the link named Review Table on the book's companion website (www.dataanalysiswith llms.com), and download the associated file. It contains a table with the structure shown in table 2.1 in .csv format.

What is the .csv format?

CSV stands for comma-separated values. It designates a specific format used to represent tabular data. Each table row is stored in a separate line, and values for different columns in the same row are separated by commas.

To analyze such data directly in the ChatGPT web interface, we first need to upload it. Click the Upload button shown in figure 2.4 (before doing so, you may also want to start a new chat). Choose the Upload From Computer option, and select the file you just downloaded (reviews_table.csv).

Figure 2.4   Click the Upload button, and choose the Upload From Computer option to upload files on disk.

After uploading the file, it should appear next to the input text field. You can now enter arbitrary questions about the data into the input text field. When generating its answers, ChatGPT will take into account and analyze the data you provided. For instance, let's ask about the number of reviews for each product category.

User: How many reviews do we have for each product category?

You should see output like that shown in figure 2.5. ChatGPT shows a table containing the answer to your question (each row counts the number of reviews for one product category) and accompanying text.

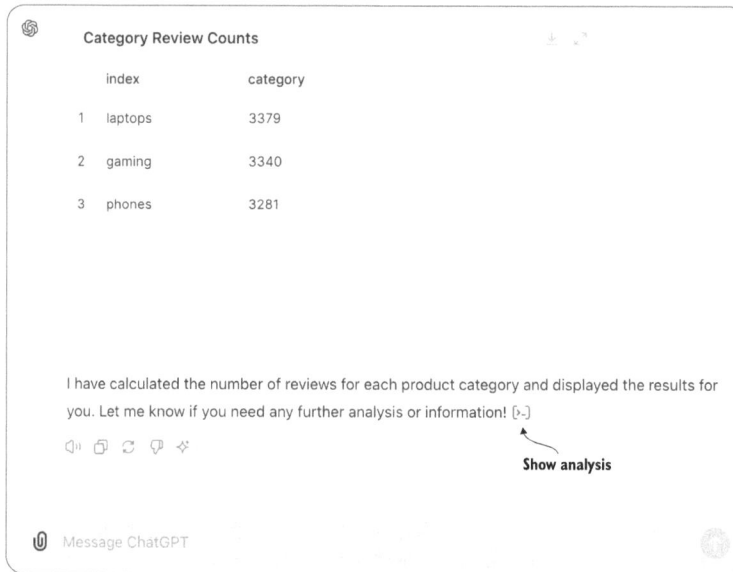

Figure 2.5   Answer generated by ChatGPT for a question about the input table. Click the Show Analysis button to see how ChatGPT determined the answer.

How did ChatGPT calculate the answer? Did it read the entire table to generate the reply directly? Not quite. In the background, ChatGPT generates and executes Python code on OpenAI's platform that analyzes the input data (in this scenario, the Python execution engine is the external tool we referred to initially). You can see the generated code by clicking the button labeled Show Analysis in figure 2.5. In fact, it is highly recommended to check the generated code instead of relying blindly on an answer. After all, despite their amazing capabilities, language models do regularly make mistakes.

Try a few more questions, check the generated code, and possibly even try a few different data sets (you can upload any tabular data on your computer, such as in Excel format). You will find that ChatGPT can handle a variety of data sets and requests.

This seems to work pretty well! Why do we need anything else? Well, there are a couple of reasons why we would like to explore other external tools for data analysis. First, there are strict limits on the size of files we can upload (512 MB at the time of writing). Uploading large data sets is not possible. Second, you may have noticed that data analysis with Python can take a few seconds, even for moderately sized data sets (e.g., the table with reviews has only 10,000 rows, which is small according to today's standards). Analyzing large data sets takes prohibitive amounts of time. Finally, uploading data to OpenAI may not be acceptable for each use case. To preserve privacy for sensitive data, users may prefer analyzing data on their own platforms. In the next section, we will see how we can use ChatGPT to analyze data outside of OpenAI's web interface.

2.4.2 Processing tables on your platform

In some scenarios, analyzing data directly in OpenAI's web interface is not an option. Instead, ChatGPT can help us use various other tools for data analysis that are directly under our control. Next, we will use a *relational database management system* (RDBMS). Such systems are specialized for handling data of the type we're interested in and tend to achieve high processing efficiency. This is just an example: the proposed approach generalizes to various other types of data-analysis systems.

Relational database management systems

A relational database management system is specialized for handling relational data: that is, data sets that contain one or multiple tables of the type in table 2.1. Most of them support variants of Structured Query Language (SQL), a language used to describe data and operations on data. For the following examples, we assume that you are familiar with the basics of SQL and RDBMSs. If you aren't, you can find a short introduction to SQL in chapter 5. To get more details, consider reading the book *Database Management Systems* by Gehrke and Ramakrishnan [2], or try the online course by this book's author at www.databaselecture.com.

We will use SQLite, one of the most popular RDBMSs. To save you the headaches of installing and configuring that system on your machine, go to the book's companion website, and follow the link to the BananaDB resource. It will lead you to a Google Colab notebook that you can use for the following steps. Figure 2.6 shows the notebook you should see after following the link.

Figure 2.6   Google Colab notebook allowing you to query the BananaDB database via SQLite. Execute the upper cell (Create Database) to create the database, replace the given SQL query (SQL Query) with a query of your choice, and then execute the lower cell (Execute Query) to see the query result. The arrow marks the Run button to execute the upper cell.

Google Colab notebooks

We will use Google Colab notebooks to enable you to try the following examples without installing software on your local machine. The following explanations assume that you're familiar with Colab Notebooks in general. If you want to brush up on your notebook skills, check out the tutorial at https://colab.research.google.com.

The notebook already contains code for creating an example database and analyzing data in it. This chapter is about getting the hang of ChatGPT's web interface. Hence, for the moment, we will not spend time discussing the code in the notebook in detail. For the rest of this chapter, it is sufficient to know what the code is doing and which specific parts of it you need to change in the following paragraphs. At a high level of abstraction, the code in this notebook creates a database with example data and allows you to execute SQL queries that analyze that data via SQLite.

You see two cells containing code in the notebook (labeled Create Database and Execute Query in figure 2.6). The upper cell (Create Database) contains code that creates a database containing an extended version of table 2.1, filling it with data for about 1,000 reviews. Let's execute that cell first by clicking the Run button in the upper-left corner of the cell (marked with an arrow in figure 2.6). After a couple of seconds, this should create an SQLite database and fill it with corresponding data. You only need to execute this cell once per session. If you do not interact with the notebook for a sufficiently long time, the environment will be reset, and you will need to execute the cell again.

We will ask ChatGPT to write SQL queries for us that refer to this database. You can execute SQL queries on the data using the lower cell in figure 2.6 (Execute Query). By default, the cell contains an SQL query counting the number of reviews in the Gaming category. Execute the cell (by clicking its Run button) to see whether everything is working. After executing the cell, you should see the number of reviews in the Gaming category: 342. We will replace the current query (`select count(*) from reviews where category = 'gaming';`) with the queries proposed by ChatGPT and then re-execute this cell to get the results for the new queries.

Okay, it's time to have ChatGPT do some data analysis for us! First, start a new dialogue by clicking the New Chat button in the ChatGPT web interface. This is important to make sure prior dialogue steps do not interfere with our new task. To use ChatGPT for writing queries, we first need to tell it a little about what our database looks like. In particular, we should describe the table structure, meaning the name of the table (Reviews) and all associated columns. In this case, the table has three columns, and we should probably add some text describing the content in those columns. When writing SQL queries, it is useful to know about the types of data in each column and ideally some information about the specific values we may find and their semantics.

Finally, another important piece of information is the specific system we use to analyze data. Although many RDBMSs support SQL, and SQL is fairly standardized, the specific subset of supported SQL features may differ across systems. Furthermore, some of these systems may support SQL syntax that slightly deviates from the SQL standard.

Having clarified what matters for writing SQL queries, let's provide ChatGPT with that information for our BananaDB example database.

User: We have an SQLite 3 database with a table (named Reviews) summarizing product reviews. The table has three columns:
- ReviewID (the integer ID of the review)
- Satisfied (1 if the reviewer is satisfied and 0 if the reviewer is not satisfied)
- Category ("laptops," "phones," or "gaming")

GPT: That's great! Having an SQLite database with a table named "Reviews"that summarizes product reviews can be quite useful. With the three columns you mentioned (ReviewID, Satisfied, and Category), you can store and retrieve valuable information about the reviews.

To help you further, I can provide you with some example SQLite queries that you can use to interact with your database. Please let me know what specific operations or information you would like to perform or retrieve from the database.

ChatGPT is upbeat about the prospect of analyzing our database and answers with a summary of the database structure that we provide in our input. Also, ChatGPT already has a sense of where this is going and proactively proposes writing some example SQL queries before we even ask it to. Let's see what ChatGPT has in store.

User: Sure! Please provide some example queries!

GPT: Certainly! Here are some example queries that you can use to interact with your SQLite database table named "Reviews":

Retrieve all reviews:
SELECT * FROM Reviews;

Retrieve satisfied reviews:
SELECT * FROM Reviews WHERE Satisfied = 1;

Retrieve unsatisfied reviews:
SELECT * FROM Reviews WHERE Satisfied = 0;

Retrieve reviews for laptops:
SELECT * FROM Reviews WHERE Category = 'laptops';

Retrieve reviews for phones:
SELECT * FROM Reviews WHERE Category = 'phones';

Retrieve reviews for gaming:
SELECT * FROM Reviews WHERE Category = 'gaming';

Count the total number of reviews:
SELECT COUNT(*) FROM Reviews;

Count the number of satisfied reviews:
SELECT COUNT(*) FROM Reviews WHERE Satisfied = 1;

Count the number of unsatisfied reviews:
SELECT COUNT(*) FROM Reviews WHERE Satisfied = 0;

These queries should give you a starting point to perform various operations on your "Reviews" table. You can modify them or combine them to suit your specific requirements.

Not bad! The queries cover quite a few natural questions; for example, about the number of reviews that fall into specific categories. In general, asking ChatGPT to propose queries is not a bad way to start analyzing a data set.

You may notice, by the way, that the web interface displays SQL queries using a specific representation. Figure 2.7 shows how the first query is displayed.

Figure 2.7   The ChatGPT web interface uses specialized markup to represent code, including SQL queries. Click the Copy Code button to copy the code (making it convenient to paste it into suitable interfaces for execution).

The SQL query is in a box, making it easy to copy it by clicking the Copy Code button. To try any of the proposed queries, copy it (as described before), and then insert it at the appropriate position in the BananaDB notebook (labeled SQL Query in figure 2.6). Finally, execute the surrounding cell in the notebook to obtain the query result.

Let's see whether we can make GPT translate our own questions into queries as well.

User: Write an SQL query to retrieve the product category with most reviews!

GPT: To retrieve the product category with the most reviews from your SQLite database table "Reviews," you can use the following SQL query:

SELECT Category, COUNT(*) AS ReviewCount
FROM Reviews
GROUP BY Category
ORDER BY ReviewCount DESC
LIMIT 1;

This query uses the GROUP BY clause to group the reviews by the "Category"column. Then, it applies the COUNT(*) function to count the number of reviews in each category. The results are ordered in descending order based on the review count using the ORDER BY clause. Finally, the LIMIT 1 clause ensures that only the category with the highest review count is returned.

The query will return the product category along with the corresponding count of reviews for that category.

We are interested in finding the product category associated with most reviews. ChatGPT translates our question into an SQL query that retrieves the corresponding result. If you execute this query on our example database, it should retrieve the Gaming category, along with the number of associated reviews.

How to deal with multiline queries

This is the first multiline SQL query generated by ChatGPT. To use that query in our Colab notebook, surround the query with triple quotes (" " ") rather than single quotes. Doing so ensures that the entire query is treated as a single string.

Strictly speaking, we asked for the category but not the associated count. Here, ChatGPT takes some liberty by adding the count to our query result. In this case, that may be acceptable and even interesting. In general, if you're using ChatGPT to translate questions into queries, make sure it does not expand your queries in ways that are not acceptable (e.g., if the output is forwarded to another tool that expects a specific input format). Let's see whether we can make ChatGPT follow our instructions more closely.

User: The query result should only return the category.

GPT: Apologies for the oversight. If you want the query to return only the category with the most reviews, you can modify the previous query by selecting only the "Category"column:

```
SELECT Category
FROM Reviews
GROUP BY Category
ORDER BY COUNT(*) DESC
LIMIT 1;
```

This updated query will retrieve the product category with the highest number of reviews from the "Reviews"table. It groups the reviews by category, orders them based on the count of reviews in descending order, and then selects only the top result using the LIMIT 1 clause. The query will return the category with the most reviews.

Perfect! ChatGPT has slightly rewritten the previous query to return only the category but not the associated count. You may notice that ChatGPT's answers contain the query and an explanation for why the query does what it is doing. Such explanations are helpful to verify that queries generated by ChatGPT are indeed correct. Next, let's drill down a bit further and see which ratio of reviewers were satisfied with their gaming products.

User: What is the ratio of positive reviews in the gaming category?

GPT: To calculate the ratio of positive reviews in the gaming category from your SQLite database table "Reviews," you can use the following SQL query:

```
SELECT (CAST(SUM(Satisfied) AS REAL) / COUNT(*)) AS PositiveRatio
FROM Reviews
WHERE Category = 'gaming';
```

This query filters the reviews specifically for the "gaming" category using the WHERE clause. Then, it calculates the sum of the "Satisfied" column, which represents the number of positive reviews, using the SUM() function. The result is then divided by the total number of reviews in the gaming category, obtained using the COUNT(*) function. The CAST() function is used to ensure that the division is performed with decimal precision.

The query will return the ratio of positive reviews (satisfied reviews) in the gaming category as a decimal value.

Executing this query, you should find that a ratio of around 50% of reviews is positive (i.e., the corresponding reviewer is satisfied).[1] Finally, let's see which product category needs improvements most urgently.

User: What is the product category with the lowest ratio of positive reviews?

GPT: To determine the product category with the lowest ratio of positive reviews from your SQLite database table "Reviews," you can use the following SQL query:

```
SELECT Category, (CAST(SUM(Satisfied) AS REAL) / COUNT(*)) AS
PositiveRatio
FROM Reviews
GROUP BY Category
ORDER BY PositiveRatio ASC
LIMIT 1;
```

This query uses the GROUP BY clause to group the reviews by the "Category" column. Then, it calculates the ratio of positive reviews for each category by dividing the sum of "Satisfied" values by the total count of reviews in that category. The results are ordered in ascending order based on the positive ratio using the ORDER BY clause. Finally, the LIMIT

---

[1] That is not surprising, given that our test data is generated with a uniform random distribution (i.e., the number of positive and negative reviews should be approximately equal).

1 clause ensures that only the category with the lowest positive ratio is returned.

The query will return the product category along with the corresponding ratio of positive reviews (satisfied reviews). The category with the lowest positive ratio will be presented.

Executing this query should return the Phones category, together with the associated ratio of positive reviews.

In this section, we have seen a second way to use ChatGPT for analyzing data: instead of applying ChatGPT directly to the data, we use it as a translation mechanism. In this case, we translate questions about the data (formulated in plain English) into SQL queries that we can then execute using a corresponding tool (an RDBMS in this scenario). In later chapters, we will also use it to translate to other formal languages.

We entered questions by hand and then copied our queries to a different interface. Clearly, this approach is not the most convenient. In chapter 5, we will see how to build frameworks that automate all those steps.

Summary

- Language models can solve various tasks, given instructions in natural language.
- Although powerful, language models can produce incorrect output.
- You can use ChatGPT via a web interface in your web browser.
- ChatGPT enables users to interact with various GPT model versions.
- To process text with ChatGPT, enter the text and a task description.
- ChatGPT can classify text, given classification categories; it can extract information from text, given corresponding questions; and it can produce text summaries according to user specifications.
- ChatGPT is not suitable for processing large data sets directly. However, it can generate code that processes large data using other tools. To produce code, enter a description of the data, the task, and the output format.

References

[1] Ji, Z., Lee, N., Frieske, R., et al. (2023). Survey of Hallucination in Natural Language Generation. *ACM Computing Surveys 55* (12), 1–38.

[2] Ramakrishnan, R. and Gehrke, J. (2002). *Database Management Systems* (3rd ed.). McGraw Hill New York.

Part 2

Data analysis with language models

A web interface is sufficient to use language models on small pieces of data. But how can we scale it up to large data sets?

In chapter 3, we look at OpenAI's Python library, a powerful library that enables you to call language models directly from Python. We discuss the most important library functions, including various parameters that can be used to fine-tune the behavior of the language model for your specific use case.

Chapter 4 discusses several mini-projects that use OpenAI's language models via the Python library to analyze collections of text documents. For instance, our projects cover classifying text documents into one of several prespecified categories, extracting specific snippets of information from text, and clustering similar text documents together.

Chapter 5 shows how to use language models to analyze structured data: data tables and graph data. Here, language models are used as an interface, translating questions about the data (in natural language) into formal queries that can be processed by specialized analysis tools. For instance, the chapter demonstrates how to use language models to build interfaces that translate questions to queries in SQL that can be processed using relational database management systems.

Chapter 6 demonstrates how language models can analyze pictures and even videos. The sample projects include using language models to answer arbitrary questions in natural language about pictures, as well as finding pairs of pictures showing the same person. This chapter also shows how to use language models to automatically caption videos based on the video content.

Chapter 7 focuses on audio data and covers speech transcription as well as speech generation. For instance, we see how to use OpenAI's models to build a voice query interface, answering spoken questions about tabular data. We also build a translation tool, translating spoken input in a first language into spoken output in a second language according to user specifications.

The OpenAI Python library

This chapter covers

- Installing the OpenAI library
- Invoking GPT models using Python
- Configuration parameters

In the last chapter, we used GPT models via the OpenAI web interface. This works well as long as we're just trying to have a conversation or classify and summarize single reviews. However, imagine trying to classify hundreds of reviews. In that case, using the web interface manually for each review becomes very tedious (to say the least). Also, perhaps we want to use a language model in combination with other tools. For instance, we might want to use GPT models to translate questions to formal queries and then seamlessly execute those queries in the corresponding tool (without having to manually copy queries back and forth between different interfaces). In all these scenarios, we need a different interface.

In this chapter, we'll discuss a Python library from OpenAI that lets you call OpenAI's language models directly from Python. This enables you to integrate calls to language models as a subfunction in your code. We will be using this library in most chapters of the book. Therefore, it makes sense to at least skim this chapter before proceeding to the following chapters.

Although the current chapter focuses on OpenAI's Python library, the libraries offered by other providers of language models (including Anthropic, Cohere, and Google) are similar.

3.1 Prerequisites

First, let's make sure we have the right environment for OpenAI's Python library. We will use the Python programming language, so make sure Python is installed. To do so, open a terminal, and enter the following command (this command should work for Linux, macOS, and Windows terminals):

```
python --version
```

If this command returns an error message, try replacing `python` with `python3` in the command and running it again. If Python is installed on your system, you should see a version number in reply (e.g., "Python 3.10.13"). If not, you will get an error message. For the following examples, you will need at least Python 3.9 (or a later version). If Python is not installed on your system, or if your version is below the required one, visit www.python.org, click Downloads, and follow the instructions to install Python. You may also want to install an integrated development environment (IDE). PyDev (www.pydev.org) and PyCharm (www.jetbrains.com/pycharm) are two of the many IDEs available for Python.

Along with Python, you will need pip, a package-management system used to install Python packages (the OpenAI library comes in the form of such a package). For recent Python versions (which you will need in any case), this program is already installed by default. Nevertheless, it can't hurt to make sure:

```
pip --version
```

Again, you should see a version number if everything is installed properly. Let's make sure pip is up to date. The following command should work on Linux, macOS, and Windows:

```
python -m pip install --upgrade pip
```

That's it! Your system is ready to install the OpenAI Python client.

What if it doesn't work?

Don't panic! If any of the previously mentioned steps fail, you may not be able to execute the following code on your local machine. However, as long as you have web access, you can use a cloud platform instead. For instance, the Google Colab platform, accessible at https://colab.research.google.com, enables you to create notebooks that can execute all of the following code samples. Figure 3.1 shows the interface after creating a cell installing the OpenAI library (upper cell) and the start of a corresponding Python program (lower cell). We will discuss library installation and usage in the following sections.

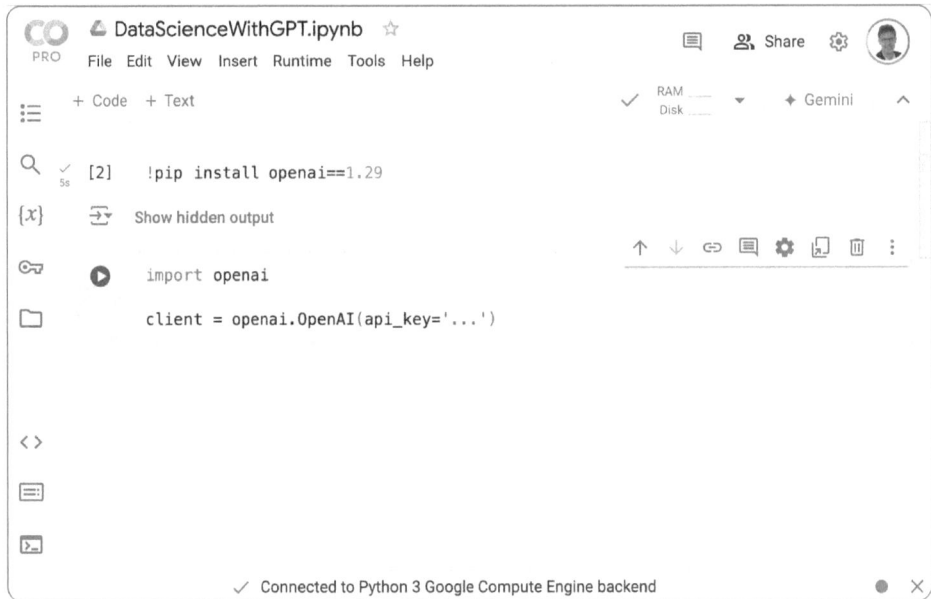

Figure 3.1   The Google Colab platform can be used to run the following examples.

3.2   *Installing OpenAI's Python library*

Time to start using GPT like a pro! Although the ChatGPT web interface, discussed in chapter 2, is useful for conversations and trying out new prompts, it is unsuitable for implementing complex data-processing pipelines. For that, OpenAI's Python library is a much better choice, enabling you to invoke language models directly from Python. First, let's install the corresponding library. Enter the following command into a terminal:

```
pip install openai==1.29
```

Can I use a different library version?

You might have noticed the reference to a specific version (version 1.29) of the OpenAI library. The code presented in this and the following chapters has been tested with this version. As the syntax differs slightly across different library versions (unless you are willing to adapt the code), install this precise version.

Every time we use the OpenAI library, we need to provide a key giving us access to the OpenAI models (this is required for billing purposes). If you have not yet created an OpenAI account, go to https://platform.openai.com, click Sign Up, and follow the instructions. If you have an account but are not currently logged in, provide your account credentials instead. Make sure to add a payment method in the Billing section, and charge it with a couple of dollars. After that, if you haven't done so yet, it is time to generate your secret key.

Go to https://platform.openai.com/account/api-keys. You should see the website shown in figure 3.2.

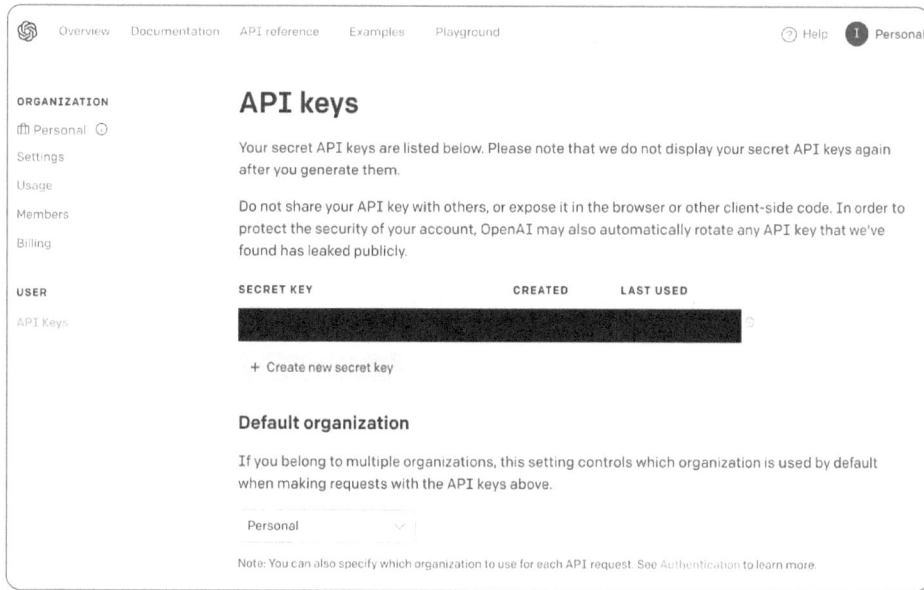

Figure 3.2 Managing secret keys for accessing the OpenAI API

Click the Create New Secret Key button. The interface will show a text string representing the key. Be sure to copy and store that key! You will not be able to retrieve the full key again after closing the corresponding window.

Whenever we use the Python library, we need to provide our secret key to link our requests to the appropriate account. The easiest way to do that is to store the secret key in an environment variable named `OPENAI_API_KEY`. OpenAI will automatically extract the key from that variable if it exists. The precise command used to set environment variables depends on the operating system. For example, the following command works for Linux and macOS (replace the three dots with your key):

```
export OPENAI_API_KEY=...
```

Alternatively, you can set the key on a per-invocation basis by prefixing your calls to Python with the corresponding assignments. For example, use the following command to call the code listing presented in the next section while setting the key at the same time (again, substitute your key for the three dots):

```
OPENAI_API_KEY=... python listing1.py
```

Finally, if none of the other options work, you can specify your access key directly in your Python code. More precisely, right after importing OpenAI's Python library, we can pass the API access key as a parameter when creating the `client` object (which we discuss in more detail later):

```
import openai
client = openai.OpenAI(api_key='...')
```

As before, replace the three dots with your OpenAI access key. The following code samples assume that the access key is specified in an environment variable and will therefore omit this parameter. If environment variables don't work for you, change the code listings by passing your access key as a parameter.

> **WARNING**   Never share your code if it contains your OpenAI access key. Among other things, having your key would enable others to invoke OpenAI's models while making you pay for it.

Assuming you have specified your access key in one way or another, we are now ready to start calling GPT models using OpenAI's Python library.

3.3   *Listing available models*

We will use the Python library to retrieve a list of available OpenAI models. Listing 3.1 shows the corresponding Python code. (You can download this and all of the following code listings from the book's companion website.) First, we import the OpenAI library (❶). Then we create a client object, enabling us to access library functions (❷). Next, we query for all available OpenAI models (❸) and print out the result (❹).

Listing 3.1   Listing available OpenAI models

```
import openai          ❶ Imports the OpenAI Python library
client = openai.OpenAI()      ❷ Creates an OpenAI client

models = client.models.list()     ❸ Gets available OpenAI models

for model in models.data:     ❹ Prints out the retrieved models
    print(model)
```

You should see a result similar to the following:

```
Model(id='dall-e-3', created=1698785189,
    object='model', owned_by='system')
Model(id='whisper-1', created=1677532384,
    object='model', owned_by='openai-internal')
Model(id='GPT-4o-2024-05-13', created=1715368132,
    object='model', owned_by='system')
Model(id='davinci-002', created=1692634301,
    object='model', owned_by='system')
Model(id='GPT-4o', created=1715367049,      ❶ GPT-4o
    object='model', owned_by='system')
...
```
❷ Fine-tuned model version
```
Model(id='curie:ft-personal-2022-01-10-16-52-53',
    created=1641833573, object='model', owned_by='trummerlab')
```

```
Model(id='davinci:ft-personal-2022-01-13-19-59-51',
    created=1642103991, object='model', owned_by='trummerlab')
Model(id='ft:gpt-3.5-turbo-0613:trummerlab::8qlJH6bV',
    created=1707585607, object='model', owned_by='trummerlab')
...
```

Each model is described by an ID (e.g., GPT-4o (**❶**)). We will use this ID to tell OpenAI which model we want to use to process our requests. Besides the ID, each model comes with a creation timestamp and information about model ownership (owned_by field). In most cases, models are owned by OpenAI (marked, for example, system or openai-internal). In some cases, however, models are owned by trummerlab (**❷**), the name of the account used by this book's author. Those models are not publicly accessible but private to the owning account. You will not see those models when executing the code using your account. They are created by a process called *fine-tuning* from the publicly available base models.

What is fine-tuning?

By default, language models such as GPT-4o are trained to be versatile, meaning they can, in principle, perform any task. But sometimes we don't want a model that is versatile but rather a model that does very well on one specific task. Fine-tuning enables us to specialize a model for a task we care about. We discuss fine-tuning in more detail in chapter 9.

3.4 Chat completion

Almost all the code in this book uses the same functionality of the OpenAI Python library: *chat completion*. With chat completion, your model generates a completion for a chat, provided as input. The input can contain various types of data, such as text and images. We will exploit those features in the following chapters but restrict ourselves to text for the moment. Chat completion is also used in the background of OpenAI's ChatGPT web interface. Given the chat history as input (which includes the latest message as well as prior messages, possibly containing relevant context), the model generates the most suitable reply.

To use chat completion from Python, we first need a format to describe the chat history. This is part of the input we're providing for chat completion. In OpenAI's Python library, chats are represented as a list of messages. Each message in turn is represented as a Python dictionary. This Python dictionary specifies values for several important properties of the message. At the very least, we need to specify two important attributes for each message:

- The role attribute, which specifies the source of a message
- The content attribute, which specifies the content of a message

Let's start by discussing the role attribute. As you know from the last chapter, a chat with GPT models is a back-and-forth series of messages, alternating between messages written by the user and messages written by the model. Accordingly, we can specify the value `user` for the `role` attribute to identify a message as written by the user. Alternatively, we can specify the value `assistant` to mark a message as generated by the language model. A third possible value for the `role` attribute is `system`. Such messages are typically used at the beginning of a chat history. They are meant to convey generic guidelines to the model, independent of the specific tasks submitted by users. For instance, a typical system message could have the content "You are a helpful assistant," but more specialized versions (e.g., "You are an assistant that translates questions about data sets into SQL queries") are also possible. We will not use `system` messages in this book, but feel free to experiment and try adding your own system messages to see if they influence the model output.

The `content` attribute specifies the content of a message. In this chapter, we will restrict ourselves to text content. In later chapters, we will see how language models can be used to process more diverse types of content. In the following code samples, we will only need to specify a single message in our chat history. This message contains instructions describing a task that the language model should solve, as well as relevant context information. For instance, the following chat history encourages the model to generate a story for us:

```
[{
    'role':'user',          ❶ Message from user
    'content':'Tell me a story!'   ❷ Task specification
}]
```

The list of messages contains only a single message. This message is marked as originating from the user (❶) and describes the previously mentioned task in its content (❷). As a reply, we would expect the model to generate a story following the input instructions.

How can we invoke a model for chat completion? This can be realized with just a few lines of Python code. First, we need to import the OpenAI Python library (❶) and create a `client` object (❷):

```
import openai          ❶ Imports the OpenAI Python library
client = openai.OpenAI()   ❷ Creates the OpenAI client
```

We will use the `client` object for all of the following invocations of the language model. The previous code appears in almost all of our code samples. Remember that you may need to pass the OpenAI access key manually as a parameter when creating the client (unless you specify your access key in an environment variable, which is the recommended approach). After creating the `client`, we can issue chat completion requests as shown here:

```
result = client.chat.completions.create(
    model='GPT-4o',          ❶ Selects a model
    messages=[{              ❷ Specifies input messages
        'role':'user',
        'content':'Tell me a story!'
        }])
```

We use the `client.chat.completions.create` function to create a new request. The `model` parameter (❶) specifies the name of the model we want to use for completion. In this case, we're selecting OpenAI's GPT-4o model, which can process multimodal data. We will use this model for most of the code samples in this book. Next, we specify the chat history as input via the `messages` parameter (❷). This is the chat history discussed before, instructing the model to generate a story.

Let's put it all together. The following listing (available as listing 2 in the chapter 3 section on the book's companion website) uses GPT-4o to generate a story.

Listing 3.2 Using GPT-4o for chat completion

```
import openai              ◄─── Imports the OpenAI Python library
client = openai.OpenAI()   ◄─── Creates an OpenAI client

result = client.chat.completions.create(  ◄─── Invokes chat completion
    model='GPT-4o',                        ◄─── Selects a model
    messages=[{                            ◄─── Specifies input messages
        'role':'user',
        'content':'Tell me a story!'
        }])
print(result)
```

Running the code should produce a result such as the following (your precise story may differ due to randomization):

```
ChatCompletion(
    id='chatcmpl-9YKmJCE8SITsKyI557T8KTuX3IxWN',
    choices=[                               ❶ List of completions
        Choice(
            finish_reason='stop',     ❷ Termination condition
            index=0,
            logprobs=None,
            message=ChatCompletionMessage(        ❸ Completion message
                content="Of course! Here's a story that ... ",
                role='assistant',
                function_call=None,
                tool_calls=None)
            )
        ],
        created=1717970051,
        model='GPT-4o-2024-05-13',
        object='chat.completion',
        system_fingerprint='fp_319be4768e',
        usage=CompletionUsage(           ❹ Token usage
            completion_tokens=810,
            prompt_tokens=12,
            total_tokens=822
        )
    )
```

Let's discuss the different components of that result. First, we have a list of completion alternatives (❶) (objects of type `Choice`). In our case, that list contains only a single entry. This is the default behavior, although we can ask for multiple alternative completions by setting the right configuration parameters (discussed in the next section). The `finish_reason` flag (❷) indicates for each completion the reason to stop generating. For instance, this can be due to reaching a length limit on generated text. The `stop` value indicates that the language model was able to generate complete output (as opposed to reaching a length limit). The actual message (❸) content is abbreviated, and in all likelihood, you will see different stories if you invoke the code repeatedly.

Besides the completions themselves, the result contains metadata and usage statistics (❹). More precisely, we find values for the following properties:

- `completion_tokens`—The number of generated tokens
- `prompt_tokens`—The number of tokens in the input
- `total_tokens`—The number of tokens read and generated

Why would we care about the number of tokens? Because pricing for most OpenAI models is proportional to the number of tokens read and generated. For instance, at the time of writing, using GPT-4o costs $5 per million tokens read and $15 per million tokens generated. Note the difference in pricing between tokens read and generated. Typically, as in this case, generating tokens is more expensive than reading tokens. The pricing depends not only on the number of tokens but also on the model used. For example, replacing GPT-4o with the GPT-3.5 Turbo model (a slightly less powerful GPT version) cuts costs by a factor of 10. Before analyzing large amounts of data with language models, choose the appropriate model size for your task and wallet.

3.5   *Customizing model behavior*

You can use various parameters to influence how the model replies to your input. These parameters can be specified in addition to the `model` and `messages` parameters when invoking the `chat.completions.create` function. In this section, we discuss different categories of parameters, classifying parameters by the aspect of model behavior they influence.

3.5.1   *Configuring termination conditions*

When we invoke a model for chat completion, it generates output until a stopping condition is met. The two parameters discussed next enable us to configure when text generation stops.

The `max_tokens` parameter specifies the maximum number of tokens (i.e., the atomic unit at which language models represent text) generated during completion. A token corresponds to approximately four characters, and a typical paragraph contains around 100 tokens. The maximum admissible value for this parameter is determined by the model used. For instance, ada, one of the smallest GPT versions, allows up to 2,049 tokens, whereas GPT-4o supports up to 128,000 tokens. Keep in mind that the maximum number of tokens supported by the model includes tokens read and tokens generated. As `max_tokens` refers only to the number of tokens generated, you should not set it higher than the maximum number of tokens supported by the model used *minus the number of tokens in the prompt.*

As a general rule, setting a reasonable value for `max_tokens` is almost always a good idea. After all, we're paying for each generated token, and setting a bound on the number of tokens enables you to bound monetary fees per model invocation.

In some scenarios, specific text patterns indicate the end of the desired output. For instance, when generating code, it can be a string specific to the corresponding programming language indicating the end of the program. On the other hand, when generating a fairy tale, it can be the string "and they lived happily ever after!" In those scenarios, we might want to use the `stop` parameter to configure the OpenAI library to stop generating output whenever a specific token sequence appears. In some cases, there is only one token sequence indicating termination. In those scenarios, we can directly assign the `stop` parameter to the corresponding string value. In other scenarios, there are multiple candidate sequences that indicate termination. In those cases, we can assign the `stop` parameter to a list of up to four sequences. Text generation terminates whenever any of those sequences is generated.

Note that you can use both of the previously mentioned parameters together. In those cases, output generation stops whenever the length limit is reached or one of the stop sequences appears (whichever happens first).

3.5.2 Configuring output generation

The parameters we just discussed enable you to choose when the output terminates. But how can you influence the output generated until that point? Here, OpenAI offers a few parameters that enable you to bias the way in which GPT models select output text.

Several parameters enable you to influence how "repetitive" the generated output should be. More precisely, those parameters allow you to influence whether generating the same tokens repeatedly is desirable or not.

The `presence_penalty` parameter enables you to penalize chat completions that use the same tokens repeatedly. The presence penalty is a value between –2 and +2 (with a default value of 0). A positive penalty encourages the model to avoid reusing the same tokens. A negative penalty, on the other hand, encourages the model to use the same tokens repeatedly. The higher the absolute value, the stronger the corresponding effect.

The `frequency_penalty` relates to the prior parameter but enables a more fine-grained penalization scheme. The `presence_penalty` parameter is based on the mere *presence* of a token. For example, we do not differentiate between a token that appears twice and one that appears hundreds of times. The frequency penalty is used as a factor, multiplying the number of prior appearances of a token when aggregating its score (which is used to determine whether the token should appear next). Hence, the more often a token was used before, the less likely it is to appear again. Similar to the presence penalty, the `frequency_penalty` parameter takes values between –2 and +2 with a default setting of 0. A positive penalty factor encourages GPT models to avoid repeating the same token, whereas a negative value encourages repetitions.

Sometimes we are only interested in one of a limited set of eligible tokens. For instance, when classifying text, the set of classes is typically determined a priori. If so, let's tell the model about it! The `logit_bias` parameter allows mapping token IDs to a bias factor. A high bias factor encourages the model to consider the corresponding token as output. A sufficiently low bias score essentially prevents the model from using the token. A sufficiently high score almost guarantees that the corresponding token will appear in the output.

Using the `logit_bias` parameter avoids generating useless output in situations where we can narrow the set of reasonable tokens. The value for `logit_bias` is a Python dictionary that maps token IDs to values between –100 and +100. Values between –1 and +1 are more typical and still give the model room to consider tokens with a low value (or to avoid using tokens that are associated with higher values). But how do we find the token IDs associated with relevant words? For that, we can use the GPT tokenizer tool, available at https://platform.openai.com/tokenizer?view=bpe. Simply enter the words you want to encourage (or ban), and the associated token IDs will be displayed. Note that multiple tokenizer variants are available, associated with different models. Select the right tokenizer for your model (because otherwise, the token IDs may be incorrect).

3.5.3 *Configuring randomization*

How do GPT models select the next output token? At a high level of abstraction, we calculate scores for all possible output tokens and then select a token based on those scores. Although tokens with higher scores tend to have better chances of being selected, we might not always want to select the token with the maximum score. For instance, think back to chapter 2, where we were able to regenerate replies for the same input, potentially leading to different results. This can be useful if the first output does not quite satisfy our requirements. If always selecting the tokens with the highest scores, regenerating an answer would be unlikely to change the output. Hence, to enable users to get diverse replies, we need to introduce a certain degree of randomization when mapping scores to output tokens.

Of course, decoupling the output too much from token scores—that is, using too much randomization—may lead to useless output (at the extreme, the output no longer connects to the input and does not follow our instructions). On the other hand, using too little randomization can lead to outputs that are less diverse than desired. Choosing the right degree of randomization for a specific scenario can take some experimentation. In each case, OpenAI offers multiple parameters that enable you to fine-tune how token scores translate to output tokens. We will discuss those parameters next.

One of the parameters most commonly used to tune randomization is the `temperature` parameter. A higher temperature means more randomization, whereas a lower temperature corresponds to less randomization. A low degree of randomization means the token with the highest score is very likely to be selected. A very high degree of randomization means tokens are (almost) selected with equal probability, independently of the scores assigned by the model. The `temperature` parameter enables you to thread the needle between those two extremes. Values for this parameter are chosen between 0 and 2 with a default of 1.

Temperature is one possibility when choosing the degree of randomization. The `top_p` parameter is an alternative approach. (It is not recommended that you alter both `temperature` and `top_p` in the same invocation of the language model.) Based on their scores, we can associate a probability of being "correct" with each possible output token. Now imagine that we are sorting those tokens in decreasing order of probability. We can reduce the degree of randomization by focusing only on the first few tokens: we neglect tokens with lower probability. How many tokens should we consider? Instead of fixing the number of eligible tokens directly, the `top_p` parameter fixes the *probability mass* of those tokens. In other words, we add tokens to the set of eligible tokens in decreasing order of probability. Whenever the sum of probability values of all selected tokens (the probability mass) exceeds the value of `top_p`, we stop adding tokens. Finally, we pick the next output token among those eligible tokens.

As the `top_p` parameter describes a probability, its values are taken from the interval between 0 and 1. Similar to temperature, choosing a higher value leads to more randomization (because even tokens with lower probability become eligible).

As soon as we are using a certain degree of randomization, it becomes useful to generate multiple answers for the same input prompt. After that, we can choose the preferred answer via postprocessing. For instance, assume that we are generating multiple SQL queries for the same input prompt. To select the preferred answer, we can try executing them on a target database and discard the queries that result in a syntax error message. Of course, we can simply call the language model repeatedly with the same prompt. However, it is more efficient to call the language model once and configure the number of generated replies. The parameter `n` determines the number of generated replies. By default, this parameter is set to 1 (i.e., only a single answer is generated). You may choose a higher value to obtain more replies. Note that using a higher value for this parameter also increases per-invocation costs (because you pay for each token generated, counting tokens across different replies).

3.5.4 Customization example

Let's try some of the parameters in our code. The following listing prompts GPT-4o to write a story, this time using some of the parameters we've discussed to customize chat completion.

Listing 3.3 Using GPT-4o for chat completion with custom parameter settings

```
import openai
client = openai.OpenAI()
```

```
result = client.chat.completions.create(
    model='GPT-4o',
    messages=[{
        'role':'user',
        'content':'Tell me a story!'
        }],
    max_tokens=512,              ❶ Limits the output length
    stop='happily ever after',   ❷ Sets a stopping condition
    temperature=1.5,             ❸ Sets temperature
    presence_penalty=0.5,        ❹ Penalizes repetitions
    logit_bias={14844:-100})         ❺ Adds bias
print(result.choices[0].message.content)
```

First, to avoid getting a lengthy story, we set the maximum number of tokens to 512 (❶). This should suffice for a few paragraphs of text. To avoid generating more content than necessary, we define a stop sequence as well: "happily ever after" (❷). We do so, hoping that any reasonable story will, of course, end with the popular expression "and they lived happily ever after." This assumption is certainly simplifying.

Next, we set the temperature to 1.5 (❸), allowing a certain degree of randomization. Having an overly repetitive story is boring. Therefore, we set a positive presence penalty (`presence_penalty=0.5`) (❹), discouraging GPT-4o from reusing the same tokens. Finally, we don't want a scary story (perhaps we want to read it to our kids), so we penalize the word *dragon* (we obtain the corresponding token ID as described in section 3.5.2) (❺).

Let's see what we get! For instance, in a sample invocation, GPT-4o generates the following story:

> *Once upon a time, in a quaint village nestled between rolling hills and dense forests, there lived a girl named Elara. She was known for her curiosity and adventurous spirit, traits that often led her to explore the uncharted parts of her village. One crisp autumn morning, Elara decided to venture into the Whispering Woods, a place shrouded in mystery and legend. The villagers often spoke of the woods as a place where magic lingered, but also one that nobody dared to enter beyond the edge. Equipped with her trusty satchel and a heart full of excitement, Elara set off with the sunrise. As she walked deeper into the woods, the whispers of rustling leaves seemed to greet her, and she felt an odd sense of familiarity. She wandered through thickets and climbed over fallen logs until she stumbled upon a hidden grove, bathed in shimmering light. In the center of the grove stood an ancient tree with silvery leaves, its trunk twisted like spiraling tendrils of smoke. Elara was mesmerized; it looked unlike any tree she had ever seen. She approached it cautiously and noticed a small, ornate chest nestled among its roots. Her heart racing, Elara opened the chest and found inside a delicate, golden locket. As soon as she touched it, the forest seemed to come alive. The whispers grew louder, forming words that she could understand. "Brave heart, you have found the Locket of Eternia," the voice murmured. "It grants the bearer one wish." Elara's mind raced with possibilities, but she knew what her heart desired most: to bring joy and prosperity to her beloved village. Clutching the locket, she whispered her wish. In an instant, a warm glow*

enveloped her, and she felt a surge of energy. The grove shimmered momentarily and then returned to its tranquil stillness. Elara knew something extraordinary had happened. As she returned home, she noticed subtle changes—the crops seemed more vibrant, the animals healthier and the village air filled with a sense of contentment. The villagers welcomed her back, their faces glowing with happiness. Elara never revealed the secret of the Whispering Woods or the Locket of Eternia to anyone. She simply smiled whenever anyone commented on the newfound prosperity of the village. She knew that sometimes, the greatest magic lies not in what is seen, but in the courage to follow one's heart. And so, Elara's village thrived, becoming a beacon of joy and harmony. All because one brave girl dared to listen to the whispers of the woods. And she lived

Happily ever after! It turns out that our stop sequence, the expression "happily ever after," was indeed used at the end of the story (and is therefore omitted in the output returned by GPT-4o). Try a few more parameter settings, and see how the result changes as a function of the configuration.

3.5.5 *Further parameters*

We have discussed the most important parameters for data-analysis purposes. You can use each of them when requesting a completion from OpenAI's GPT models. Note that there are more parameters beyond the ones mentioned in this chapter. OpenAI's API reference documentation (https://platform.openai.com/docs/api -reference/completions) describes all parameters in detail.

Summary

- You can use OpenAI's language models via a Python API. Other providers offer similar libraries for accessing their models.
- To use OpenAI's library, create a client object.
- You can use OpenAI's models to complete chats. Chats to complete are specified as a list of messages.
- Each chat message is characterized by content and a role. Roles can be one of `user`, `assistant`, or `system`.
- Obtain chat completions via the `chat.completions.create` function.
- You can configure models using various parameters:
  - The `max_tokens` parameter limits the number of tokens generated.
  - `stop` lets you define phrases that stop text generation.
  - You can penalize or encourage specific tokens via `logit_bias`.
  - `presence_penalty` penalizes repetitive output.
  - `frequency_penalty` penalizes repetitive output.
  - `temperature` chooses the degree of randomization.
  - `top_p` determines the number of output tokens considered.
  - n chooses the number of generated completions.

Analyzing text data

Text data is ubiquitous and contains valuable information. For instance, think of newspaper articles, emails, reviews, or perhaps this book you are reading! However, analyzing text via computational means was difficult until only a few years ago. After all, unlike formal languages such as Python, natural language was not designed to be easy for computers to parse. The latest generation of language models enables text analysis at almost human levels for many popular tasks. In some cases, the performance of language models for text analysis and generation has even been shown, on average, to surpass the capabilities of humans [1].

In this chapter, we will see how to use large language models to analyze text. In certain ways, analyzing text data is a very "natural" application of language models. They have been trained on large amounts of text and can be applied directly for text analysis (i.e., without referring to external tools for the actual data analysis). This chapter covers several popular flavors of text analysis: classifying text documents, extracting tabular data from text, and clustering text documents into groups of semantically similar documents. For each of these use cases, we will see example code and discuss variants and extensions.

Classification, information extraction, and clustering are three important types of text analysis but by no means the only ones you may need in practice. However, working through the examples in this chapter will enable you to create custom data-processing pipelines for text data based on language models.

4.1 Preliminaries

Let's make sure your system is set up properly for the example projects. The following examples use OpenAI's GPT model series, accessed via OpenAI's Python library. This library was discussed in detail in chapter 3. Make sure to follow the instructions in chapter 3 to be able to execute the example code.

> **WARNING** OpenAI's Python library is changing quickly. The code in this chapter has been tested with version 1.29 of the OpenAI Python library but may not work with different versions.

Besides the OpenAI library, we will use the popular `pandas` library. `pandas` is a popular library for handling tabular data (which we will use as input and output format). We will only use basic functionality from that library and explain the corresponding commands as they occur in the code. Make sure `pandas` is installed (e.g., try `import pandas` in the Python interpreter); if it isn't, install it by entering the following command in the terminal:

```
pip install pandas==2.2
```

Finally, for the last section in this chapter, you will need the clustering algorithms from the `scikit-learn` library. Run the following command in the terminal to install the appropriate version:

```
pip install scikit-learn==1.3
```

The following sections contain code for three mini-projects that use language models for text analysis. No need to type in the code—you can find all the code on the book's companion website in the resource section for this chapter. Although you can execute the code on your own data, this book comes with a couple of sample data sets we use in the examples (also on the companion website). And now it's time to use language models for text classification!

4.2 Classification

So here you are, planning your Saturday evening and deliberating whether to go and see the newest installation of your favorite movie franchise. But is it worth it? Your social media feeds keep filling up with comments from your friends (and your friend's friends), expanding on their movie experiences. You could browse through them manually, reading each one to get a better sense of whether the majority opinion about the movie is positive or negative. But who has time to do that? Can't language models help us to automate this task?

Indeed they can. What we have here is an instance of one of the most classic text-processing problems: we have a text and want to classify it, mapping it to one of a fixed set of categories. In this case, the text to classify is a movie review. We want to classify it as positive (i.e., the writer thinks it was a great movie, and you should go see it!) or negative (save your money!). That means we have two categories. Table 4.1 shows extracts from a few example reviews with the associated class labels. A review praising a movie as "well realized" is clearly positive, whereas one describing the movie as "obviously weak, cheap" is negative. You can find these and a few other reviews in a corresponding file on the book's companion website.

Table 4.1   **Extracts from movie reviews and associated class labels**

Review	Class
First of all this movie is a piece of reality very well realized artistically. ...	Positive
Re-titled "Gangs, Inc.", this is an obviously weak, cheap mobster melodrama. ...	Negative

Classifying movie reviews is only one of many use cases for text classification. As another example, imagine trying to sort through your email inbox. Wouldn't it be nice to automatically classify emails based on their content (e.g., using custom categories such as Work, Hobby, Childcare, etc.)? That's yet another instance of text classification, this time with more than two categories. As a final example, imagine that you're creating a website that enables users to leave free-text comments. Of course, you don't want to show potentially offensive comments and would like to filter them out automatically. Again, that means you're classifying text comments into one of two categories (Offensive and Inoffensive). We will now see how language models can easily be used for each scenario.

4.2.1   *Overview*

We'll focus on classifying movie reviews (or, really, any type of review) into Positive (great movie!) and Negative (stay home!) reviews. For that, we'll use OpenAI's language models. We'll assume that we have collected reviews to classify in a file on disk. The code we develop will iterate over all reviews, classify each using the language model, and return the classification result for each review.

But how can we classify reviews? We will use OpenAI's Python library, presented in chapter 3. For each review to classify, we will first generate a prompt. The prompt describes a task to a language model. In our case, that task assigns a review to one of our two categories (Positive or Negative). For instance, consider the following prompt as an example:

```
This movie is a piece of reality very well realized ...    ❶ Review
Is the sentiment positive or negative?                     ❷ Question
Answer ("Positive"/"Negative"):    ❸ Output format
```

This prompt contains the review to classify (❶), a question describing the classification task (❷), and a final statement describing the desired output format (❸). We will construct prompts of this type for each review, send the prompt to the language model, and (hopefully) get back one of the two possible answers (Positive or Negative). Figure 4.1 illustrates the high-level classification process for each review.

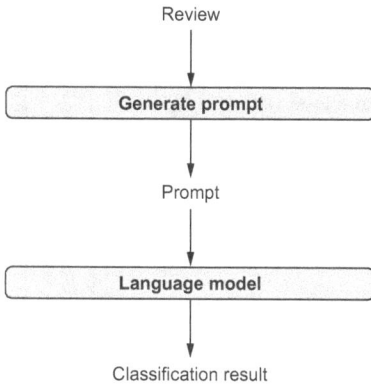

Review

Generate prompt

Prompt

Language model

Classification result

Figure 4.1 **For each review, we generate a prompt that contains the review, together with instructions describing the classification task. Given the prompt as input, the language model outputs a class label for the review.**

4.2.2 Creating prompts

Given a review, we generate a prompt instructing the language model to classify it. All the prompts we generate for classification follow the same prompt template.

Reminder: What is a prompt template?

We briefly mentioned prompt templates in chapter 1. A prompt template is a text that contains placeholders. By substituting actual text for these placeholders, we obtain a prompt that we can send to the language model. We also say that a prompt *instantiates* a prompt template if the prompt can be obtained by substituting the template's placeholders.

The example prompt from the previous section instantiates the following prompt template:

```
[Review]                                  ❶  Review (placeholder)
Is the sentiment positive or negative?    ❷  Question
Answer ("Positive"/"Negative"):           ❸  Output format
```

Our template contains only a single placeholder: the text of the review to classify (❶). For each review, we will replace this placeholder with the actual review text. We also instruct the language model on what to do with the review text (❷) (check whether the underlying sentiment is positive or negative) and define the output format (❸). The latter step is important because there may be many ways to express the underlying sentiment: for example, "P" for positive and "N" for negative, or a longer answer such as "The review is positive." If we don't explicitly tell the language model to use a specific output format, it may choose any of these possibilities! In our scenario, we ultimately want to aggregate the classification results to learn the majority opinion (do most people like the movie or not?), and aggregating the results from each review becomes much simpler if all the classifications follow the same output format.

The following function follows the template to generate a prompt for a given review (specified as the input parameter `text`):

```
def create_prompt(text):
    task = 'Is the sentiment positive or negative?'
    answer_format = 'Answer ("Positive"/"Negative")'
    return f'{text}\n{task}\n{answer_format}:'
```

The result of the function is the prompt, instantiating the template for the input review.

4.2.3 Calling the model

Next, we send generated prompts to a language model to obtain a solution. More precisely, we are using OpenAI's GPT-4o model, OpenAI's latest model at the time of writing. As this is one of OpenAI's chat models, optimized for multistep interactions with users, we use the chat completions endpoint to communicate with the model. As discussed in more detail in chapter 3, this endpoint expects as input a history of prior messages (in addition to the specific model name). Here, we have only one prior "message": the prompt. We classify it as a `user` message, encouraging the model to solve whatever task is described in the message. For instance, we can send prompts to the language model and collect the answers using the following piece of code (assuming that `prompt` contains the previously generated prompt text):

```
import openai
client = openai.OpenAI()

response = client.chat.completions.create(
    model='gpt-4o',
    messages=[
        {'role':'user', 'content':prompt}
        ]
    )
```

However, using this code directly is problematic. OpenAI's GPT models are hosted online and accessed remotely. This creates opportunities for failed attempts to reach the corresponding endpoint: for example, due to a temporary connection loss. Because of that, it is good practice to allow for a couple of retries when calling the model. In particular, when processing large data sets requiring many consecutive calls to OpenAI's models, the chances of at least one unsuccessful call increase. Instead of interrupting computation with an exception, it is better to wait a few seconds before starting another try. Here is a completed version of the previous code—a function that calls the language model with automated retries:

```
import openai
client = openai.OpenAI()

def call_llm(prompt):
    for nr_retries in range(1, 4):
        try:
            response = client.chat.completions.create(
                model='gpt-4o',
                messages=[
                    {'role':'user', 'content':prompt}
                    ]
                )
            return response.choices[0].message.content
        except:
            time.sleep(nr_retries * 2)
    raise Exception('Cannot query OpenAI model!')
```

The `call_lm` function allows up to three retries with an increasing delay between them. This delay is realized by a call to the `time.sleep` function (using Python's `time` library) whenever an exception (indicating, for instance, a temporary connection loss) is encountered. After three retries, the function fails with an exception (assuming, pessimistically, that whatever problem prevents us from contacting OpenAI will not be resolved any time soon). Whenever the call succeeds, the function returns the corresponding result.

4.2.4 *End-to-end classification code*

It's time to put it all together! The next listing shows the code that matches the classification process we've discussed. It also contains the function for generating prompts (❷) and the one for calling the language model (❸).

Listing 4.1 **Classifying input text by sentiment (positive, negative)**

```
import argparse        ❶ Imports libraries
import openai
import pandas as pd
import time

client = openai.OpenAI()

def create_prompt(text):        ❷ Generates classification prompts
    """ Generates prompt for sentiment classification.

    Args:
        text: classify this text.

    Returns:
        input for LLM.
    """
    task = 'Is the sentiment positive or negative?'
    answer_format = 'Answer ("Positive"/"Negative")'
```

```
        return f'{text}\n{task}\n{answer_format}:'

def call_llm(prompt):                            ❸ Calls the large language model
    """ Query large language model and return answer.

    Args:
        prompt: input prompt for language model.

    Returns:
        Answer by language model.
    """
    for nr_retries in range(1, 4):
        try:
            response = client.chat.completions.create(
                model='gpt-4o',
                messages=[
                    {'role':'user', 'content':prompt}
                ]
            )
            return response.choices[0].message.content
        except:
            time.sleep(nr_retries * 2)
    raise Exception('Cannot query OpenAI model!')

def classify(text):                 ❹ Classifies one text document
    """ Classify input text.

    Args:
        text: assign this text to a class label.

    Returns:
        name of class.
    """
    prompt = create_prompt(text)
    label = call_llm(prompt)
    return label

if __name__ == '__main__':       ❺ Reads text, classifies, and writes result

    parser = argparse.ArgumentParser()            ❻ Defines command-line arguments
    parser.add_argument('file_path', type=str, help='Path to input file')
    args = parser.parse_args()

    df = pd.read_csv(args.file_path)         ❼ Reads input
    df['class'] = df['text'].apply(classify)     ❽ Classifies text
    statistics = df['class'].value_counts()      ❾ Generates output
    print(statistics)
    df.to_csv('result.csv')
```

First, let's discuss the libraries used in listing 4.1 (❶). We will reuse those libraries for the following projects, so it makes sense to have a closer look at them (and why we need them here). We want to start our code from the command line, specifying relevant parameters (e.g., the path of the input data) as arguments. The `argparse` library features useful functions to specify and read out such command-line arguments. Next, we need the `openai` library, discussed in chapter 3, to call OpenAI's language model from Python. The `pandas` library supports standard operations on tabular data. Of course, tabular data is not our focus in this chapter. However, we will store text documents and related metadata as rows in tables, so the `pandas` library comes in handy. Finally, as discussed previously, we use the `time` library to implement delayed retries when calling the language model.

4.2.5 Classifying documents

The classification of a single text document (❹) combines the two functions discussed previously. Given an input text to classify, the code first creates a corresponding prompt (call to `create_prompt`) and then generates a suitable reply via a call to the language model (call to `call_llm`). The result is assumed to be the class label and is returned to the user.

Now we put it together (❺). This part of the code is executed when invoking the Python module from the command line and uses the functions we've introduced. The initial `if` condition (❺) ensures that the following code is only executed when invoking the module directly (instead of importing it from a different module).

First (❻), we define command-line arguments. We need only one argument here: a path to a .csv file containing the data to classify. We assume that each row contains one text document and that the text to classify is contained in the `text` column. We parse command-line arguments and make their values available in the `args` variable.

Next, we load our input data from disk (❼). We assume that data is stored as a .csv file (comma-separated value): that is, a header line with column names, followed by lines containing data (fields are separated by commas, as the name suggests). Here, the `pandas` library comes in handy and enables us to load such data with a single command. The `df` variable then contains a `pandas` DataFrame containing data from the input file. We retrieve the DataFrame `text` column (❽) and apply the previously defined `classify` function to each row (using `pandas`' `apply` method). Finally (❾), we generate and print out aggregate statistics (the number of occurrences for each answer generated by the model) and write the resulting classifications into a file (result.csv).

4.2.6 Running the code

On the book's companion website, download the file reviews.csv. This file contains a small number of movie reviews that we can use for classification. The file contains two columns: the review text and the associated sentiment (`neg` for negative sentiment and `pos` for positive sentiment). Of course, our goal is to detect such sentiments automatically. However, having the ground truth also enables us to assess the quality of the classifications.

You can test the code for classification as described next (the following commands have been tested on a Linux operating system). Using a terminal, change to the directory containing a Python module (listing1.py) with the code in listing 4.1. Then, run the following command (replacing `python` with the name of your Python interpreter, such as `python3`, if needed):

```
python listing1.py reviews.csv
```

Here, we assume that the input file (reviews.csv) is stored in the same repository as the code (otherwise, you have to substitute the corresponding path for the filename). Typically, the code should not take more than a few seconds to execute (slightly more if your connection is unstable, requiring retries). If execution succeeds, the only output you will see summarizes the number of labels assigned for each of the two possible classes.

After executing the code, you will find a result.csv file in the same repository. In addition to the columns of the input file, the result file contains a new `class` column. This column contains the classification results (positive and negative). Compare the label assigned by our classifier to the ground-truth sentiment. You will find that the classification is consistent in a majority of cases. Not bad for a few lines of Python code, right?

4.2.7 *Trying out variants*

At this point, it is a good idea to play a bit more with the code and the data to get a better sense of how it works. For instance, try writing a few movie reviews yourself! For which reviews is the classification reliable, and where is it challenging? Also try a few variants of the prompt. Which instructions lead to better accuracy, and which degrade performance? To take just one example variation, try removing the part of the prompt that defines the output format precisely (the line `Answer ("Positive"/"Negative")`). Now try running the program with the changed prompt. What happens? In all likelihood, you will see more than two labels in your classification result (in the output of the program), including, for instance, abbreviations (e.g., "P" and "N") as well as overly detailed answers (e.g., during testing, GPT-4o generated replies such as "The sentiment of this review is positive."). In chapter 9, we evaluate the effect of different prompts on the model's output quality.

You may also want to vary the model used for extraction. How about using one of the smaller model versions, such as GPT-3.5 (which is significantly cheaper per token processed)? And how about the model configuration? Listing 4.1 only uses two parameters (the model name and the message history), both of which are required. However, in chapter 3, we saw various configuration parameters that can be applied here. For instance, try changing the `temperature` parameter (e.g., setting `temperature` to 0 will give you more deterministic results), or limit the length of the desired output! In rare cases, GPT models may generate output text that is longer than the desired classification result (which consists of a single token). You can avoid that by limiting the output length using the `max_tokens` parameter. At the same time, instead of restricting the output format only via instructions in the prompt, you may increase the likelihood of the two possible results (positive and negative) using the `logit_bias` parameter. We discuss model tuning further in chapter 9.

As yet another variant, try changing the classification task! For instance, it is relatively easy to classify using a different set of categories. All it takes is changing the instructions in the prompt (outlining all answer options as before). By changing a few lines of code, you can even obtain a versatile classification tool that enables users to specify the classification task and corresponding classes as additional command-line arguments. For example, beyond movie reviews, you can use this tool to categorize newspaper articles into one of several topic categories or to classify emails as either Urgent or Nonurgent. By now, you are hopefully convinced that language models enable text classification with relatively high quality and moderate implementation overheads. Time to broaden our scope to different tasks!

4.3 Text extraction

Imagine that, given your expertise in data analysis with language models, you recently landed a highly sought-after job at Banana (a popular company producing various consumer electronics). The moment you sit down at the desk of your new office, emails from enthusiastic students inquiring about summer internships start rolling in. Having a summer intern would be nice, but how do you choose the best match? Ideally, you would like to compile a table comparing all applicants in terms of their GPA, their degree, the name of the company at which they did their most recent internship (if any), and so on. But combing through emails to compile that table manually seems tedious. Can't you automate that?

Of course you can. Let's use language models to analyze emails to extract all the relevant factors to choose our lucky summer intern. What we have here is, again, a standard problem in text analysis: information extraction! In information extraction, we generally extract structured information (e.g., a data table) from text. Here, we consider emails (from applicants) as text documents. For each email, we want to extract a range of attributes: for example, name, GPA, and (current or most recent) degree. For instance, consider the following extract from an email from one of the hopeful applicants:

```
Hi!
My name is Martin, I would love to do a summer internship at Banana!
A bit about myself: I am currently working on a Bachelor of Computer Science
at Stanford University, my current GPA is 4.0.
```

Considering the three previously mentioned attributes, we can extract the name of the applicant ("Martin"), his GPA ("4.0"), and his degree ("Bachelor of Computer Science"). If analyzing emails from multiple applicants, we can represent the result as a data table, as shown in table 4.2. In the next section, we discuss how we can accomplish information extraction using language models.

Table 4.2   Extracted information about applicants for summer internships

Name	GPA	Degree
Martin	4.0	Bachelor of Computer Science
Alice	4.0	Master of Software Engineering
Bob	3.7	Bachelor of Design

4.3.1 Overview

Again, we'll assume that our emails are stored on disk (in a tabular data file where each row contains one email). We'll iterate over emails and use the language model to extract all relevant attributes. Instead of hard-coding relevant attributes, we will allow users to specify those attributes on the command line (that way, you can easily reuse the code if your criteria for summer internships should change). As we use language models for text analysis (which are good at interpreting natural language), there is no need to specify attributes in any kind of formal language. Simply specify the attribute names (or, optionally, a short description in natural language), and the language model should be able to figure out what to extract. The output of our code will be a tabular data file (in .csv format) that contains content similar to table 4.2: the output table has one column for each extracted attribute and one row for each analyzed email.

So how can we extract attributes from a given email? Again, we want to generate a prompt that describes the extraction task to the language model. For instance, the following prompt should help us extract all relevant attributes from the previous email:

❶ Task description
```
Extract the following properties into a table:
name,GPA,Degree
```

❷ Text to analyze
```
Text source: My name is Martin, I would love to do a summer
internship at Banana! A bit about myself: I am currently
working on a Bachelor of Computer Science at Stanford
University, my current GPA is 4.0.
```

❸ Output format
```
Mark the beginning of the table with <BeginTable> and the end with
<EndTable>. Separate rows by newline symbols and separate fields by pipe
symbols (|). Omit the table header and insert values in the attribute
order from above. Use the placeholder <NA> if the value for an attribute
is not available.
```

The prompt consists of three parts: a task description, including a specification of the attributes to extract (❶); the source text for extraction (❷); and the desired output format, including values to use if the source text does not contain any information on specific attributes (❸). Sending this prompt to the language model should yield text that contains the desired extraction results.

The output from the language model is, first, a text string. Ultimately, we want to output a structured data table. That means we still need some postprocessing to extract values for all relevant attributes (name, GPA, and degree) from the output text. Figure 4.2 illustrates the steps of the extraction process (for a single text document).

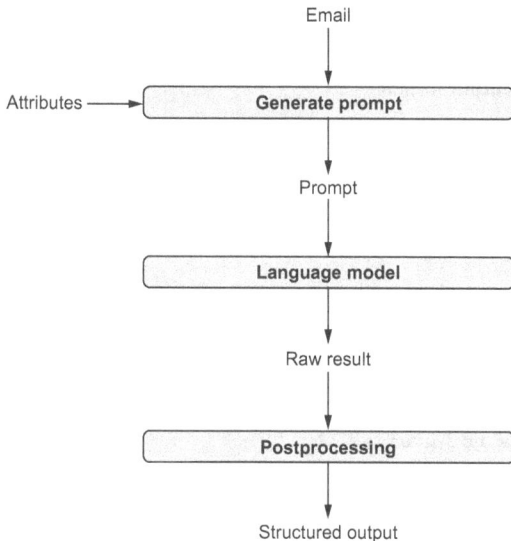

Figure 4.2 **For each email, we generate a prompt that contains the email and a description of the extraction task. This description references the attributes to extract specified by the user. Given the prompt as input, the language model generates an answer text containing extracted attribute values. Via postprocessing, we extract those values from the raw answer text.**

4.3.2 Generating prompts

We want to generate prompts that instantiate the following prompt template:

❶ Task description
```
Extract the following properties into a table:
[List of attributes]
```

❷ Text to analyze
```
Text source: [Email]
```

❸ Output format
```
Mark the beginning of the table with <BeginTable> and the end with <EndTable>.
Separate rows by newline symbols and separate fields by pipe symbols (|).
Omit the table header and insert values in the attribute order from above.
Use the placeholder <NA> if the value for an attribute is not available.
```

The prompt template contains a task description (❶), the source text for extraction (❷), and a specification of the output format (❸). Note that this prompt now contains two placeholders (the template we used in the previous section contained only a single placeholder): the list of attributes to extract and the source text for extraction.

We will generate prompts using the following code:

```
def create_prompt(text, attributes):
    parts = []
```

❶ Generates a task description
```
    parts += ['Extract the following properties into a table:']
    parts += [','.join(attributes)]

    parts += [f'Text source: {text}']       ❷ Adds source text
```
❸ Adds a description of the output format
```
    parts += [
        ('Mark the beginning of the table with <BeginTable> '
        'and the end with <EndTable>.')]
    parts += [
        ('Separate rows by newline symbols and separate '
        'fields by pipe symbols (|).')]
    parts += [
        ('Omit the table header and insert values in '
        'the attribute order from above.')]
    parts += [
        ('Use the placeholder <NA> if the value '
        'for an attribute is not available.')]
    return '\n'.join(parts)
```

This function takes as input the text to analyze (which we certainly want to include in the prompt) along with a list of attributes we want to extract. After generating the task description (❶), including the list of attributes to extract, the function adds the source text (❷), as well as a specification of the desired output format (❸). The prompt concatenates these parts.

4.3.3   Postprocessing

Compared to the previous project (text classification), our prompt has changed to adapt to the new task (text extraction). Even with a different prompt, we can still reuse the same function as in the last section to obtain an answer from the language model. On the other hand, we need to do a little more work than before to process the raw answer using the language model. For classification, we directly used the reply from the language model as the final result. In our current scenario (text extraction), we generally will want to extract values for multiple attributes for a single input text. As the output text from the language model contains values for all extracted attributes, we need to extract values for specific attributes from the raw answer text.

For instance, we might receive the following raw answer text from the language model:

```
| Martin | 4.0 | Bachelor of Computer Science |
```

To extract values for each attribute, we can split the raw text using pipe symbols as field delimiters (while removing the first and last pipe symbols in the answer). Ideally, we want to expand our scope beyond the specific use case we are currently considering (extracting information on applicants from emails). In some scenarios, we may extract multiple rows from the same text (imagine a scenario where multiple applicants together submit a group email—but that's admittedly a less likely case). To support such use cases, we may also have to split the raw answer into text associated with different rows. To do that, we can use the newline symbol as row delimiters (as rows are split by newline symbols).

We can do all these things with the following function:

```
import re

def post_process(raw_answer):
    table_text = re.findall(            ❶ Extracts table data
        '<BeginTable>(.*)<EndTable>',
        raw_answer, re.DOTALL)[0]

    results = []
    for raw_row in table_text.split('\n'):    ❷ Splits by row
        if raw_row:                      ❸ Splits by field
            row = raw_row.split('|')
            row = [field.strip() for field in row]
            row = [field for field in row if field]
            results.append(row)
    return results
```

The input to this function is raw text produced by the language model for a single text document. The output is a list of rows (where each result row is, again, represented as a list). To get from input to output, we first need to extract the part of the raw answer that contains the actual table data (❶). Answers generated by GPT-4o may contain a preamble or additional explanations beyond the extracted table (e.g., "Sure, here is the table you wanted: ..."). We need to separate the data we are interested in. Fortunately, that's easy as long as GPT-4o is following our instructions (which, typically, it does): the data we're interested in should be contained between two markers (`<BeginTable>` and `<EndTable>`). Hence, the regular expression `'<BeginTable>(.*)<EndTable>'` exactly matches the part of the output we're interested in. We retrieve it using Python's `re.findall` function, which, given a string and regular expression as input, returns a list of matching substrings. We use the `re.DOTALL` flag to ensure that the dot within the regular expression matches all characters and newlines (because the table may contain multiple lines). From the resulting matches, we take the first one. Note that this implicitly assumes at least one table in GPT's output. Although that is typically the case, think about how to make the function more robust toward answers from the language model that do not comply with our instructions in the prompt.

Having extracted the table data in a text representation, we first split it into data associated with specific rows (❷) and data associated with specific cells (❸). After some cleanup (the Python function `strip` removes whitespace), we add the resulting cell values to our result list. This list of rows (where each row is, again, represented as a list) is returned.

4.3.4 *End-to-end extraction code*

Listing 4.2 shows the completed Python code. The code structure is similar to listing 4.1, and some of the functions are shared among the two listings (rather than omitting repeated functions, this book aims to provide you with self-contained code so you don't have to piece together code from multiple pages). In particular, the code uses the same libraries as before (**❶**) and invokes the language model via the same function (**❸**). You will recognize the function for creating prompts (**❷**) and the one for postprocessing raw output from the language model (**❹**), introduced earlier.

Listing 4.2   Extracting user-defined attributes from text

```
import argparse       ❶ Imports relevant libraries
import openai
import pandas as pd
import re
import time

client = openai.OpenAI()


def create_prompt(text, attributes):          ❷ Generates prompts
    """ Generates prompt for information extraction.

    Args:
        text: extract information from this text.
        attributes: list of attributes.

    Returns:
        input for LLM.
    """
    parts = []
    parts += ['Extract the following properties into a table:']
    parts += [','.join(attributes)]
    parts += [f'Text source: {text}']
    parts += [
        ('Mark the beginning of the table with <BeginTable> '
        'and the end with <EndTable>.')]
    parts += [
        ('Separate rows by newline symbols and separate '
        'fields by pipe symbols (|).')]
    parts += [
        ('Omit the table header and insert values in '
        'the attribute order from above.')]
    parts += [
        ('Use the placeholder <NA> if the value '
        'for an attribute is not available.')]
    return '\n'.join(parts)


def call_llm(prompt):                          ❸ Invokes the language model
```

```
    """ Query large language model and return answer.

    Args:
        prompt: input prompt for language model.

    Returns:
        Answer by language model.
    """
    for nr_retries in range(1, 4):
        try:
            response = client.chat.completions.create(
                model='gpt-4o',
                messages=[
                    {'role':'user', 'content':prompt}
                ]
            )
            return response.choices[0].message.content
        except:
            time.sleep(nr_retries * 2)
    raise Exception('Cannot query OpenAI model!')


def post_process(raw_answer):                    ❹ Postprocesses model output
    """ Extract fields from raw text answer.

    Args:
        raw_answer: raw text generated by LLM.

    Returns:
        list of result rows.
    """
    table_text = re.findall(
        '<BeginTable>(.*)<EndTable>',
        raw_answer, re.DOTALL)[0]

    results = []
    for raw_row in table_text.split('\n'):
        if raw_row:
            row = raw_row.split('|')
            row = [field.strip() for field in row]
            row = [field for field in row if field]
            results.append(row)
    return results


def extract_rows(text, attributes):              ❺ Extracts data tables from text
    """ Extract values for attributes from text.

    Args:
        text: extract information from this text.
        attributes: list of attributes to extract.

    Returns:
        list of rows with attribute values.
    """
```

```
    prompt = create_prompt(text, attributes)
    result_text = call_llm(prompt)
    result_rows = post_process(result_text)
    return result_rows

if __name__ == '__main__':
    parser = argparse.ArgumentParser()
    parser.add_argument('file_path', type=str, help='Path to input file')
    parser.add_argument('attributes', type=str, help='Attribute list')
    args = parser.parse_args()

    input_df = pd.read_csv(args.file_path)
    attributes = args.attributes.split('|')

    extractions = []
    for text in input_df['text'].values:
        extractions += extract_rows(text, attributes)

    result_df = pd.DataFrame(extractions)
    result_df.columns = attributes
    result_df.to_csv('result.csv')
```

❻ **Extracts information and writes the result**

❼ **Iterates over text**

The main function (❻) reads two input parameters from the command line:

- A path to a .csv file containing the text to analyze
- A list of attributes to extract, separated by pipe symbols

After opening the input file (using the `pandas` library), we iterate over all input text documents (❼). Note that we expect the input text in the `text` column in the input file. To perform the actual extraction, we use the `extract_rows` function (❺). Given input text and a list of attributes to extract, this function generates a suitable prompt, obtains a raw answer from the language model, and postprocesses the raw answer to get structured output (which it returns). After iterating over the input text (❼), we store the final result in a file named result.csv (this file will be overwritten if it already exists).

4.3.5 *Trying it out*

You can find the code from listing 4.2 as listing2.py on the companion website. You can also download the file biographies.csv there, giving you a small data set to experiment on with your extractor (this is a bit different from our motivating scenario, but publicly available data on email applications is sparse). This file contains biographies of five famous people, as well as the associated names, with one person per row. Change into the directory containing listing2.py (as well as the data), and run

```
python listing2.py biographies.csv
   "name|city of birth|date of birth"
```

The first parameter is the data set (if it is not in the same directory, adapt the path accordingly). The second parameter is the list of attributes to extract. We use the pipe symbol again to separate attributes. Note that we only identify attributes via their names; no need to refer to predefined categories. The language model can understand attribute semantics based on the name alone.

After executing the code (which should not take more than a minute), you will find the results stored in a file named result.csv. For example, executing the code on the sample data could yield the following table:

```
    name       city of birth     date of birth
0   Sergey Mikhailovich Brin    Moscow      August 21, 1973
1   Martin Luther King Jr.    Atlanta, Georgia     January 15, 1929
2   Anne E. Wojcicki    <NA>     July 28, 1973
3   Maria Salomea Skłodowska-Curie    Warsaw     7 November 1867
4   Alan Mathison Turing    Maida Vale, London     23 June 1912
```

Even if you execute the same code on the same data, you may see slight variations (due to randomization when generating model output). Each row in that file (besides the header row) represents an extraction. We are extracting name, birth city, and birth date. Hence, we expect one extracted row per biography (and that is what happens in our sample run). Note that there are missing values: for Ann E. Wojcicki, the biography snippet does not contain the city of birth. The language model reacts appropriately and inserts a corresponding placeholder ("<N/A>"), instead of a concrete value.

4.4 Clustering

You're a few weeks in at your new job at Banana. The job is great, but there is one problem: your inbox keeps overflowing with emails! It's not only applications from hopeful summer interns (we took care of that in the last section). Those emails cover a variety of different topics, and making sure to read all relevant emails takes a lot of your time. Looking closer, you notice that many of the emails are redundant. For example, you observe that many emails try to draw attention to the same company events. For a moment, you ponder using your code for text classification (discussed in section 4.2) to categorize emails into several categories (e.g., associated with specific company events). After that, you can read only a few emails from each category to have a full overview of what's happening at Banana. Alas, there is one problem: it is hard to come up with and maintain an exhaustive list of topics because those topics will keep changing over the course of your employment. Instead, it would be nice to automatically group different emails that are somewhat similar because, for instance, they discuss the same event. That way, you wouldn't have to come up with a list of topics in advance.

What we want is to group similar emails into clusters. That's yet another classical text-processing problem: text clustering. If you want to bring related text documents together without knowing the set of categories beforehand, clustering methods are probably the way to go! In this section, we will see how to use language models for text clustering.

4.4.1   *Overview*

Clustering is a classical approach in computer science. Clustering methods predate language models and advanced text analysis by quite a bit. However, traditionally, clustering focuses on elements that are expressed as vectors. We want to bring together (in the same cluster) vectors that have a small distance from each other (and, of course, there are various distance metrics that we can apply for vectors). However, that's not really the case here: in our scenario, we want to assign similar emails (or, in general, similar text documents) to the same cluster. So how do we get from documents to vectors?

The answer is *embeddings*. An embedding represents a text document as a (typically high-dimensional) vector. That's exactly what we're looking for! Of course, this approach only makes sense if we map text documents to vectors that have something meaningful to say about the content of the documents. Ideally, we want documents with similar vectors (i.e., vectors with a small distance according to our preferred distance metric) to also have similar content. This means we cannot use naive methods to map text documents to vectors. Instead, we need an approach that considers the semantics of the text and takes them into account when generating a vector representation.

Fortunately, language models can help! Providers like OpenAI offer language models that take text as input and produce embedding vectors as output. So, having a collection of text documents to cluster, we can calculate embedding vectors for all of them and apply any classical clustering algorithm to the resulting vectors. Figure 4.3 illustrates this process. Next, we discuss how to implement it.

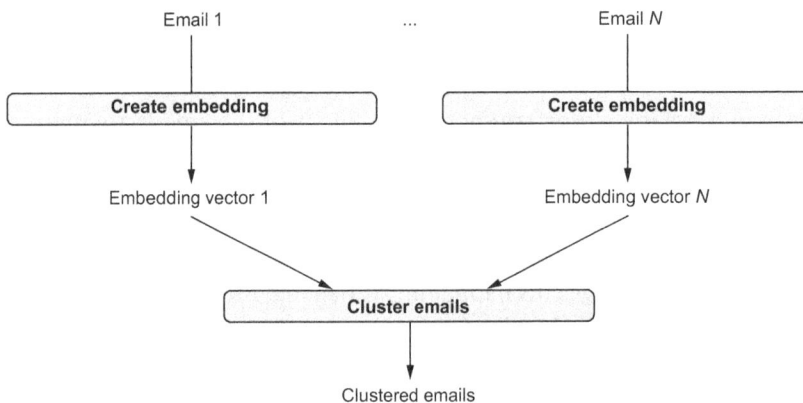

Figure 4.3   **Clustering emails. We first calculate embedding vectors for all emails. Then we cluster those vectors to assign emails with similar content to the same cluster.**

4.4.2   *Calculating embeddings*

For the examples discussed so far, we have used OpenAI's chat completions endpoint. For clustering, we will use OpenAI's embedding endpoint instead. The goal of embedding is to create a vector that compresses the semantics of a text. Different models can be used to calculate embeddings. The dimension of the vector depends on the model used. For the following code, we will use the `text-embedding-ada-002` model. You can try substituting other models for this one (you can find a list of OpenAI models for calculating embeddings at https://platform.openai.com/docs/guides/embeddings) to compare the output quality.

For instance, we can generate embeddings for text documents as follows:

```
import openai
client = openai.OpenAI()

response = client.embeddings.create(
    model='text-embedding-ada-002',
    input=text)
```

Here you see an extract from the corresponding response:

```
CreateEmbeddingResponse(
    data=[
        Embedding(embedding=[                    ❶ Embedding vector
            -0.005983137525618076, -0.000303583248751238, ...],
            index=0, object='embedding')],
    model='text-embedding-ada-002',    ❷ Model that generated embeddings
    object='list',
    usage=Usage(prompt_tokens=517, total_tokens=517))   ❸ Usage statistics
```

The extract only shows values for the first few vector dimensions (❶) (whereas the full vector has over 1,000 dimensions). Besides the embedding vector, the response contains the model name (❷) and usage statistics (❸). Unlike earlier, usage statistics only refer to the number of tokens in the prompt (which is also the total number of tokens processed). Unlike text completion, the language model only reads tokens but does not generate them.

The most relevant part for us is, of course, the embedding vector itself. You can access that embedding vector via the following command:

```
response.data[0].embedding
```

Most of the time, invoking the language model once should provide you with the embedding you are searching for. Of course, when calculating embedding vectors for a large number of emails, we may run into problems (i.e., failed connection attempts) every once in a while. This is why the final version of our embedding function again contains a retry mechanism:

```
import openai
client = openai.OpenAI()

def get_embedding(text):
    for nr_retries in range(1, 4):
        try:
            response = client.embeddings.create(
                model='text-embedding-ada-002',
                input=text)
            return response.data[0].embedding
```

```
        except:
            time.sleep(nr_retries * 2)
    raise Exception('Cannot query OpenAI model!')
```

Given a text as input, we try up to three times to get a corresponding embedding vector (increasing the delay between retries after each failed attempt). This is the function we will use.

4.4.3   *Clustering vectors*

To cluster vectors (representing documents), we will use the k-means clustering algorithm. K-means is a very popular clustering algorithm that works by iteratively refining the mapping from vectors to clusters. Unlike other clustering algorithms, the algorithm requires you to specify the number of clusters in advance. In our example scenario, that means choosing how fine-grained the partitioning of emails by their content should be.

How does the k-means algorithm work?

The k-means algorithm takes as input a set of elements to cluster and a target number of clusters. It works by iteratively refining the mapping from elements to clusters until a termination criterion (e.g., a maximum number of iterations or minimal changes in cluster assignments between consecutive iterations) is met. The k-means algorithm associates each cluster with a vector (representing the center of that cluster). In each iteration, it assigns each vector to the cluster with the nearest center. Then, it recalculates the vectors associated with clusters (by averaging over the vectors of all elements currently assigned to the cluster).

We will be using the k-means implementation in the `scikit-learn` library. Follow the instructions in the first section of this chapter to ensure that this library is installed (import clustering methods via `from sklearn.cluster import KMeans`). After importing the library, we can invoke the k-means implementation with the following (concise) piece of code:

```
def get_kmeans(embeddings, k):
    kmeans = KMeans(n_clusters=k, init='k-means++')
    kmeans.fit(embeddings)
    return kmeans.labels_
```

The function takes a list of embedding vectors and the number of target clusters as input and then clusters those vectors using the k-means implementation. The result of clustering is labels associated with each embedding vector. Those labels indicate the ID of the associated cluster.

4.4.4   *End-to-end code for text clustering*

The following listing shows the complete code for clustering text documents via embedding vectors. You will recognize the functions for calculating embedding vectors (❶) and clustering them (❷).

Listing 4.3   Clustering text documents using language models

```
import argparse
import openai
import pandas as pd
import time

from sklearn.cluster import KMeans

client = openai.OpenAI()

def get_embedding(text):                              ❶ Calculates embedding vectors
    """ Calculate embedding vector for input text.

    Args:
        text: calculate embedding for this text.

    Returns:
        Vector representation of input text.
    """
    for nr_retries in range(1, 4):
        try:
            response = client.embeddings.create(
                model='text-embedding-ada-002',
                input=text)
            return response.data[0].embedding
        except:
            time.sleep(nr_retries * 2)
    raise Exception('Cannot query OpenAI model!')

def get_kmeans(embeddings, k):                        ❷ Clusters embeddings
    """ Cluster embedding vectors using K-means.

    Args:
        embeddings: embedding vectors.
        k: number of result clusters.

    Returns:
        cluster IDs in embedding order.
    """
    kmeans = KMeans(n_clusters=k, init='k-means++')
    kmeans.fit(embeddings)
    return kmeans.labels_

if __name__ == '__main__':                            ❸ Reads text and writes out clusters
    parser = argparse.ArgumentParser()
    parser.add_argument('file_path', type=str, help='Path to input file')
    parser.add_argument('nr_clusters', type=int, help='Number of clusters')
    args = parser.parse_args()

    df = pd.read_csv(args.file_path)

    embeddings = df['text'].apply(get_embedding)
    df['clusterid'] = get_kmeans(list(embeddings), args.nr_clusters)

    df.to_csv('result.csv')
```

The main function of listing 4.3 (❸) reads data from a file on disk. Again, we assume that data is contained in a .csv file and focus on the text column. First, we iterate over text documents and generate corresponding embeddings (by invoking the get_embedding function, discussed previously). Then, we cluster embedding vectors via the get_kmeans function. The cluster IDs become an additional column in the result table written to disk.

4.4.5 *Trying it out*

Time to try clustering via embedding vectors! You can find the code from listing 4.3 on the book's companion website (listing3.py), as well as a suitable data set (textmix.csv). This data set contains a mix of text snippets from two sources: a collection of poems and a repository of emails. We'll try to separate the two via clustering: we expect emails and poems to be assigned to different clusters.

Change into the directory containing the code and data, and run the following command in the terminal:

```
python listing3.py textmix.csv 2
```

Here, textmix.csv is the name of the input file, and 2 is the number of target clusters (in this specific case, two seems like a reasonable choice, whereas determining the right number of clusters can be more difficult in other scenarios). The result will be stored in the file result.csv. It contains all the columns from the input file, as well as an additional column with the cluster ID (because we only use two clusters, this ID is either 0 or 1). Running the command, you will likely see a result that places emails in one cluster while putting poems in the other.

You may want to try different models to see differences in run time and result quality. You can also try different input text and vary the number of clusters. Besides that, you may want to implement some of the other use cases for embedding vectors, which are mentioned at the beginning of this section. For instance, how about implementing a retrieval interface that maps a natural language statement to the most closely related document (by comparing the embedding vectors of questions and documents)?

4.4.6 *Other use cases for embedding vectors*

So far, we have used vectors to identify similar documents via clustering. But this is not the only use case for embedding vectors! To name just a few examples, embedding vectors are often used to facilitate the retrieval of text documents related to a natural language question. Here, we compare an embedding vector associated with the question to embedding vectors associated with documents. Documents with similar vectors are more likely to be useful in answering the question.

For instance, we hope that the embedding vectors for the question "What is a Transformer model?" and the text "The Transformer is a neural network architecture, often used for language models" are similar due to related topics. If so, we can identify the document most relevant to the question by comparing embedding vectors. More precisely, we calculate embedding vectors once for each document that may be useful to answer questions. Then, whenever a new question is received, we calculate the associated embedding vector and retrieve documents with similar embedding vectors. We can then generate an answer based on those documents.

Another use case for embedding vectors is outlier detection. To identify text documents from a set that are strikingly different from other documents in the same set, we can compare their embedding vectors. Again, we only need to calculate embedding vectors once for each document. In doing so, we avoid having to use language models to compare documents. Instead, we simply compare embedding vectors (which is very fast).

In summary, although we have focused on clustering, there are many use cases for embedding vectors. This makes it worthwhile to learn how to generate and use them!

Summary

- You can apply language models directly to analyze text data.
- Prompts typically contain text to analyze, along with instructions. Instructions describe the task to solve as well as the output format.
- You can use chat completion for classification, extraction, and question answering.
- Raw model output may need postprocessing to change the format.
- Language models can transform a text into embedding vectors. You can create embedding vectors via the embedding endpoint. Comparing embedding vectors is relatively efficient.
- You can use embeddings for clustering, retrieval, and outlier detection.

References

[1] Katz, D. M., Bommarito, M. J., Gao, S., et al. (2024). GPT-4 Passes the Bar Exam. *Philosophical Transactions of the Royal Society A: Mathematical, Physical and Engineering Sciences 382*(2270), 1–17.

Analyzing structured data

A significant percentage of the world's information is stored as structured data. Structured data essentially means data stored in a standardized format. For example, data tables (e.g., think of the data you would find in an Excel spreadsheet) and data describing entities and their relationships as graphs (such as a data set describing a social network) are popular types of structured data.

Tools for processing structured data have been available for many decades. After all, structured data has a standardized format optimized to make it easy for computers to process. So why do we need large language models for that? The problem with existing tools for processing structured data is their interface. Typically, each tool (or, at the very least, each category of tools for specific types of structured data) supports its own formal query language.

Using this language, users can often perform a wide range of analysis operations on structured data. But learning such query languages takes time! Wouldn't it be nice if all those systems could be queried using a single language, ideally in natural language (e.g., plain English)?

This is where language models come into play. Large language models can translate questions in natural language into a wide range of formal languages. So we can use them as a universal interface to various data-analysis tools supporting a wide range of structured data types. In this chapter, we will build natural language query interfaces for different types of structured data. Such interfaces enable us (or others) to analyze data by typing questions in natural language. The system then translates our questions into formal queries, executes them, and presents us with results.

5.1 *Chapter outline*

In this chapter, we will be creating several natural language query interfaces. In general, a natural language query interface answers questions about data formulated in natural language. This chapter considers different types of structured data. First, we will create natural language interfaces that answer questions about tabular data. After that, we will create one that answers questions about graphs.

The principle is the same in both cases. We assume that data is processed using a data type–specific tool for data processing. For instance, for tabular data, we will use a relational database management system (RDBMS). To analyze graphs, we will use a system for managing graph data. Then we will use the large language model to translate questions in natural language into the query language supported by the specific tool. For instance, for an RDBMS, this is typically the Structured Query Language (SQL). Graph database management systems support a variety of graph data–specific query languages. We will use the Cypher query language (a language describing analysis operations on graph data). We will discuss both languages in more detail in the following sections.

To translate questions into formal queries, the language model needs access to the question (of course), some information about the target language (e.g., do we want to write SQL or Cypher queries?), and some information about the structure of the data we are trying to query. For instance, the structure of tabular data is characterized by the names of tables, the headers of the columns that appear in those tables (hopefully providing some hints on the semantics of data stored within them), and the data types of each column (are we storing integer values or strings?), among other things. By providing the language model with all of these pieces of information, including them in the prompt, the model should be able to produce a formal query that captures the semantics of our question.

We can process that query using a specialized tool to produce a query result. Assuming the query translation was correct, this result will represent an answer to the original question. Figure 5.1 illustrates the whole process.

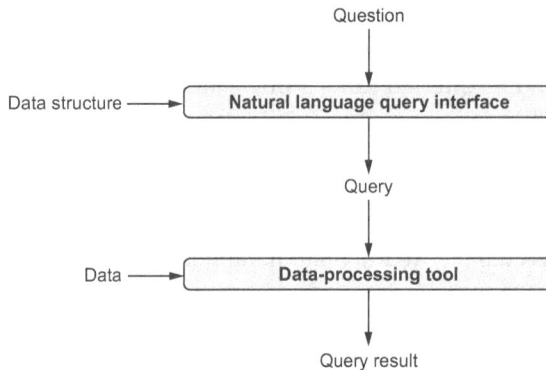

Figure 5.1   A natural language query interface translates questions in natural language into formal queries, taking into account the data structure. Formal queries are then processed on data by a specialized tool, generating a query result.

Why do we need external tools?

We have seen that language models can solve a variety of tasks. So why not simply use language models to analyze structured data directly? Why do we rely on external tools to do so and use the language model merely as a translator?

The primary reason is efficiency. Using large language models is expensive, and, at least for large data sets, the size of the data can easily exceed the maximum input size of the language model. Hence, relying on existing tools that can deal with large structured data sets seems like a better idea.

WARNING   In the following sections, we use language models to write commands for data processing. Although language models work astonishingly well in many cases, never rely on them to generate correct results in every single scenario. In some cases, language models may write incorrect queries. Other times, they may write commands to change or delete your data or alter your system setup. Always keep a backup of important data before enabling data access via language models.

5.2   *A natural language query interface for analyzing game sales*

We're back at Banana, where you realize that your boss happens to be a computer games enthusiast. Your boss not only likes to spend the evenings playing but also loves analyzing data about computer games. Having recently obtained a data set about computer game sales, your boss is seeking to extract interesting statistics. SQL is the language of choice for analyzing tabular data, but your boss does not feel comfortable writing SQL queries. Knowing about your expertise with regard to language models and data analysis, your boss asks whether it would be possible to build an interface that translates questions about computer games into corresponding SQL queries.

After thinking about it, you realize that this could be a fun project that can be realized easily with language models. Let's get started!

5.2.1 Setting up an SQLite database

Before we can analyze tabular data using SQL queries, we first must load that data into an RDBMS, a tool for processing data tables efficiently. In this subsection, we'll see how to load data about computer games into SQLite, a popular RDBMS.

As a first step, make sure SQLite is installed. We will be using SQLite version 3 in this section. You can check whether SQLite 3 is installed by typing the following in your terminal:

```
sqlite3 --version
```

If you receive a message like this one, no further installation is necessary:

```
3.33.0 2020-08-14 13:23:32 fca8...
```

If you see an error message, go to www.sqlite.org/download.html. Select the version that is consistent with your operating system, download all the relevant files, and follow the instructions to install SQLite. In case of problems, click the SQLite Installation item in the chapter 5 section of the book's companion website. You will find detailed instructions for how to install SQLite on different platforms. Afterward, run the previous command to ensure that SQLite is installed properly.

Next, we want to create a relational database using SQLite. A relational database is essentially a collection of data tables. You can think of each data table as a simple spreadsheet. We have named table columns associated with a data type and (possibly many) table rows that contain values for each of the columns. For instance, table 5.1 contains information about video games, and each row represents one game. The table has four columns: Name, Platform, Year, and Genre. Three of the columns (Name, Platform, and Genre) contain strings (i.e., text). The column Year contains numbers (representing the year in which a game was released).

Table 5.1 Sample of data table. Each table row describes one video game.

Name	Platform	Year	Genre
Wii Sports	Wii	2006	Sports
Super Mario Bros.	NES	1985	Platform
Mario Kart Wii	Wii	2008	Racing
Wii Sports Resort	Wii	2009	Sports
Pokemon Red/Pokemon Blue	GB	1996	Role-Playing

Table 5.1 shows a small sample of a data set you can find on the book's companion website (look for the Games item in the chapter 5 section). We will use that data set in the following sections to create a natural language query interface, enabling users to analyze it with natural language commands. But first, we need to load that data into the SQLite database system.

TIP   We'll go over all the steps required to load tabular data into SQLite. This is useful if you want to load data other than that discussed here. If you don't want to create your own database, you can skip this section and download games.db from the book's companion website instead.

Let's start the SQLite command-line interface. Enter the following command in the terminal, and press Enter:

```
sqlite3 games.db
```

This command creates a new database stored in the file games.db. At the same time, it opens the SQLite command-line interface. Now we can instruct the SQLite tool to load the data set we will use in the following sections. First we have to tell SQLite a little about the structure of the data. We want to load an extended version of table 5.1 containing additional columns. Run the following command to describe the structure of the data:

```
CREATE TABLE games(                       ❶ Table name
rank int, name text, platform text,                ❷ List of table columns
year int, genre text, publisher text, americasales numeric,
eusales numeric, japansales numeric, othersales numeric,
globalsales numeric);
```

This command describes the structure of a single table named games (❶) (because it will store information about video games); in parentheses, we specify the full list of columns in the table (separated by commas) (❷). Each column is defined by the column name (e.g., rank, name, or genre) followed by the column type. For example, int means the column stores integer numbers, whereas text means the column stores text data. All table rows must provide values for each column of the appropriate data type.

After defining the table structure, we can load data into the table from the .csv file under Games on the book's website. Download the file if you haven't already. We will assume that the file is stored in the folder /Downloads/videogames.csv for the following commands. Simply replace that path with the file path on your system. Load the data using the following command (still in the SQLite interface):

```
.mode csv                             ❶ Sets CSV mode
.import /Downloads/videogames.csv games   ❷ Imports the data
```

The first command prepares SQLite to load data from a .csv file (which applies to the file we want to load) (❶). The next command (❷) imports the data: the first parameter is the path to the file we want to load data from, and the second parameter is the name of the data table we want to load the file into. In this case, we reference the table whose structure we defined before (games). To test whether the data was loaded successfully (which should be the case if you don't see an error message), run the following command in SQLite:

```
SELECT count(*) FROM games;
```

You should see the result 16599 if all the data was loaded. If you see a lower number, check for error messages in the SQLite output. You can quit the SQLite console via the command .quit (don't forget to prefix your command with a dot to make it work). For the following sections, we will assume that the data has been loaded and is stored in an SQLite file called games.db.

5.2.2   SQL basics

Sure, we can use the language model to translate questions to SQL queries (which are understood by SQLite). But can we trust its translations? Thinking more about it, you realize that it wouldn't hurt to have at least some SQL basics to verify the output of the language model before presenting the interface to your boss. That's what we'll do in this section. A full introduction to SQL is, of course, beyond the scope of this book. Have a look at the website www.databaselecture.com to get a more detailed introduction by this book's author. We'll discuss a few SQL basics in this section that help implement our natural language query interface.

SQL queries are used to analyze data tables. Query results may be derived from a single table or by combining data from multiple tables. In our example database, created in the last section, we have a single table. Using SQL queries, we can, for instance, count rows with certain properties (e.g., all games by the same publisher), filter data (e.g., only show games that were released in 2017), or perform various aggregate operations (e.g., for each publisher, calculate the average earnings per game).

An SQL query generally describes a table to generate (using data that is already available in the database). Most example queries in this section have the following structure:

```
SELECT [Columns or Aggregates]    ❶ SELECT clause
FROM [List of tables]             ❷ FROM clause
WHERE [List of conditions]        ❸ WHERE clause
```

The FROM clause (❷) (the code following the FROM keyword and before the WHERE keyword) describes the source data used for analysis. For instance, the FROM clause can contain a list of table names separated by commas. In our example database, we have only a single table to process (for advanced queries, the same table name may appear multiple times in the FROM clause, creating different copies of the same table). The queries we will encounter in the following sections will contain a single entry in the FROM clause: the games table.

The WHERE clause (❸) defines predicates on the tables that appear in the FROM clause. For instance, it may contain a condition restricting the scope to games from a certain publisher. The WHERE clause can contain simple conditions (i.e., conditions that can be expressed by an equality or inequality on a table column) as well as complex conditions (connecting multiple simple conditions by AND or OR operators). Those conditions are used to filter rows from the tables in the FROM clause. Rows that do not satisfy the condition in the WHERE clause are discarded and do not appear in the query result.

Finally, we specify the columns of the desired result table in the SELECT clause (❶). More precisely, we specify a list of column definitions separated by commas. Columns may be defined by a column name (a column that appears in one of the tables in the FROM clause) or by a more complex expression: for example, an arithmetic expression connecting multiple columns. Alternatively, we can specify aggregates such as count(*) in the SELECT clause (the latter aggregate counts the number of rows). The query result contains a table with the specified columns, filling them with content corresponding to the column definition.

For instance, let's say we want to count all games published in 2017. In this case, our query result should contain a single column with a count aggregate. Also, our WHERE clause should contain a filter condition restricting our scope to games from 2017. Our FROM clause contains, of course, the name of the only table in our database (games). The following query generates the desired result:

```
SELECT Count(*)
FROM games
WHERE year = 2017
```

To make things a little more complex, let's assume that we want to calculate the combined number of sales in Europe and Japan for all games released in 2017 by a specific publisher (Activision). Our desired query result contains two columns: the name of the game and the sales count. As our data table features two columns with sales in Europe and sales in Japan (eusales and japansales, as per our table definition in the previous section), we can describe the desired result column by adding them (eusales + japansales). Because we want to restrict our scope to games from 2017 and from Activision, we can use a complex predicate in the WHERE clause: year = 2017 AND publisher = 'Activision'. Note the use of apostrophes around the name Activision—we need to use apostrophes to delimit strings in query conditions instead of numbers. The following query generates the desired result:

```
SELECT name, eusales + japansales
FROM games
WHERE year = 2017 AND publisher = 'Activision'
```

Optionally, when specifying aggregates, we can calculate those aggregates for different groups of rows defined by shared values in certain columns. To do so, we add a final GROUP BY clause to the previous query template, followed by a comma-separated list of columns used to form groups. For instance, let's assume that we want to calculate game sales for each genre (such as strategy or action) separately. We can use the following query to return one row with aggregates for each category of games (note that we add the genre column in the SELECT clause as well to ensure that we can associate numbers with the correct genre):

```
SELECT genre, name, eusales + japansales
FROM games
WHERE year = 2017 AND publisher = 'Activision'
GROUP BY genre
```

The SQL primer in this section is clearly insufficient to write your own SQL queries, except for a few simple cases. However, we don't really want to write our own SQL queries—we want to rely on the language model instead! This introduction should enable you to understand queries generated by the language model at a high level of abstraction. And observing how the language model maps questions to queries may be a good way to get started with learning SQL yourself. In the next section, we will start by creating a simple translator, translating questions into SQL queries on the games database.

5.2.3 Overview

Having acquired a few SQL basics to check the output of the language model, we will now work on our text-to-SQL translator. We will use our translator via the command line. We specify a question as input and ideally want an SQL query, translating our question as output. If we run the output query in SQLite, we should get the answer to our original question. Of course, this interface is manual and not very convenient to use. Ideally, we would like it to execute queries automatically and show the corresponding results directly in our query interface. We will create such an interface in the following section. For now, we just focus on the core problem of translating questions into queries. Also, for the moment, our only goal is to translate questions about computer games. Therefore, we will hardcode the structure of the target database. Again, we will generalize that in our next project.

Internally, to translate the input question, we will first create a prompt. This prompt describes the translation task and contains all relevant details for translation (e.g., the structure of our target database). Sending this prompt to the language model should result, in most cases, in a correctly translated SQL query. We may still need to do a little work to extract this query from potentially overly verbose output generated by the language model. Let's discuss these steps in more detail, starting with the prompts.

5.2.4 Generating prompts for text-to-SQL translation

What information do we need to convey to the language model for a successful translation? Clearly, we need to specify the question we want to translate. Also, we need to specify the target system (SQLite) and describe the structure of the target database. For the moment, we hardcode the database structure. We can simply provide the language model with the table definition (`create table...`) that we used in section 5.2.1. The language model will understand how this command maps to a table structure. By sending a prompt with instructions for translation to the model containing all of the previously mentioned types of information, the language model should be able to produce a corresponding SQL query.

Let's use the following prompt template:

```
Database:                                    ❶ Database description
CREATE TABLE games(rank int, name text, platform text,
year int, genre text, publisher text, americasales numeric,
```

```
eusales numeric, japansales numeric, othersales numeric,
globalsales numeric);
Translate this question into SQL query:    ❷ Task description
[Question]                                 ❸ Question to translate
```

This prompt template contains all the pieces of information described earlier. First, it describes the target database (❶) by providing the SQL commands used to create the associated tables (in this case, a single table). Note that this is not a placeholder because, for the moment, our query interface only needs to work for one database (whose structure we hardcode in the template). Next, the prompt template contains a task description (❷): the goal is to translate questions into SQL queries. Finally, the template contains the question to translate (❸). Here, we use a placeholder (indicated by square brackets). This enables us to use the same prompt template for various questions our boss may ask about the data.

The following code generates prompts according to the previous template:

```
def create_prompt(question):
    parts = []
```

❶ **Adds the database description**

```
    parts += ['Database:']
    parts += ['create table games(rank int, name text, platform text,']
    parts += ['year int, genre text, publisher text, americasales numeric,']
    parts += ['eusales numeric, japansales numeric, othersales numeric,']
    parts += ['globalsales numeric);']
```

❷ **Adds the task description**

```
    parts += ['Translate this question into SQL query:']
    parts += [question]           ❸ Adds the question to translate
    return '\n'.join(parts)       ❹ Returns the concatenation
```

Given the question to translate as input, the code adds the description of the database (❶), then instructions for translation (❷), and finally the question to translate (❸). The result is the concatenation of all the prompt parts (❹).

5.2.5   Complete code

The next listing contains the full code for our natural language query interface. It uses the prompt-generation function discussed earlier (❶), as well as the function invoking the language model (❷) that we already know from prior chapters.

Listing 5.1   Translating questions about video games into SQL queries

```
import argparse
import openai
import re
import time

client = openai.OpenAI()
```

```
def create_prompt(question):                    ❶ Generates a prompt for translation
    """ Generate prompt to translate question into SQL query.

    Args:
        question: question about data in natural language.

    Returns:
        prompt for question translation.
    """
    parts = []
    parts += ['Database:']
    parts += ['create table games(rank int, name text, platform text,']
    parts += ['year int, genre text, publisher text, americasales numeric,']
    parts += ['eusales numeric, japansales numeric, othersales numeric,']
    parts += ['globalsales numeric);']
    parts += ['Translate this question into SQL query:']
    parts += [question]
    return '\n'.join(parts)


def call_llm(prompt):                           ❷ Invokes the language model
    """ Query large language model and return answer.

    Args:
        prompt: input prompt for language model.

    Returns:
        Answer by language model.
    """
    for nr_retries in range(1, 4):
        try:
            response = client.chat.completions.create(
                model='gpt-4o',
                messages=[
                    {'role':'user', 'content':prompt}
                    ]
                )
            return response.choices[0].message.content
        except:
            time.sleep(nr_retries * 2)
    raise Exception('Cannot query OpenAI model!')


if __name__ == '__main__':                      ❸ Reads a query and translates it to SQL

    parser = argparse.ArgumentParser()
    parser.add_argument('question', type=str, help='A question about games')
    args = parser.parse_args()

    prompt = create_prompt(args.question)       ❹ Generates a prompt
    answer = call_llm(prompt)                   ❺ Generates an answer
```
❻ **Extracts an SQL query from the answer**
```
    query = re.findall('''''sql(.*)''''', answer, re.DOTALL)[0]

    print(f'SQL: {query}')
```

This listing reads a question about computer games from the command line (❸). Using the input question, it generates a prompt (❹) that instructs the language model to translate the question into an SQL query. It sends the prompt to the language model and receives its answer (❺).

The raw answer from GPT-4o typically contains explanations interleaved with the SQL query we are ultimately interested in. To get the query alone, we have to extract it from the raw answer (❻). Here, we exploit the fact that GPT-4o encloses SQL queries between the markers ```sql and ``` (when interacting with GPT models via the ChatGPT web interface, the content between those markers is rendered as a code box). The regular expression ```sql(.*)``` matches the SQL query between the markers, using the Python function `re.findall` to return a list of matches for this regular expression (the `re.DOTALL` flag is required to ensure that the dot matches all characters, including newlines, which may appear in SQL queries). We use the first of those matches as our query (i.e., we implicitly assume that at least one match is returned and that the first match is suitable).

5.2.6 *Trying it out*

Okay! Time to try our text-to-SQL translator! In the terminal, switch to the directory containing the Python code. We will assume that the code is stored in a file called listing1.py (which you can download from the companion website). Run the following command:

```
python listing1.py "How many games are stored?"
```

As a result, you should obtain the following SQL query:

```
SELECT COUNT(*) FROM games;
```

Is that query correct? Let's find out: in the terminal, switch to the repository containing the SQLite database file (games.db). Then, open the database via the SQLite command-line interface:

```
sqlite3 games.db
```

Now we can finally try the query generated by our text-to-SQL translator. Enter the query, and press Enter. You should see the number of games stored in the database: 16,599.

You may want to try a few other questions. For example, see whether you can count the number of games by specific publishers or games of a specific genre! Chances are, for most questions referring to this simple database, GPT-4o should be capable enough to provide an accurate translation. Your boss will be happy.

The interface we created in this section is still limited in various ways. First, you have to reexecute the program for each new question. Second, you have to manually copy and execute each translated query into the database system interface. Third, and most importantly, if you ever want to switch to a different data set, you will have to manually change your prompt template. In the next section, we'll see how to overcome these restrictions.

5.3 A general natural language query interface

Your boss is happy with the new natural language interface and regularly shares interesting insights about computer game sales with you. However, you can't help but wonder whether this use case alone exploits the full potential of your approach. For instance, the human resources unit at Banana regularly deals with complex questions on tables storing employee information. Couldn't we generalize our natural language interface to help them as well? In this section, we'll generalize the natural language query interface to work with arbitrary databases without requiring any changes to the code itself. Furthermore, we will make the interface more convenient by executing the translated queries directly and avoiding restarts between different questions on the same data.

5.3.1 Executing queries

As a first step, let's see how we can execute translated queries directly from Python. This will avoid tediously copying queries from one interface to another. In Python, we can execute queries on an SQLite database using the `sqlite3` library.

Let's assume that the variable `data_path` stores the path to the database file. To execute queries on that database, we must first create a connection:

```
import sqlite3

with sqlite3.connect(data_path) as connection:
    ...
```

We can now execute SQL queries on the database via the `connection` object. Let's assume that the SQL query we want to execute is stored in the variable `query`. After connecting to the database, we first create a cursor object (enabling querying and result retrieval) and then use it to execute the query:

```
import sqlite3

with sqlite3.connect(data_path) as connection:
    cursor = connection.cursor()
    cursor.execute(query)
```

After execution, we can get a list of result rows by calling `cursor.fetchall()`. We'll put everything together in a function that takes two parameters—the path to the database and a query to execute on it—as input, returning the query result in a string representation:

```
def process_query(data_path, query):
    with sqlite3.connect(data_path) as connection:    ❶ Connects to the database
        cursor = connection.cursor()                  ❷ Creates the cursor
        cursor.execute(query)        ❸ Executes a query
        table_rows = cursor.fetchall()    ❹ Retrieves the query result
        ❺ Transforms to a list of strings
        table_strings = [str(r) for r in table_rows]
        return '\n'.join(table_strings)        ❻ Concatenates result rows
```

After connecting to the target database (**❶**), the function creates a cursor (**❷**), executes the input query (**❸**), and retrieves the query result (**❹**). After casting the result tuples into a string representation (**❺**), we concatenate the result rows, separated by newline symbols (**❻**).

5.3.2 *Extracting the database structure*

We want an interface that works for arbitrary SQLite databases without having to change the code. This means we need to extract the structure of the current database (information about its tables and columns) automatically.

For SQLite, we can extract the structure of a database by executing SQL queries. These queries access a special table: the *schema table*. This table is created automatically (i.e., we do not need to create it by hand). Among other things, this table contains the SQL commands used to create other tables in a database. We can use them as a concise description of the database structure, suitable as input to the language model.

We can access the schema table via the table name `sqlite_master`. This table contains a column named `sql` with information about queries used to create objects inside the database. Specifically, we are interested in SQL commands used to create tables. Those queries contain crucial information for query translation, including the names and types of the columns that belong to the table created by the query. The following query retrieves all SQL statements used to create tables in the current database:

```
select sql from sqlite_master where type = 'table';
```

So all we need to do is execute this query from Python. Fortunately, we already know how to do that from the previous section. Given the path to a database, the following function returns a text describing the queries used to create all the tables in the database:

```
import sqlite3

def get_structure(data_path):
    with sqlite3.connect(data_path) as connection:      ❶ Connects to the database
        cursor = connection.cursor()                    ❷ Creates a cursor
        cursor.execute("select sql from sqlite_master where type =
            'table';")                                  ❸ Accesses schema table
        table_rows = cursor.fetchall()                  ❹ Retrieves results
        table_ddls = [r[0] for r in table_rows]         ❺ Retrieves SQL strings
        return '\n'.join(table_ddls)                    ❻ Concatenates SQL strings
```

Again, we create a connection (**❶**) and a corresponding cursor object (**❷**). Next, we issue a query to the schema table to retrieve all SQL queries used to create tables in the current database (**❸**). We fetch the results (**❹**) and extract the SQL strings from the query result (**❺**). Note that this part of the function differs slightly from the generic function for executing queries, discussed in the previous section. By extracting the values for the first (and, for this specific query, only) field of each row, we get rid of unnecessary delimiters between rows that would otherwise show up in our output (and, later, in our prompts). The result is the concatenation of all the result rows (**❻**).

5.3.3 Complete code

Listing 5.2 shows the complete code for our generic natural language query interface (you can download it from the book's companion website as listing 2 in the chapter 5 section). The code uses the function for extracting the database structure (**❶**), discussed earlier. The function for generating prompts (**❷**) is a slight variant of the one used for our previous database-specific query interface. Instead of a hardcoded description of the database structure, it takes a description of the database as input and inserts it into the prompt. The function for invoking the language model (**❸**) has not changed compared to the prior interface version. The function `process_query` (**❹**) was discussed in section 5.3.1.

Listing 5.2 Generic text-to-SQL query interface

```python
import argparse
import openai
import re
import sqlite3
import time

client = openai.OpenAI()

def get_structure(data_path):                    ❶ Extracts the database structure
    """ Extract structure from SQLite database.

    Args:
        data_path: path to SQLite data file.

    Returns:
        text description of database structure.
    """
    with sqlite3.connect(data_path) as connection:
        cursor = connection.cursor()
        cursor.execute("select sql from sqlite_master where type = 'table';")
        table_rows = cursor.fetchall()
        table_ddls = [r[0] for r in table_rows]
        return '\n'.join(table_ddls)

def create_prompt(description, question):        ❷ Creates a prompt for translation
    """ Generate prompt to translate a question into an SQL query.

    Args:
        description: text description of database structure.
        question: question about data in natural language.

    Returns:
        prompt for question translation.
```

```
    """
    parts = []
    parts += ['Database:']
    parts += [description]
    parts += ['Translate this question into SQL query:']
    parts += [question]
    return '\n'.join(parts)


def call_llm(prompt):                          ❸ Invokes the language model
    """ Query large language model and return answer.

    Args:
        prompt: input prompt for language model.

    Returns:
        Answer by language model.
    """
    for nr_retries in range(1, 4):
        try:
            response = client.chat.completions.create(
                model='gpt-4o',
                messages=[
                    {'role':'user', 'content':prompt}
                    ]
                )
            return response.choices[0].message.content
        except:
            time.sleep(nr_retries * 2)
    raise Exception('Cannot query OpenAI model!')


def process_query(data_path, query):           ❹ Processes a query on a database
    """ Processes SQL query and returns result.

    Args:
        data_path: path to SQLite data file.
        query: process this query on database.

    Returns:
        query result.
    """
    with sqlite3.connect(data_path) as connection:
        cursor = connection.cursor()
        cursor.execute(query)
        table_rows = cursor.fetchall()
        table_strings = [str(r) for r in table_rows]
        return '\n'.join(table_strings)


if __name__ == '__main__':

    parser = argparse.ArgumentParser()
    parser.add_argument('dbpath', type=str, help='Path to SQLite data')
    args = parser.parse_args()
```

```
data_structure = get_structure(args.dbpath)    ❺ Reads data structure

while True:                                     ❻ Answers questions until the user quits
    user_input = input('Enter question:')
    if user_input == 'quit':
        break

    prompt = create_prompt(data_structure, user_input)
    answer = call_llm(prompt)
    query = re.findall('''''sql(.*)''''', answer, re.DOTALL)[0]
    print(f'SQL: {query}')

    try:                                        ❼ Processes the query on the database
        result = process_query(args.dbpath, query)
        print(f'Result: {result}')
    except:
        print('Error processing query! Try to reformulate.')
```

After reading the command-line arguments, the natural language query interface extracts the structure of the database (❺). Next, we loop (❻) until the user terminates the interface. In each iteration, we first read input from the keyboard (leaving the loop if the user enters quit) and then create a prompt and invoke the language model.

After translating the input question to a query, we execute that query directly (❼). Of course, the translation may be incorrect and result in a query that does not execute on the target database. In that case, SQLite may throw an error, and we must ensure that our program does not terminate. This is why we surround the call to the query-processing function with a try-catch block.

5.3.4 *Trying it out*

Time to try our natural language query interface! Our interface now works for arbitrary databases. But we don't have another database, so we'll use it again on the games database. In the terminal, switch to the directory containing the games.db file, and run the following command (let's assume the code is stored in a file named listing3.py):

```
python listing3.py games.db
```

The command will open an input box in which we can enter questions about the data. Following is an example of interaction with the natural language query interface:

```
Enter question:How many games are stored in total?
SQL: SELECT COUNT(*) FROM games;
Answer: (16599,)
Enter question:How many games did Activision create?
SQL: SELECT COUNT(*) FROM games WHERE publisher = 'Activision'
Answer: (975,)
Enter question:Name one game that was released in 2017!
SQL: SELECT name
FROM games
```

```
WHERE year = 2017
LIMIT 1
Answer: ('Phantasy Star Online 2 Episode 4: Deluxe Package',)
Enter question:How many games were released for each genre?
SQL: SELECT genre, COUNT(*) as num_games
FROM games
GROUP BY genre
Answer: ('Action', 3316)
('Adventure', 1286)
('Fighting', 848)
('Genre', 1)
('Misc', 1739)
('Platform', 886)
('Puzzle', 582)
('Racing', 1249)
('Role-Playing', 1488)
('Shooter', 1310)
('Simulation', 867)
('Sports', 2346)
('Strategy', 681)
Enter question:Which three games sold more copies in Japan than in Europe?
SQL: SELECT name
FROM games
WHERE japansales > eusales
ORDER BY japansales DESC
LIMIT 3;
Answer: ('Name',)
('Pokemon Red/Pokemon Blue',)
('Pokemon Gold/Pokemon Silver',)
Enter question:Break down game sales in America by the platform!
SQL: SELECT platform, sum(americasales) AS total_sales
FROM games
GROUP BY platform
Answer: ('2600', 90.59999999999992)
('3DO', 0)
('3DS', 78.86999999999996)
('DC', 5.43)
('DS', 390.7099999999977)
('GB', 114.32000000000001)
('GBA', 187.54000000000033)
('GC', 133.46000000000004)
('GEN', 19.27)
('GG', 0)
('N64', 139.02000000000015)
('NES', 125.94000000000005)
('NG', 0)
('PC', 93.2800000000005)
('PCFX', 0)
('PS', 336.509999999998)
('PS2', 583.8399999999925)
```

```
('PS3', 392.2599999999998)
('PS4', 96.79999999999998)
('PSP', 108.98999999999975)
('PSV', 16.200000000000006)
('Platform', 0.0)
('SAT', 0.7200000000000001)
('SCD', 1)
('SNES', 61.22999999999998)
('TG16', 0)
('WS', 0)
('Wii', 507.7099999999991)
('WiiU', 38.31999999999999)
('X360', 601.0499999999992)
('XB', 186.6900000000008)
('XOne', 83.19000000000003)
Enter question:quit
```

As you see, we can ask a wide range of questions and obtain reasonable answers. Besides the answer, the system also prints out the query. Knowing a little about SQL enables us to verify whether the query accurately translates the question.

5.4 A natural language query interface for graph data

Word spreads at Banana about your text-to-SQL interface, and multiple colleagues use it to analyze their tabular data sets. A new colleague of yours is working with large graphs, modeling connections between colleagues in Banana's internal social network. This data is represented not as a table but as a graph, a data format particularly suitable for modeling connections between entities (in this case, people). The colleague reaches out to ask whether it would be possible to expand your interface to query such data too. Knowing that language models should, in principle, be able to handle a variety of formal query languages, you are optimistic and agree to look into it.

5.4.1 What is graph data?

Like relational data, graphs are a particularly popular type of structured data. A graph generally consists of a collection of nodes connected by edges. Nodes can be associated with properties, and edges are labeled. For instance, social networks are often represented as graphs. Here, nodes represent people, and edges represent friendships and relationships. Graphs are also a natural representation of road or subway networks. In this case, nodes represent cities or subway stations, whereas edges represent roads or rails connecting them.

Figure 5.2 shows an example graph representing a subway network. It represents stations of the New York City subway as nodes (hence, nodes are labeled `Station`). Edges represent direct connections and are labeled with the associated subway line. Nodes are associated with a `name` property, assigning nodes to the name of the corresponding station.

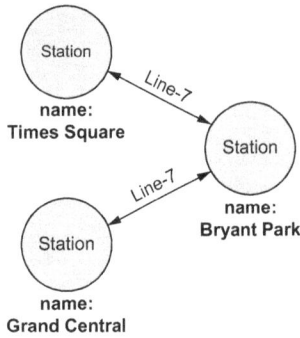

Figure 5.2   An example graph representing a small part of the subway network in New York City. Nodes, drawn as circles, represent subway stations and are associated with a property, assigning them to the name of the represented subway station. Edges, drawn as arrows, represent direct connections via specific subway lines. Edges are labeled by the subway line connecting the stations.

The fact that graphs can be used to model various types of data has motivated a variety of specialized systems called *graph database systems* for graph data processing. These systems support graph-specific query languages (not SQL), enabling users to formulate complex questions about the underlying data. Graph database systems are optimized for processing large graphs efficiently.

Next, we will use language models to translate questions in natural language into queries formulated in the graph database management system. We will see that this scenario requires only small modifications compared to our approach for translating questions into SQL queries.

5.4.2   *Setting up a Neo4j database*

We will use the Neo4j system, a database system specialized for graph data. You don't even have to install anything on your local machine. Neo4j comes with an online demo that we will use next.

First, go to https://neo4j.com/sandbox/ in your web browser. Click the Launch the Free Sandbox button. This should open a login form, in which you can decide to create a new account or use existing accounts (e.g., a Google account). Figure 5.3 shows the screen you should see next.

Here, we can select one of several example databases to try Neo4j. We will be using the `Movies` database. This database contains information about movies and the actors who played in them (representing movies and actors as nodes). Click the `Movies` database and then the Create button to create an instance of the database and prepare it for querying. Creating the database may take a few minutes. Afterward, you can open the `Movies` database and access the query interface.

Figure 5.4 shows the Neo4j query interface. Click the database icon in the upper-left corner to see an overview of the database. The database contains multiple types of labels (i.e., node types), including `People` and `Movies`. It also contains relationship types such as `ACTED_IN` and `DIRECTED`, labeling the edges in our graph. For instance, these two relationship types allow us to keep track of who played in which movie (`ACTED_IN`) and who directed which movie (`DIRECTED`). Properties are associated with nodes and assign keys to values. The database overview reports on property keys such as `name` (assigning an actor to a name) and `title` (assigning movies to titles).

Select the Movies database.

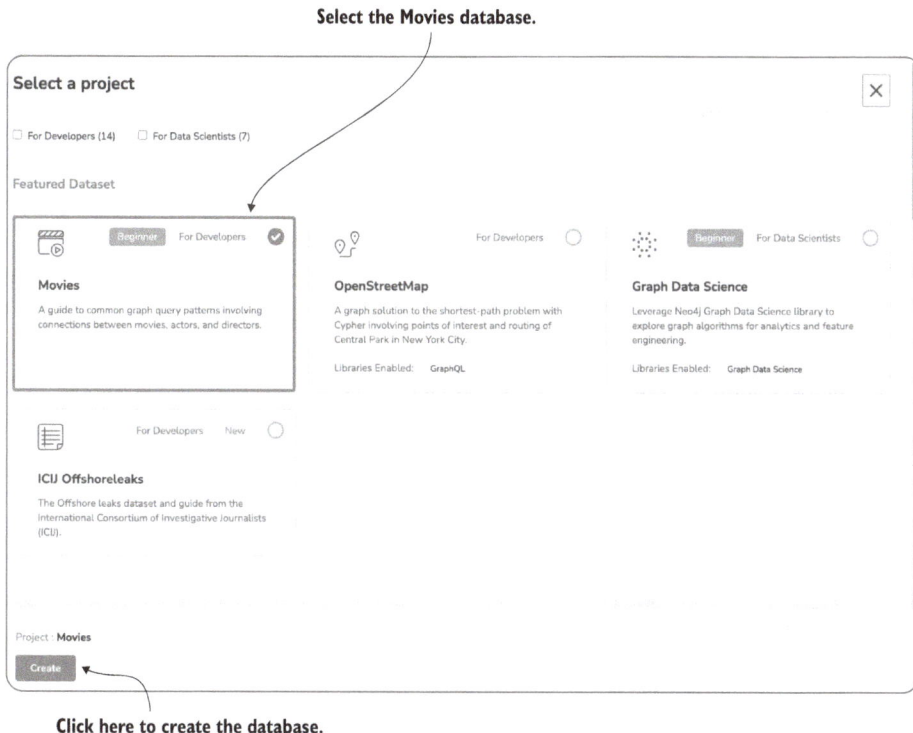

Figure 5.3   Select the movies database, and click Create to create a corresponding instance.

You can enter queries in the text box at the top of the screen and submit them by clicking the button to the right of the text box.

5.4.3   *The Cypher query language*

Neo4j supports the Cypher query language. Although a full introduction to Cypher is beyond the scope of this book (instead, have a look at the Neo4j documentation, available at https://neo4j.com/docs/cypher-manual/current/introduction/), we will quickly go over the basics. The purpose of this introduction is to enable you to understand, at least in simple cases, the semantics of the queries generated by the language model.

A simple type of Cypher query uses a MATCH statement describing a subgraph to find. For instance, we may simply want to find all nodes of a certain type. The query for finding the names of all the people in our Movies database is the following:

```
MATCH (p:Person)    ❶ Pattern to match
RETURN p.name       ❷ Result to return
```

The MATCH statement describes a pattern to match (❶). In this case, that pattern consists of single nodes of type Person. The MATCH statement assigns nodes or edges that appear within the pattern to variables. In this case, we introduce the variable p and assign it to nodes matching the pattern. The RETURN statement (❷) describes

Click here to see
database information.

Enter queries here.

Submit query here.

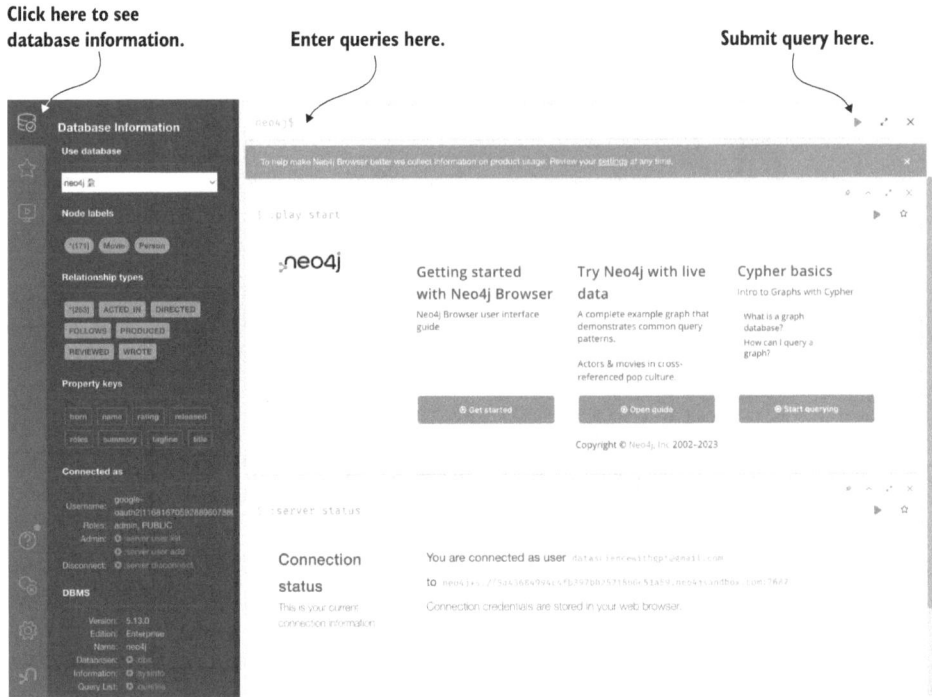

**Figure 5.4   Click the database icon (upper-left corner) to access information about the current graph
database, including the types of nodes and edges.**

the query result based on matched patterns. Here, we instruct the system to return
the name property for each node matching the pattern.

Patterns can extend beyond a single node. For instance, we may want to find the
titles of all movies starring the actor Tom Cruise. In this case, the pattern we are
looking for consists not of a single node but rather of two connected nodes. We are
searching for a node of type Movie connected via an edge of type ACTED_IN to a node
of type Person whose name property is set to "Tom Cruise." This can be accomplished
by the following Cypher query:

❶ **Matches movies starring Tom Cruise**

```
MATCH (p:Person name: 'Tom Cruise')-[:ACTED_IN]->(m:Movie)
RETURN m.title                              ❷ Returns the movie title
```

The expression (p:Person name: 'Tom Cruise') (❶) matches all nodes of type
Person whose name property is set to "Tom Cruise." The expression (m:Movie)
matches all nodes of type Movie. Finally, we connect those two with the expression -[:ACTED_IN]->. This expression represents a directed connection (hence the
arrow shape) between the first node (representing Tom Cruise) and the second node
(representing an arbitrary movie). The type of the connection is restricted to ACTED_IN
(excluding, for instance, movies directed by Tom Cruise in which he did not act).
Finally, note that the MATCH expression assigns parts of this pattern to variables again.

Tom Cruise will be represented by variable p, and the movies he played in will be represented by variable m. The RETURN expression (❷) retrieves the title property of the movie node.

Finally, let's see how Neo4j can calculate aggregates (similar to SQL):

❶ **Matches movies starring Tom Cruise**

```
MATCH (p:Person name: 'Tom Cruise')-[:ACTED_IN]->(m:Movie)
RETURN count(*)                          ❷ Returns the number of movies
```

This query is similar to the one before and simply counts the number of movies featuring Tom Cruise as an actor (❶). The RETURN statement (❷) contains a corresponding aggregate. If you enter the query, you should obtain "3" as the query result (so, clearly, the example database is incomplete).

5.4.4 *Translating questions to Cypher queries*

We will use a similar approach to the one we used for translating questions to SQL queries. Primarily, we need to change the prompt to our language model. Instead of instructing the language model to translate to SQL, we will instruct it to translate to Cypher. Fortunately, language models like GPT-4o have been pretrained with a large and diverse set of training data. As we will see in the remainder of this section, this pretraining data must have included Cypher queries as well, and that's why we can use language models for translation. As always, there are no absolute guarantees, and Cypher queries generated by the language model may not accurately translate our questions. However, at least for simple queries, the translation is typically correct.

5.4.5 *Generating prompts*

To translate questions into Cypher queries, we need to include several pieces of information in the prompt. First, this includes the question we want to translate. Second, this must include a description of the database structure. In the case of SQL, the database structure is defined, for instance, by table and column names. In the case of a Neo4j database, we want to include information about node and edge types, as well as the names of the most relevant properties. This is essentially the information shown on the left side of figure 5.4.

To keep things simple, we'll focus on the example database introduced previously, containing information about movies. This means we hardcode the database structure. Of course, similar to our text-to-SQL interface, it is possible to extend the interface to handle arbitrary graph databases.

We will use the following prompt template:

```
Neo4j Database:              ❶ Database description
Node labels: Movie, Person
Relationship types: ACTED_IN, DIRECTED,
FOLLOWS, PRODUCED, REVIEWED, WROTE
Property keys: born, name, rating, released
roles, summary, tagline, title
[Question]                   ❷ Question to translate
Cypher Query:                ❸ Specification of the target language
```

This prompt template contains a description of the database (❶). This description includes a specification of the database type (a Neo4j database), as well as a list of node labels, relationship types, and properties. Note that we hardcode the database structure in this prompt template. If using the interface on a different database, this part of the prompt must be replaced. Next, the prompt template specifies the question to translate (❷). This is a placeholder, as we want to enable users to ask various questions about the data. The prompt ends with a specification of the target language for query translation (❸). This implicitly instructs the language model to translate the question to a Cypher query.

The following piece of code instantiates this prompt template for an input question:

```
def create_prompt(question):
    parts = []
    parts += ['Neo4j Database:']
    parts += ['Node labels: Movie, Person']
    parts += ['Relationship types: ACTED_IN, DIRECTED,']
    parts += ['FOLLOWS, PRODUCED, REVIEWED, WROTE']
    parts += ['Property keys: born, name, rating, released']
    parts += ['roles, summary, tagline, title']
    parts += [question]
    parts += ['Cypher Query:']
    return '\n'.join(parts)
```

5.4.6   *Complete code*

The following listing uses the function for generating prompts (❶), discussed previously, and reuses the function for calling GPT-4o (❷) (with repeated retries, if necessary).

Listing 5.3   Translating text questions into Cypher queries for Neo4j

```
import argparse
import openai
import re
import time

client = openai.OpenAI()

def create_prompt(question):                      ❶ Generates prompts for translation
    """ Generate prompt to translate a question into Cypher query.

    Args:
        question: question about data in natural language.

    Returns:
        prompt for question translation.
    """
    parts = []
    parts += ['Neo4j Database:']
```

```
    parts += ['Node labels: Movie, Person']
    parts += ['Relationship types: ACTED_IN, DIRECTED,']
    parts += ['FOLLOWS, PRODUCED, REVIEWED, WROTE']
    parts += ['Property keys: born, name, rating, released']
    parts += ['roles, summary, tagline, title']
    parts += [question]
    parts += ['Cypher Query:']
    return '\n'.join(parts)


def call_llm(prompt):                              ❷ Calls the LLM
    """ Query large language model and return answer.

    Args:
        prompt: input prompt for language model.

    Returns:
        Answer by language model.
    """
    for nr_retries in range(1, 4):
        try:
            response = client.chat.completions.create(
                model='gpt-4o',
                messages=[
                    {'role':'user', 'content':prompt}
                    ]
                )
            return response.choices[0].message.content
        except:
            time.sleep(nr_retries * 2)
    raise Exception('Cannot query OpenAI model!')


if __name__ == '__main__':

    parser = argparse.ArgumentParser()
    parser.add_argument('question', type=str, help='A question about movies')
    args = parser.parse_args()

    prompt = create_prompt(args.question)     ❸ Creates a prompt
    answer = call_llm(prompt)                 ❹ Generates an answer
    ❺ Extracts Cypher queries
    query = re.findall('```cypher(.*)```', answer, re.DOTALL)[0]

    print(f'Cyper Query: {query}')
```

Given a question about the database as input, the code generates a corresponding prompt (❸), obtains an answer from the language model (❹), and finally extracts the Cypher query from that answer (❺). The regular expression used for extraction differs slightly because GPT includes Cypher queries using the pattern ```cypher ... ```. We finally print out the extracted query.

5.4.7 *Trying it out*

You can find listing 5.3 on the book's companion website. Download it, and use it from the command line like so:

```
python listing3.py "How many movies are stored?"
```

You should obtain a query such as the following as output:

```
MATCH (m:Movie)
RETURN COUNT(m) AS numberOfMovies
```

You can now enter this query into the Neo4j interface to get the corresponding result (which is 38). Try a few more queries to get a better sense of the capabilities of the language model. As you see, with just a few changes to the prompt template, we transformed our text-to-SQL interface into a text-to-Cypher interface that works well in most cases.

Summary

- Structured data follows a standard format, making it easier to parse. Examples of structured data include tabular data and graphs.
- Structured data is often processed via specialized tools.
- Relational database management systems process tabular data and typically support SQL queries.
- Graph data management systems process data representing graphs.
- Language models translate natural language to many formal query languages.
- Besides a question, prompts for query translation specify the database structure.
- Copy your database before executing queries generated by language models.
- Do not blindly trust your language model to generate accurate queries.

Analyzing images and videos

In the previous chapters, we have seen how to analyze text and structured data. Does that cover everything? Not even close! By far, the largest portion of data out there comes in the form of images and videos. For instance, videos alone account for an impressive two-thirds of the total data volume exchanged over the internet! In this chapter, we will see how language models can also help us extract useful insights from such data types.

The following sections introduce a couple of small projects that process images and video data. GPT-4o is a natively multimodal model; we can use it for all these tasks. First, we will see how to use GPT-4o to answer free-form questions (in natural language) about images. Second, we will use GPT-4o to build an automated picture-tagging application, automatically tagging our holiday pictures with the people who appear in them.

Finally, we will use GPT-4o to automatically generate titles for video files. The goal of these mini-projects is to illustrate features for visual data processing offered by the latest generation of large language models. After working through those projects, you should be able to build your own applications for image and video data processing in various scenarios.

6.1 Setup

You will need to install one more Python package to run the example code. Specifically, you need OpenCV, a library for image processing. In the terminal, run the following command to install OpenCV:

```
pip install opencv-python==4.8.1.78
```

We will use this library to, for example, read images from disk and split videos into frames.

Next, you need to install one more library, enabling you to send requests directly to OpenAI's web services (which you will use to send pictures stored locally to OpenAI):

```
pip install requests==2.31.0
```

Well done! If you didn't encounter any error messages running these commands, your system is now configured for image and video data analysis using GPT-4o. Let's start with our first project in the next section.

6.2 Answering questions about images

Neural networks for detecting objects (such as cars) in images have been around for many years. So what's the big deal about processing images with GPT-4o?

The primary limitation of classical models for image processing is that they need to be trained for specific analysis tasks. For example, let's say you have a neural network that is really good at detecting pictures of cats. You can use that to filter out cat pictures from your personal collection. However, maybe you're not into cats in general but are specifically interested in golden Persian cats. Unless your model is trained to detect that specific type of cat, you're out of luck and need to label enough example pictures yourself. Doing that is tedious, and you may end up not using the model and instead going through the pictures by hand. The big deal about image processing with GPT-4o (and similar models) is that it solves a wide range of tasks with images based on just a description of the task (in natural language).

We will use that to build a generic question-answering system for images. As a user, you will formulate arbitrary questions in natural language and point to a picture, and the system will generate a text answer. For example, asking the system to detect "golden Persian cats" in a picture should work out of the box without needing task-specific training data.

6.2.1 *Specifying multimodal input*

In this section, we will create a system that takes two inputs:

- A URL leading to an image on the web
- A natural language question about the image

The output is an answer to the question (as text). Internally, the system uses GPT-4o to process the question on the input image. It generates multimodal prompts, combining multiple types of data (here, text and images). Figure 6.1 shows an example prompt: it contains one image (of an apple) and a question about the image (whether the image shows a banana). The correct answer is "No" in this case.

Is this a banana ("Yes","No")?

Figure 6.1   Multimodal prompt containing an image and text. The prompt instructs the language model to decide whether the picture shows a banana. In this case, the expected output is "No" (otherwise "Yes").

How can we create such prompts for GPT-4o? We can reuse the chat completions endpoint for that. As a reminder, this endpoint takes as input a list of prior messages exchanged between the user and (potentially) the system. For our visual question-answering system, we only need a single message (that originates from the user).

Unlike the prior code, messages can now contain multimodal content. In this specific case, this content consists of one text snippet (the question asked by the user) and one image (specified as a URL for the moment). This is the message we will use in the following code (question is a variable containing the question text, and image_url is the URL to the image):

```
{'role':'user', 'content':[
    {'type':'text', 'text':question},        ❶ Question text
    {'type':'image_url', 'image_url':{
        'url':image_url}}                     ❷ Image URL
    ]
}
```

First, note the role attribute identifying the message as generated by the user. Second, the message content is specified as a list of Python dictionaries. Each of those dictionaries describes one element of the message. As we are now considering multimodal data—that is, images and text—we need to clarify the type (or *modality*) of each input element. This is accomplished by setting the `type` attribute to either `text` or `image_url`. The actual content is specified using either the `text` attribute (❶) or (in the case of an image) the `image_url` attribute (❷). GPT-4o is flexible enough to understand that the question refers to the image and to process both appropriately.

> **TIP**   Whereas the input contains a single picture, the content of a message may contain multiple elements of the same type: for example, multiple images. We will exploit that capability for the project in the next section.

6.2.2   *Code discussion*

The following listing shows the complete code for our visual question-answering system. Taking the image URL and a question as input (❸), the actual magic (i.e., visual question-answering) happens in the `analyze_image` function (❶).

Listing 6.1   Answering questions about images via language models

```
import argparse
import openai
import time

client = openai.OpenAI()

def analyze_image(image_url, question):          ❶ Answers question about an image
    """ Use language model to answer questions about image.

    Args:
        image_url: URL leading to image.
        question: question about image.

    Returns:
        Answer generated by the language model.
    """
    for nr_retries in range(1, 4):
        try:
            response = client.chat.completions.create(
                model='gpt-4o',
                messages=[                        ❷ Multimodal content
                    {'role':'user', 'content':[
                        {'type':'text', 'text':question},
                        {'type':'image_url', 'image_url':{
                            'url':image_url
                            }
                        }]
                    }]
                )
            return response.choices[0].message.content
```

```
        except:
            time.sleep(nr_retries * 2)
    raise Exception('Cannot query OpenAI model!')


if __name__ == '__main__':

    parser = argparse.ArgumentParser()          ❸ Input parameters
    parser.add_argument('imageurl', type=str, help='URL to image')
    parser.add_argument('question', type=str, help='Question about image')
    args = parser.parse_args()

    answer = analyze_image(args.imageurl, args.question)
    print(answer)
```

As you see, all it takes is a few lines of Python code to answer questions about images! The function `analyze_image` (❶) contains but a single call to GPT-4o, using the message described in the previous subsection (❷). The fact that we now provide multimodal input does not change the format of the answer. Again, we get an object containing a message generated by the language model. Although the input may now be multimodal, the output is text. As we instructed the language model to generate an answer to the input question (❸) (i.e., exactly what the user is looking for), the output is directly printed out for the user.

6.2.3 *Trying it out*

Time to test our visual question-answering system! You're back at Banana (a producer of various consumer electronics, including laptops and smartphones, introduced in chapter 2) and looking for a new company logo. You want to base your logo on a picture of a banana. Searching the web, you find large repositories with images of fruit. But which of them are bananas? Instead of going through images by hand, you would much rather delegate that task to a language model. Luckily, you can directly use the code from the previous section by specifying the URL of each fruit picture, together with the question "Is this a banana ("Yes","No")?" This means you're using the visual question-answering system essentially as a classification method (which is only one of many possible use cases). You can then write a simple script, iterating over all relevant URLs and retaining the ones where the answer is "Yes."

On the book's companion website, you will find the code from listing 6.1 as well as pictures of fruit (look for the links labeled Fruit 1 to Fruit 5). Download the code, change to the containing repository in the terminal, and run the following code:

```
python [URL] 'Is this a banana ("Yes","No")?'
```

In this command, replace [URL] with the URL of the image (you can obtain a suitable URL by, for example, copying the Fruit 1 link on the book's website).

Object classification is relatively easy, particularly for objects as common as bananas. So you should see accurate results for most examples. Try a few different fruits and possibly other images of your choice. The range of questions you can ask is virtually unlimited (putting aside the rather generous input length limit of 128,000 tokens, about 300 pages of text).

A word of caution may be in order when it comes to processing costs. Processing images via GPT-4o can be expensive! The precise cost depends on the image size and the degree of detail used for image processing. You can control the degree of precision using the `detail` parameter. For instance, choose a low degree of precision using the following specification of image URLs (in the model input):

```
{'type':'image_url', 'image_url':{'url':image_url, 'detail':'low'}}
```

Set the `detail` attribute to `low` to pay a cost equivalent to 85 tokens per image (i.e., the cost equivalent of processing a text with 85 tokens using GPT-4o). If you set the degree of detail to `high` (the default), the cost consists of a fixed amount of 85 tokens and a variable amount that depends on the image size. To calculate the variable cost component, we first scale the image to a size (in pixels) of 2,048 × 2,048 (while maintaining the aspect ratio). This scaling step only applies to pictures with a size beyond 2,048 × 2,048 pixels. The second scaling step is performed in any case. It scales the shorter side of the image to a size of 768 pixels. Now consider the minimum number of 512 × 512 pixel squares needed to cover the image after the second scaling step. The variable cost component is proportional to the number of squares multiplied by a factor of 170 tokens (the cost per square, set by OpenAI).

For instance, let's say we want to process an image of size 1,024 × 1,024 pixels with high precision. In that case, we can skip the first scaling step, as the image still fits within a 2,048 × 2,048 pixel square. The second scaling step, however, is performed in any case. It scales the image to a size of 768 × 768 pixels. To cover a square with a length of 768 pixels on both sides, we require four squares of size 512 × 512 pixels. That means that to process our image, we pay the following:

- 85 tokens (the fixed cost component)
- 4 × 170 tokens = 680 tokens (the variable cost component)

In total, we therefore pay 85 + 4 × 170 = 765 tokens. Given current prices, this corresponds to $0.003825 (i.e., less than one cent). Although that may seem acceptable, always keep costs in mind when processing large repositories of images via language models.

> **TIP** To find the price for processing images with a specific resolution, you can also use the OpenAI price calculator: https://openai.com/pricing.

6.3   *Tagging people in images*

Imagine the following situation: you just came back from a (well-deserved) holiday with friends, and, of course, you have taken a large number of pictures. You want to send your friends the pictures in which they appear. But how to do that efficiently? You could go through the pictures by hand and tag each friend individually. But having just come back from vacation, your email inbox is overflowing, and you don't have time to go through holiday pictures. What can you do?

6.3.1   Overview

In this section, we will create a small application that automatically tags people in images. Users provide three inputs:

- The path of a directory containing the pictures to tag
- The path of a directory containing pictures of the people to look for
- The path to an output directory into which tagged pictures are written

To keep things simple, we will use filenames to represent tags. We assume that pictures showing people to look for are named after the person they show. For example, let's say we have images named Joe.png and Jane.png in our directory containing the people to look for. Given a picture to tag, we will simply change the filename by prefixing it with the names of people that appear in it.

For instance, assume we have an image called beach.png in which both Joe and Jane appear. Then, in the output directory, we will create two files called Joebeach.png and Janebeach.png, showing that both appear in the beach picture. If we want to send out all pictures showing the same person, such as Joe, we can search for all files whose name satisfies the regular expression Joe*.png (with * representing arbitrary strings).

Internally, as a first step, we need to load pictures representing people to look for, as well as the pictures to tag. We will consider each pair of a person to look for and a picture to tag. For example, if we are looking for five people and have 10 pictures to tag, that makes 50 pairs to consider. For each of these pairs, we use GPT-4o to decide whether the corresponding person appears in the picture to tag.

To make that happen, we will need multimodal prompts containing text and two pictures. The first picture shows the person to look for, and the second picture shows the picture to tag. Via text, we can instruct the language model to compare the pictures to decide whether the same person appears. Whenever we find a match—that is, a combination of a person and a picture in which that person appears—we will copy the corresponding picture to the output folder, prefixing its name with the name of the person.

Figure 6.2 shows an example prompt. On the left, we have a picture of Jane, one of the people we are looking for. On the right side, we have a picture to tag. The text instructions ask the language model to compare the two pictures, producing the answer "Yes" if they show the same person (and "No" otherwise). In this case, the pictures do not show the same person, and the correct answer should be "No."

6.3.2   Encoding locally stored images

In the previous section, we used GPT-4o to analyze images on the web. Now we are talking about our private holiday pictures. We may not want to make all of them publicly accessible on the web. So how can we share them with GPT-4o alone?

We may have to convert images into a format suitable for GPT-4o. GPT-4o supports a wide range of image formats, including PNG, JPEG, WEBP, and GIF. For any format, the image file size is currently limited to 20 MB. To upload pictures of the supported types to GPT-4o, we first need to encode them using a base64 encoding.

Do the images show the same person ("Yes"/"No")?

Figure 6.2   Multimodal prompt containing two images and text: the prompt instructs the language model to check whether the two pictures show the same person (expected answer: "Yes") or not (expected answer: "No").

What is base64 encoding?

The base64 encoding is a way to encode binary data as a printable string. As the name base64 suggests, the alphabet we use for the string is based on 64 characters. This means we can represent each character using six bits (because six bits allow representing $2^6 = 64$ possible characters). As computers store data at the granularity of bytes (i.e., 8 bits), it is convenient to encode groups of three bytes (i.e., 24 bits) together. Using base64 encoding, three bytes can be used to represent four characters (as $24/6 = 4$).

In Python, we can use the `base64` library to encode binary data in the base64 format. The following code opens an image file stored at `image_path` and encodes it using base64 format:

```
with open(image_path, 'rb') as image_file:
    encoded = base64.b64encode(image_file.read())
```

We have transformed the binary image data into a string in base64 format. Before sending such images to GPT-4o, we still need to make one final transformation: we must represent the string using the UTF-8 encoding.

What is UTF-8 encoding?

UTF-8 is a way to represent string data. It is extremely popular and used by about 98% of sites on the web. UTF-8 can represent over a million characters, covering a variety of languages. We can represent those characters using a fixed number of bytes: four bytes to represent each character. However, this is inefficient because it does not exploit the fact that certain characters are much more common than others. If we encode common characters with fewer bytes while reserving many-byte representations for the less common ones, we can represent the same text with fewer bytes. This is what UTF-8 does, and because different characters may need a different number of bytes for representation, it is also called a *variable-length standard*. At the same time, UTF-8 is designed to be backward-compatible with the older ASCII standard, using the same encoding as ASCII for the first 128 characters.

To transform our base64 string encoding of the image into UTF-8, we can use Python's `decode` function. Assuming that the image is still encoded in the `encoded` string variable, we can do so using the following code:

```
image = encoded.decode('utf-8')
```

The resulting image, encoded as UTF-8 text string, is suitable as input for GPT-4o. Next, we will see how we can upload images in this format to the OpenAI platform. After uploading them, we can include references to those pictures in our prompts. Images are generally specified as components of the prompt:

```
{'type':'image_url', 'image_url':{'url':image_url}}
```

Here, `image_url` represents the URL that leads to the image to analyze. Previously, we used publicly accessible URLs for that. Now we are analyzing private images that we will send to OpenAI to be used only to process specific requests. Assuming that `image` still represents the image encoded as a string, we can set the image URL as follows:

```
image_url = {'url':f'data:image/png;base64,{image}'}
```

This code assumes that the image is of type PNG (if not, replace the string `png` with the appropriate format identifier such as `jpeg`). The URL combines metadata about the image (such as the image type and encoding) with a string suffix representing the picture itself.

6.3.3 *Sending locally stored images to OpenAI*

We will use this project as an opportunity to demonstrate an alternative way to interact with GPT models. Doing so will give us insights into how OpenAI's Python library works internally. So far, we have been using Python wrappers that send requests to OpenAI's platform in the background. To send our local images to GPT-4o, we will create those requests ourselves.

We use Python's `requests` library to create HTTP requests, sending our prompts (with text and images) to GPT-4o and collecting the answer. More precisely, we will be sending HTTP Post requests. This is the type of request accepted by the OpenAI platform. Such requests can be sent via the `requests.post` method.

Our requests will contain all relevant information needed by GPT-4o to solve the task we are interested in (in this case, verifying whether two images show the same person). First, we need to include headers in the request. We will use the following headers:

```
headers = {
    'Content-Type': 'application/json',
    'Authorization': 'Bearer ...'
}
```

You see that we're specifying headers as a Python dictionary. For our use case, we only need to store two properties: the type of our payload (we plan to send JSON content) and our access credentials (the three dots represent our OpenAI access key).

Next, we need to specify the payload—that is, the content that we primarily want to send via the request:

```
payload = {
    'model': 'gpt-4o',        ❶ Model specification
    'messages': [
        {'role': 'user', 'content': ...}    ❷ First message
        ],
    'max_tokens':1     ❸ Output length
    }
```

You may notice that the payload contains exactly the fields we would typically specify in our invocations to the `completions.create` method. That is not a coincidence, as the latter method creates requests with a similar payload internally. First, the payload specifies the model (❶): gpt-4o (to be able to process multimodal input prompts). We specify a list of messages with a single entry (❷). This message is marked as originating from the user (`'role':'user'`), and its content, abbreviated by three dots, will contain text instructions and images. Finally, we limit the answer length to a single token (`'max_tokens':1`) (❸). That makes sense because we are searching for a binary result: either the same person appears in multiple input images (expected answer: "Yes") or not (expected answer: "No").

Having generated headers and a payload, we can invoke GPT-4o using the following code:

```
response = requests.post(
        'https://api.openai.com/v1/chat/completions',
        headers=headers, json=payload)
```

As the first parameter, the invocation of `requests.post` specifies the URL to send the request to. In this case, `'https://api.openai.com/v1/chat/completions'` indicates that we want to perform a task of type `Completion`, using one of OpenAI's chat models (which applies to GPT-4o). We use the headers and payload created previously.

The response contains the GPT-4o result object. We can access the answer (indicating whether two images show the same person) via the following code snippet:

```
response.json()['choices'][0]['message']['content']
```

6.3.4 *The end-to-end implementation*

We are now ready to discuss the end-to-end implementation! Listing 6.2 contains code for tagging people in pictures. Have a look at the main function (❹) first. As discussed previously, users specify three directories as command-line parameters (❺): a directory containing pictures to tag, a directory containing people to use for tagging, and an output directory.

As a first step, we load all images to tag as well as all images of the people to search for. We use the load_images function (❶) for that. This function retrieves a list of all files in the input directory and then considers those ending with the suffix .png (i.e., we consider all PNG images). As discussed previously, we need to encode images as strings (via base64 encoding) that are ultimately represented via the UTF-8 encoding. The result of load_images is a Python dictionary mapping filenames to the associated, encoded images. This dictionary is returned as the result of the function.

Listing 6.2 Tagging people in pictures stored locally

```
import argparse
import base64
import os
import requests
import shutil


def load_images(in_dir):                    ❶ Loads images from disk
    """ Loads images from a directory.

    Args:
        in_dir: path of input directory.

    Returns:
        directory mapping file names to PNG images.
    """
    name_to_image = {}
    file_names = os.listdir(in_dir)
    for file_name in file_names:
        if file_name.endswith('.png'):
            image_path = os.path.join(in_dir, file_name)
            with open(image_path, 'rb') as image_file:
                encoded = base64.b64encode(image_file.read())
                image = encoded.decode('utf-8')
                name_to_image[file_name] = image

    return name_to_image


def create_prompt(                          ❷ Creates a multimodal prompt
    person_image, image_to_label):
    """ Create prompt to compare images.

    Args:
        person_image: image showing a person.
```

```
        image_to_label: image to assign to a label.

    Returns:
        prompt to verify if the same person appears in both images.
    """
    task = {'type':'text',
            'text':'Do the images show the same person ("Yes"/"No")?'}
    prompt = [task]
    for image in [person_image, image_to_label]:
        image_url = {'url':f'data:image/png;base64,{image}'}
        image_msg = {'type':'image_url', 'image_url':image_url}
        prompt += [image_msg]

    return prompt


def call_llm(ai_key, prompt):                    ❸ Generates an answer for the prompt
    """ Call language model to process prompt with local images.

    Args:
        ai_key: key to access OpenAI.
        prompt: a prompt merging text and local images.

    Returns:
        answer by the language model.
    """
    headers = {
        'Content-Type': 'application/json',
        'Authorization': f'Bearer {ai_key}'
    }
    payload = {
        'model': 'gpt-4o',
        'messages': [
            {'role': 'user', 'content': prompt}
            ],
        'max_tokens':1
        }
    response = requests.post(
        'https://api.openai.com/v1/chat/completions',
        headers=headers, json=payload)
    return response.json()['choices'][0]['message']['content']


if __name__ == '__main__':      ❹ Tags images with people

    parser = argparse.ArgumentParser()                  ❺ Command-line parameters
    parser.add_argument('peopledir', type=str, help='Images of people')
    parser.add_argument('picsdir', type=str, help='Images to tag')
    parser.add_argument('outdir', type=str, help='Output directory')
    args = parser.parse_args()

    people_images = load_images(args.peopledir)
    unlabeled_images = load_images(args.picsdir)

    for person_name, person_image in people_images.items():      ❻ Over people
```

```
for un_name, un_image in unlabeled_images.items():          ❼ Over images
    prompt = create_prompt(person_image, un_image)
    ai_key = os.getenv('OPENAI_API_KEY')
    response = call_llm(ai_key, prompt)
    description = f'un_name versus person_name?'
    print(f'description -> response')

    if response == 'Yes':                  ❽ Copies image in case of a match
        labeled_name = f'person_name[:-4]un_name'
        source_path = os.path.join(args.picsdir, un_name)
        target_path = os.path.join(args.outdir, labeled_name)
        shutil.copy(source_path, target_path)
```

After applying the `load_images` function to each of the two input directories, we end up with two Python dictionaries. One maps filenames of images showing people (which, by convention, are the names of those people) to the corresponding encoded image. The other maps the filenames of images to be tagged to the encoded images.

Our goal is to match each picture to be tagged to all people that appear in it. As we use prompts comparing only two pictures at once, we need to look at each combination of a person and of an image to tag. That is why we use a double-nested `for` loop: one iterates over people (❻) and the other over images to tag (❼).

For each combination of an image to tag and a person, we create a multimodal prompt using `create_prompt`. This function (❷) assembles both encoded pictures, together with text instructions, into a prompt. The text instructions ("Do the images show the same person ("Yes"/"No")?") define the task as well as the expected output format ("Yes" or "No"). Each prompt is sent to GPT-4o via `call_llm`. As discussed previously, this function (❸) uses the requests API to send locally stored images, together with text instructions, to GPT-4o. If GPT-4o answers "Yes," the currently considered person appears in the currently considered image to tag.

If the person appears in the image (❽), we tag the image as follows. We use the name of the person (the name of the associated picture file without the .png suffix) and prepend it to the name of the file to tag. Next, we copy the file to tag to the output directory using the new filename (which indicates the tagging result).

6.3.5 *Trying it out*

Let's try it! If you have real vacation pictures to tag, you can use them. Otherwise, you will find suitable test data on the book's companion website. Look for the Tagging link to access a zipped file; download this file and unzip its contents. After decompression, you should see three subdirectories in the resulting folder:

- *people*—A folder containing pictures of people (in this case, actors from the *Avengers* series). Filenames contain the names of the corresponding actors.
- *pics*—Another set of pictures (in this case, more pictures of the same actors as in the people folder) to tag with the names of actors.
- *processed*—An empty folder that can be used as the output directory.

We'll assume that the decompressed folder is stored under the path /tagging (e.g., the path /tagging/people then leads to the subfolder with pictures of people to search for). Execute the code by running the following command from the terminal:

```
python listing2.py /tagging/people  /tagging/pics /tagging/processed
```

> **TIP**   If you are invoking the code on a Windows platform, you will have to adapt these paths. In particular, you will have to replace / with \.

During processing, the implementation prints updates on whether specific people appear in specific pictures. The sample data contains two people to look for and four images to tag. This means processing should not take more than a few minutes (typically less than two).

After processing finishes, look in the output folder. You should see pictures to tag, prefixed with the names of people appearing in them. Not bad for a few lines of Python code!

6.4   Generating titles for videos

Besides many pictures (which we can now automatically tag, thanks to the code outlined in the previous section!), you also took quite a few videos on vacation. Automatically assigned filenames are not very informative. Which video is the one showing you swimming in the ocean? It would be great to assign meaningful captions to those videos and help you find the ones you're looking for faster. But who has time to manually label videos? Again, we can use language models to do that task automatically.

6.4.1   Overview

We will develop a system that automatically assigns suitable titles to videos. This system uses GPT-4o in the background. To assign titles to videos, we will submit multimodal prompts containing video frames (i.e., images) together with text instructing the language model to come up with a title. Figure 6.3 shows an example prompt.

Generate a concise title for the video.

Figure 6.3   Multimodal prompt for video processing: based on a selection of video frames, the language model is instructed to generate a suitable title.

It consists of multiple video frames (we only see the first and the last frame in figure 6.3; the three dots represent the ones in between) and the text instructions "Generate a concise title for the video." Note that we have to pay for each video frame we're submitting to GPT-4o. That means video data processing via GPT-4o quickly becomes expensive!

As an answer, GPT-4o should send back a reasonable title. In the example shown in figure 6.3, this can be a reference to cars and, potentially, even a reference to the location (shown as white text in the frames).

6.4.2 Encoding video frames

First we need to discuss video formats. In the last section, we saw how to encode images stored locally. Now we will expand that to videos. Ultimately, our goal is to extract a sequence of frames. However, videos are typically not stored as a sequence of frames but using more efficient encodings. For us, that means we first have to extract images from a video.

We will use the OpenCV library for that. OpenCV is the Open Source Computer Vision Library. It provides various functionalities for computer vision as well as for image and video processing in general. Of course, we will use GPT-4o to do the computer vision part. Nevertheless, OpenCV will be useful for extracting frames from videos. If you haven't done so already, now would be a good time to set up OpenCV by following the instructions in section 6.1.

Let's assume that the installation has worked and you can access OpenCV from Python. The corresponding Python library is called `cv2` (a name you will often see as a prefix in the following code snippets).

To work with a video stored locally, we first need to open the corresponding file. Run this code to open a video stored under the path `video_path`:

```
video = cv2.VideoCapture(video_path)
```

Using the variable `video`, we can now read the video's content via the `read` method:

```
success, frame = video.read()
```

The result consists of tuples with two components: a `success` flag and a video frame. The `success` flag indicates whether we were able to read another frame. That's no longer the case once we reach the end of the video. In that case, we do not obtain a valid frame, and the `success` flag is set to `False`.

Let's assume that we are able to read another frame. In that case, we will turn the frame into an image we can send to GPT-4o. OpenCV has us covered and provides the corresponding functionality:

```
_, buffer = cv2.imencode('.jpg', frame)
```

The `imencode` function turns a video frame into an image of the corresponding type. Here, we transform the frame into a JPEG picture. From the resulting tuple, the second component (`buffer`) is interesting for our purposes. It contains a binary representation of the corresponding picture.

That's a situation we know from the previous section: we have a binary representation of an image and want to turn it into a suitable format for GPT-4o. Again, we first encode the image as a string via base64 encoding and then represent that string via UTF-8:

```
encoded = base64.b64encode(buffer)
frame = encoded.decode('utf-8')
```

The resulting `frame` is encoded properly to be included as part of a GPT-4o prompt. Once you're done processing the video, close the corresponding video capture object using the following code:

```
video.release()
```

Next, we will put everything together to generate video titles for arbitrary videos.

6.4.3 *The end-to-end implementation*

Listing 6.3 generates titles for videos stored locally. The only input parameter is the path to the video. Given that, the implementation extracts some of the video frames (❹) and then generates a prompt instructing GPT-4o to generate a video title based on a sample of frames. After sending this prompt to the language model, the answer contains a proposed video title.

Listing 6.3   Generating a video title via language models

```
import argparse
import cv2
import base64
import openai
import time

client = openai.OpenAI()

def extract_frames(video_path):        ❶ Extracts video frames
    """ Extracts frames from a video.

    Args:
        video_path: path to video file.

    Returns:
        list of first ten video frames.
    """
    video = cv2.VideoCapture(video_path)
    frames = []
    while video.isOpened() and len(frames) <= 10:
        success, frame = video.read()
        if not success:
            break

        _, buffer = cv2.imencode('.jpg', frame)
        encoded = base64.b64encode(buffer)
```

```
        frame = encoded.decode('utf-8')
        frames += [frame]

    video.release()
    return frames

def create_prompt(frames):
    """ Create prompt to generate title for video.

    Args:
        frames: frames of video.

    Returns:
        prompt containing multimodal data (as list).
    """
    prompt = ['Generate a concise title for the video.']
    for frame in frames[:10]:
        element = {'image':frame, 'resize':768}
        prompt += [element]
    return prompt

def call_llm(prompt):
    """ Query large language model and return answer.

    Args:
        prompt: input prompt for language model.

    Returns:
        Answer by the language model.
    """
    for nr_retries in range(1, 4):
        try:
            response = client.chat.completions.create(
                model='gpt-4o',
                messages=[
                    {'role':'user', 'content':prompt}
                    ]
                )
            return response.choices[0].message.content
        except:
            time.sleep(nr_retries * 2)
    raise Exception('Cannot query OpenAI model!')

if __name__ == '__main__':

    parser = argparse.ArgumentParser()
    parser.add_argument('videopath', type=str, help='Path of video file')
    args = parser.parse_args()

    frames = extract_frames(args.videopath)
    prompt = create_prompt(frames)
    title = call_llm(prompt)
    print(title)
```

❷ **Creates multimodal prompt**

❸ **Queries the language model**

❹ **Titles videos**

The code extracts video frames using `extract_frames` (❶). As discussed previously, this function uses the OpenCV library to open the video for frame extraction and proceeds to read each frame consecutively. We will only use up to 10 frames to generate a video title. That's why extraction ends after at most 10 frames (or fewer if the video is very short). Each extracted frame is encoded according to GPT-4o's requirements (i.e., JPEG images encoded as strings). The result of the function is a list of encoded frames.

During prompt generation (❷), we combine relevant text instructions ("Generate a concise title for the video.") with the first 10 frames from the video. To send those images, along with instructions, to GPT-4o, we use a Python wrapper again (❸). Alternatively, we can create requests ourselves (as in the previous project). The response of the language model should contain a suitable title for our video.

Of course, we are only sending the first few frames of the video. If the video content changes drastically after those few frames, the title may not be optimal. The reason we only send 10 frames is computation fees. Keep in mind that you're paying for each picture submitted in the prompt! Sending all frames of larger videos is typically prohibitively expensive. That's why we content ourselves with sending only a small subset of video frames.

6.4.4   *Trying it out*

Let's try our video title generator! On the book's companion website, this chapter's section includes a Cars link that will guide you to a short video from a traffic camera showing traffic on a busy road. Download the video to your local machine.

Open the terminal, and change to the directory containing the code for this chapter. We'll assume that the video was downloaded into the same directory (if not, replace the name of the video, cars.mp4, with the full path leading to it).

Run the following command:

```
python listing3.py cars.mp4
```

After a few seconds of computation time, you should see a proposal for a video title: for example, "Traffic Conditions on I-5 at SR 516 and 188th Street" (the precise title may vary across different runs due to randomization).

Note that the title integrates information—the name of the location—that is only available in the form of text in the video. Using GPT-4o to extract text from images may be useful in various scenarios: for example, to extract data from forms.

Summary

- GPT-4o processes images as well as text.
- Prompts can integrate text snippets and images.
- GPT-4o supports multiple image formats.
- Images can be specified via a public image URL.
- Locally stored images can be uploaded to OpenAI.
- GPT-4o processes images in string encoding.
- Processing images is costly compared to processing text. The cost of image processing may depend on the image size. Processing images with a low degree of detail reduces costs.
- The `base64` library can encode images as strings.
- Decompose videos into their frames to send them to GPT-4o.
- The OpenCV library can be used to extract frames from videos.

Analyzing audio data

This chapter covers

- Transcribing audio data
- Translating audio data
- Generating speech

Watch any credible science fiction TV show or movie, and you won't see people typing to interact with their computers! Whether it's *Star Trek* or *2001: A Space Odyssey* (both released in the 1960s), people speak to (not type into) their machines. And there are good reasons for that! For most users, voice is the most natural form of communication (because that's the one they start with). No wonder people imagined speaking with computers long before that was technically feasible.

Reality has now caught up with science fiction, and voice assistants, including the likes of Amazon's Alexa, Google's Assistant, and Microsoft's Cortana (among many others), are ubiquitous. The newest generation of speech recognition (and speech generation) models have reached near-human levels of proficiency. And voice-based interaction with computers is, of course, only one use case for this amazing technology.

In this chapter, we will use OpenAI's latest models for speech transcription, translation, and speech generation for several mini-projects. First, we will see that transcribing voice recordings to text takes just a few lines of Python code. After that, we'll look at more complex applications, starting with a voice-based version of our natural language database query interface from chapter 5. Whereas we previously had to type in questions, we can now simply speak them, and the system will produce an answer. Finally, we will see how to build a simultaneous translator that turns our voice input into voice output in a different language.

7.1 Preliminaries

Before we can start with all of those cool projects, we need to perform a few setup steps. First, you will need to record voice input via your computer. For that to work, you first need some kind of microphone. Most laptops nowadays have a built-in microphone. It doesn't have to be a professional microphone; any way of recording sound on your computer will do. But beyond the microphone, you also need software that can be activated from Python to turn audio recordings into files. For that, we will use Python's `sounddevice` library. Run the following command in the terminal to install this library in the correct version:

```
pip install sounddevice==0.4
```

This library interacts with Python's `scipy` library, which you should also install. Run the following command in the terminal:

```
pip install scipy==1.11
```

Together, those libraries will enable you to record voice input (which you can then transcribe, translate, or summarize using OpenAI's models).

We have covered the input side, but what about the output? For some of the following projects, we not only want to listen to audio but also generate it! To generate speech, we will use OpenAI's generative AI models again. But after generating speech stored in an audio file, we still need suitable libraries to play speech on our computer from Python. We will use the `playsound` library for that. Run this command in the terminal to install this library in the correct version:

```
pip install playsound==1.3
```

On certain operating systems (in particular, macOS), you additionally have to install the `PyObjC` library using the following command:

```
pip install PyObjC==10.0
```

If you haven't done so already when working through the last chapter, install the `requests` library (enabling you to send requests directly to OpenAI's API):

```
pip install requests==2.31.0
```

Well done! If you didn't encounter any error messages running these commands, your system is now configured to process audio data with OpenAI's Transformer models. Let's start with our first project in the next section.

7.2   Transcribing audio files

Having recently started your job at Banana, you are overwhelmed by the number of meetings. There are just too many meetings to attend, but you don't want to miss anything important! Fortunately, Banana has the good sense to create audio recordings of all employee meetings as a general rule (with the consent of all participants). But listening to all the recordings of those meetings is still too time-consuming.

It would be great to have transcripts of meetings, enabling you to quickly search for anything relevant to your unit via a simple text search. Unfortunately, Banana doesn't offer such transcripts out of the box, and none of your colleagues are willing to take notes during those meetings. Would it be possible to create such transcripts automatically? In this section, we will see that it's not only possible but actually easy to create such an automated transcription service.

7.2.1   Transcribing speech

For transcribing speech to text, we will use OpenAI's Whisper model. Unlike the models we have used so far (in particular, GPT models), Whisper is specifically targeted at audio transcriptions.

What is the Whisper model?

Whisper is a Transformer model trained on large numbers of audio recordings (more than 680,000 hours of recordings, to be precise!). Whisper was trained on a multilingual audio corpus and therefore supports a broad range of input languages that it transcribes to English (i.e., you get speech transcription and translation in a single step).

Similar to the GPT variants, we will access Whisper via OpenAI's Python library. This means no additional setup is required on your local machine (assuming that you have installed OpenAI's Python library, as described in chapter 3).

In this section, we will use the Whisper model to transcribe an audio file to disk. Let's assume that our audio file is initially stored on disk. Whisper supports a wide range of file formats: MP3, MP4, MPEG, MPGA, M4A, WAV, and WEBM. At the time of writing, the file size is limited to 25 MB. Given such a file, let's assume that its file path is stored in the variable `audio_path`. Now all it takes to transcribe its content to text are the following few lines of Python code:

```
import openai
client = openai.OpenAI()

with open(audio_path, 'rb') as audio_file:    ❶ Opens the audio file
```

❷ **Transcribes the content**
```
transcription = client.audio.transcriptions.create(
    file=audio_file, model='whisper-1')
```

As a first step (❶), we need to open our audio file. For that, we can use Python's `open` command. Note the use of the `rb` flag as a parameter of the `open` command. This flag indicates to Python that we want to read the file (`r`) and that we are opening a binary file (`b`). A binary file is a file that does not contain readable characters. Sound files, such as the one we are trying to open here, generally qualify as binary files. After processing the first line, the file content is accessible via the variable `audio_file`.

As a second step (❷), we perform the actual transcription. We now use a different endpoint, specialized for audio data processing. From that endpoint, we invoke the transcription service (`transcriptions.create`) using two parameters:

- `file`—A reference to the file to transcribe
- `model`—The name of the model for transcription

We refer to the previously opened file (`audio_file`) and select `whisper-1` as our transcription model. The result of transcription is an object containing the transcribed text and metadata about the transcription process. We can access the transcribed text via the `text` field (i.e., via `transcription.text`).ents. After decompression, you should see three subdirectories in the resulting folder:

As you see, transcribing text takes just a few lines of Python code! In the next subsection, we will use this code to build a simple transcription service.

7.2.2 *End-to-end code*

Listing 7.1 shows the code for a simple transcription program. The actual transcription happens in the `transcribe` function (❶). This is essentially the code we discussed in the previous section. Given the path to an audio file as input, it returns the transcribed text.

Listing 7.1 Transcribing audio files to text

```
import argparse
import openai

client = openai.OpenAI()


def transcribe(audio_path):          ❶ Transcribes audio to text
    """ Transcribe audio file to text.

    Args:
        audio_path: path to audio file.

    Returns:
        transcribed text.
    """
    with open(audio_path, 'rb') as audio_file:
```

```
    transcription = client.audio.transcriptions.create(
        file=audio_file, model='whisper-1')
    return transcription.text

if __name__ == '__main__':           ❷ Main function

    parser = argparse.ArgumentParser()
    parser.add_argument('audiopath', type=str, help='Path to audio file')
    args = parser.parse_args()

    transcript = transcribe(args.audiopath)
    print(transcript)
```

The main function (❷) reads the path to an audio file (which should contain speech) as input. After invoking the `transcriptions.create` function, it prints the transcribed text on the screen.

7.2.3   *Trying it out*

To try it, we first need an audio file with recorded speech. You can use any such file (including a recording of your company meetings, if available) as long as it complies with the format and size restrictions outlined in section 7.2.1. However, keep in mind that you pay per minute of audio data processed! At the time of writing, using Whisper via the OpenAI library costs $0.006 per minute (you can find more up-to-date information about pricing at https://openai.com/pricing). Processing long recordings can therefore be expensive.

If you don't want to use your own recording, have a look at the book's companion website. You can find a short recording in the Audio item in this chapter's section. Download this recording to use it for transcription (by default, the filename should be QuoteFromTheAlchemist.mp3).

Listing 7.1 is also available on the book's companion website (item listing1.py in the chapter 7 section). After downloading it, switch to the corresponding repository in the terminal. Assuming that you downloaded the audio file into the current directory, run the following command in the terminal to transcribe the sample file:

```
python listing1.py QuoteFromTheAlchemist.mp3
```

If everything goes well, you should see the following output in the terminal (for the sample file from the website, that is):

```
Two years ago, right here on this spot,
I had a recurrent dream, too.
```

Click the sample file to listen to it yourself; you will find the transcript to be accurate! Next, we will integrate speech transcription into more complex applications.

7.3   *Querying relational data via voice*

Analyzing tabular data is fun! A significant part of your job at Banana consists of poring over data tables, extracting insights, and preparing corresponding reports and visualizations. You're using the text-to-SQL interface from chapter 5 to automatically translate text questions to formal queries (written in SQL), execute them, and present the query results. This makes analyzing data easier and is faster than writing complex SQL queries from scratch.

However, there is a problem: you think better when pacing back and forth in your office while analyzing data. But typing queries forces you back to your desk every time. Can't we modify our query interface to accept spoken, as opposed to typed, input? It turns out that indeed, we can! In this section, we will see how to use OpenAI's models to enable a simple voice query interface for tabular data.

7.3.1 Preliminaries

We will build a voice query interface that processes spoken questions on tabular data. It is an extension of the query interface discussed in chapter 5. We assume that spoken questions refer to data stored in SQLite, a popular system for processing queries on relational data. See chapter 5 for a short introduction to SQLite and installation instructions. To try the following code, you will first need to install the SQLite database system.

The SQLite system processes queries formulated in SQL, the structured query language. Fortunately, you won't need to write SQL queries yourself (we will use a language model to write those SQL queries for us). However, language models are not perfect and may occasionally produce incorrect queries. To recognize those cases, it is useful to have a certain degree of SQL background. You will find a short introduction to SQL in chapter 5. For more details, have a look at www.databaselecture.com.

Our voice query interface processes spoken questions, so you need to ensure that your microphone is working. Also, to execute the following code, make sure your voice query interface has all the required permissions to access the microphone.

7.3.2 Overview

Our voice query interface processes spoken questions on tabular data stored in an SQLite database. For instance, having loaded a database with data about computer game sales, we can ask questions such as the following:

- "How many games did Activision sell in 2023?"
- "How many action games were released between 2019 and 2021?"

On receiving a spoken question, the voice query interface performs the following steps:

1. Transcribes the spoken question into text
2. Translates the text question into an SQL query
3. Processes the SQL query on the data using SQLite
4. Displays the query result to the user

Figure 7.1 illustrates the different processing steps in more detail. The process is executed for each spoken question.

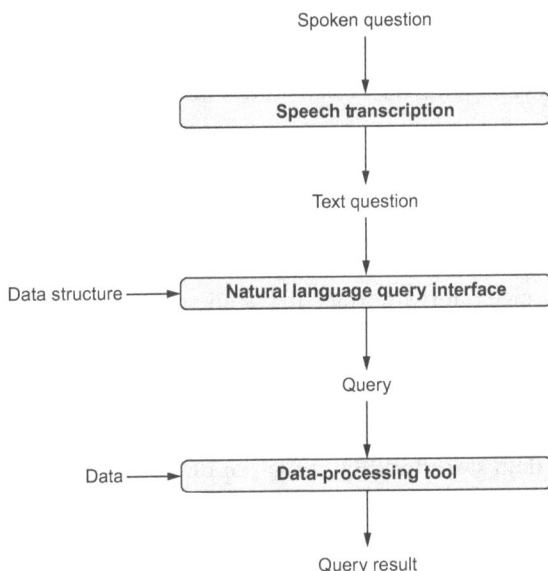

Figure 7.1   Our voice query interface transcribes spoken questions into text, translates text questions into SQL queries, and finally processes those queries and displays the query result.

7.3.3   *Recording audio*

For our transcription application, we assumed that an audio recording was already available. For our new project, we want to issue voice queries repeatedly. That means we have to record them ourselves. How can we do that in Python? First, we need to import two libraries for precisely that purpose:

```
import sounddevice        ❶  Records audio
import scipy.io.wavfile   ❷  Stores .wav files
```

The `sounddevice` library (❶) contains many useful functions to record audio input from a microphone. What will we do with our recordings? We will store them as .wav files on disk. In the previous section, we saw how to transcribe audio data stored in that format. This is where the second library (❷), `scipy`, comes into play: it enables us to store the recordings in .wav format on disk.

When recording, we need to make two important choices:

- At what sample rate should we read input from the microphone?
- How many seconds of speech should we record?

We will record for a duration of 5 seconds. Five seconds should suffice for most voice queries. You can try different settings if the recording tends to terminate too soon or if you find yourself waiting often after finishing your voice queries. A more sophisticated implementation would record continuously or stop recording after a speaking pause is detected. To keep things simple in terms of the recording mechanism, we will just record for a predetermined amount of time for each voice query.

For the sampling rate—that is, the number of audio data points stored per second—we will choose 44,100 Hertz. This is the standard for CD-quality recordings. The total number of *frames*—the number of audio data points received in total—is then 44,100 times the number of seconds we want to record (in our case, that's 5 seconds). We store the number of frames and the sampling rate in auxiliary variables:

```
sample_rate = 44100
nr_frames = 5 * sample_rate
```

Now we're ready to record using the `rec` function of the `sounddevice` library:

```
recording = sounddevice.rec(                    ❶ Sets up recording
    nr_frames, samplerate=sample_rate, channels=1)
sounddevice.wait()                              ❷ Waits for recording to finish
```

The first command (❶) starts a recording from the input microphone, providing as input the total number of frames to record as well as the sampling rate. The number of channels (the third parameter in our invocation) depends on the microphone used for the recording. If your microphone has more than one channel, try a higher value here. After starting the recording, we just need to wait until the predetermined recording time has passed. We accomplish that via the `wait` command (❷).

After executing the previous code, the variable `recording` contains the recorded audio data. As discussed earlier, we want to store the recording as a .wav file on disk. All it takes is a single command from the `scipy` library:

```
scipy.io.wavfile.write(output_path, sample_rate, recording)
```

That's it! We have recorded a few seconds of audio input and stored it in a file on disk.

7.3.4 *End-to-end code*

Listing 7.2 shows the code for our voice query interface. Beyond our default libraries, `openai` and `argparse`, we import (❶) the libraries for audio processing (`sounddevice` and `scipy`), as well as the `sqlite3` library (which we will need for processing SQL queries) and the `time` library. The latter library is required to wait for a specified amount of time (for voice input). Next, we will discuss the functions introduced in listing 7.2.

Listing 7.2   Querying an SQLite database using voice commands

```
import argparse      ❶ Imports libraries
import openai
import re
import scipy.io.wavfile
import sounddevice
import sqlite3
import time
```

```
client = openai.OpenAI()

def get_structure(data_path):                    ❷ Extracts the database schema
    """ Extract structure from SQLite database.

    Args:
        data_path: path to SQLite data file.

    Returns:
        text description of database structure.
    """
    with sqlite3.connect(data_path) as connection:
        cursor = connection.cursor()
        cursor.execute("select sql from sqlite_master where type = 'table';")
        table_rows = cursor.fetchall()
        table_ddls = [r[0] for r in table_rows]
        return '\n'.join(table_ddls)

def record(output_path):                          ❸ Records audio
    """ Record audio and store in .wav file.

    Args:
        output_path: store audio recording there.
    """
    sample_rate = 44100
    nr_frames = 5 * sample_rate
    recording = sounddevice.rec(
        nr_frames, samplerate=sample_rate, channels=1)
    sounddevice.wait()
    scipy.io.wavfile.write(output_path, sample_rate, recording)

def transcribe(audio_path):              ❹ Transcribes audio
    """ Transcribe audio file to text.

    Args:
        audio_path: path to audio file.

    Returns:
        transcribed text.
    """
    with open(audio_path, 'rb') as audio_file:
        transcription = client.audio.transcriptions.create(
            file=audio_file, model='whisper-1')
        return transcription.text

def create_prompt(description, question):         ❺ Creates a text-to-SQL prompt
    """ Generate prompt to translate question into SQL query.

    Args:
        description: text description of database structure.
        question: question about data in natural language.

    Returns:
```

```
            prompt for question translation.
        """
    parts = []
    parts += ['Database:']
    parts += [description]
    parts += ['Translate this question into SQL query:']
    parts += [question]
    parts += ['SQL Query:']
    return '\n'.join(parts)


def call_llm(prompt):                            ❻ Translates to SQL
    """ Query large language model and return answer.

    Args:
        prompt: input prompt for language model.

    Returns:
        Answer by language model.
    """
    for nr_retries in range(1, 4):
        try:
            response = client.chat.completions.create(
                model='gpt-4o',
                messages=[
                    {'role':'user', 'content':prompt}
                    ]
                )
            return response.choices[0].message.content
        except:
            time.sleep(nr_retries * 2)
    raise Exception('Cannot query OpenAI model!')


def process_query(data_path, query):             ❼ Processes the SQL query
    """ Processes SQL query and returns result.

    Args:
        data_path: path to SQLite data file.
        query: process this query on database.

    Returns:
        query result.
    """
    with sqlite3.connect(data_path) as connection:
        cursor = connection.cursor()
        cursor.execute(query)
        table_rows = cursor.fetchall()
        table_strings = [str(r) for r in table_rows]
        return '\n'.join(table_strings)


if __name__ == '__main__':      ❽ Processes the voice queries
    parser = argparse.ArgumentParser()
```

```
parser.add_argument('dbpath', type=str, help='Path to SQLite data')
args = parser.parse_args()

data_structure = get_structure(args.dbpath)

while True:     ❾ Main loop
    user_input = input('Press enter to record (type quit to quit).')
    if user_input == 'quit':
        break

    audio_path = 'question.wav'     ❿ Transcribes voice input
    record(audio_path)
    question = transcribe(audio_path)
    print(f'Question: {question}')

    prompt = create_prompt(data_structure, question)     ⓫ SQL translation
    answer = call_llm(prompt)
    query = re.findall(''"`'sql(.*)"`'', answer, re.DOTALL)[0]
    print(f'SQL: {query}')

    try:                                      ⓬ Executes the SQL query
        answer = process_query(args.dbpath, query)
        print(f'Answer: {answer}')
    except:
        print('Error processing query! Try to reformulate.')
```

We process voice queries that refer to data in a relational database. To translate voice commands into formal queries formulated in SQL, we need to know a little about the database structure. In particular, we need to know the names of the data tables and their columns (i.e., we need to know the database schema). The function get_structure (❷) retrieves the commands used to create the database schema. These commands contain the names of tables and columns, as well as the data types associated with the table columns. We will use those commands as part of a prompt, instructing the language model to translate questions into SQL queries.

Before we can translate questions, we first need to record them from the microphone. This is where the function record (❸) comes into play. It uses the sounddevice library to record 5 consecutive seconds of audio input from the microphone. The resulting audio recording is stored as a .wav file on disk at a path specified as function input (parameter output_path). Strictly speaking, storing the audio input as a file is not necessary (we can process it directly in memory). However, storing audio input on disk can be useful for debugging purposes. If our system fails to translate voice input to appropriate queries, we can listen to the audio file ourselves to assess the level of background noise and overall audio quality. If the microphone is not set up properly (a common problem), our audio files will contain nothing but silence.

After recording input from the microphone, we first want to transcribe voice input to text. We use the transcribe function (❹) for that. Given a path to an audio file (in this case, recorded audio input from the microphone), it returns a transcript generated using OpenAI's Whisper model (the same one we used previously).

Next, we want to translate questions into formal SQL queries. Of course, we will use language models for that task. The `create_prompt` function (**❺**) generates a suitable prompt. The prompt contains the previously extracted description of the database, the transcribed question, and the task description. The `call_llm` function (**❻**) calls GPT-4o to translate questions, given the previously mentioned prompt as input. Finally, the `process_query` function (**❼**) processes the resulting queries on the database and returns the query result.

Time to put it all together! Our voice query interface takes the path to an SQLite database file as input (**❽**). After extracting the database schema, we enter the main loop (**❾**). Each iteration processes one voice query (unless the user enters `quit`, in which case the program terminates). To keep things simple, we wait for the user to press the Enter key before recording voice input (a more sophisticated version would record continuously). After that, we record voice input from the microphone. We print out the transcribed question and store the recording itself as question.wav on disk (**❿**). Next, we translate the transcribed text into a query (**⓫**), execute it (**⓬**) (we need exception handling here in case of incorrect queries!), and show the result to users.

7.3.5 *Trying it out*

Listing 7.2 is listing 2 in the chapter 7 section on the book's website. Download the code, and switch to the containing folder in your terminal.

Beyond the code, we also need an SQLite database to try our voice query interface. We discuss in chapter 5 how to set up an example database containing information about computer game sales. We assume this database is stored in the same folder as your code and named games.db (of course, you are free to use any SQLite database you like to try the voice query interface). Now enter the following command in the terminal:

```
python listing1.py games.db
```

Update the path to the database file to the one you want to access. Depending on your operating system and security settings, you may be asked to enable microphone access for your application. After enabling microphone access, press Enter, and ask a question! For instance, using the games database, you may ask "How many games were sold in 2007?" or "How many games were released for each genre?" You should see output like the following:

```
Press enter to record (type quit to quit).
Question: How many games were released for each genre?
SQL: SELECT genre, COUNT(*) as num_games
FROM games
GROUP BY genre
Answer: ('Action', 3316)
('Adventure', 1286)
('Fighting', 848)
('Genre', 1)
```

```
('Misc', 1739)
('Platform', 886)
('Puzzle', 582)
('Racing', 1249)
('Role-Playing', 1488)
('Shooter', 1310)
('Simulation', 867)
('Sports', 2346)
('Strategy', 681)
```

This output includes the transcribed question, the translated SQL query, and the query result (or an error message if the query cannot be executed). Clearly, it's a long way from a voice question to a query result! A mistake in recording, transcription, or translation will lead to incorrect results. Before trusting the query result, be sure to check the additional output to verify that the system did not make any mistakes.

> **TIP**   If your voice interface only produces nonsense, check the recordings in question.wav. If you don't hear anything, make sure your application has access to your microphone. By default, applications typically have no access to the microphone (making it harder to spy on you with malicious software). You need to update your security settings to enable access.

7.4   *Speech-to-speech translation*

The Banana branch in Paris has started looking into language models and potential applications for data science tasks. You have grown your reputation as the local expert on the topic, and your manager asks you to advise the French team on how to get started. There is just one tiny problem: you don't speak any French. On hearing that Banana Paris conducts most staff meetings in French, you are about to decline the assignment. But after thinking about it, you realize that this may not be a dealbreaker after all. Although you don't speak any French, GPT-4o certainly does! Would it be possible to use language models to translate for you?

You can indeed use language models to translate between various languages. In this section, we will create a translator tool that takes spoken input in a first language and produces spoken output in a second language. Because the tool produces spoken output, you don't even need to learn the French pronunciation. Simply speak English and wait for the tool to produce a spoken translation. That way, you can collaborate with your French colleagues while simultaneously demonstrating the capabilities of state-of-the-art language models!

7.4.1   *Overview*

Our translator tool processes spoken input. As before, we will use OpenAI's Whisper model to transcribe input speech to text. Then, we will use the GPT-4o model to translate the text to a different language. For our example scenarios, we use French as the target language. However, due to the amazing flexibility of models like GPT-4o, our tool won't be restricted to that! Our tool will enable users to specify the target language as input, to be used as a text snippet in the prompt instructing the language model for the translation.

After generating a text translation, we still want to generate a spoken version. It turns out that we can use yet another OpenAI model to transform text into spoken output in various languages. Figure 7.2 shows the complete processing pipeline, starting with spoken input in a first language and ending with spoken output in a second.

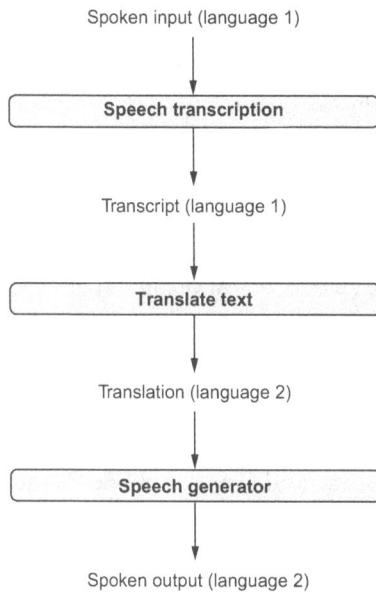

Spoken input (language 1)

Speech transcription

Transcript (language 1)

Translate text

Translation (language 2)

Speech generator

Spoken output (language 2)

Figure 7.2 Our translator tool records spoken input in a first language, transcribes input to text, translates that text into a second language, and finally generates spoken output.

7.4.2 Generating speech

The pipeline in figure 7.2 requires several transformations. We already saw how to transcribe spoken input to text in the previous sections. Translating text via language models is relatively straightforward (ask GPT-4o to translate from one language to another, and it will do so). We are still missing a way to transform written text (e.g., in French) into spoken output. We discuss how to do that next.

OpenAI (as well as other providers) offers several text-to-speech (TTS) models. Such models take written text as input and produce a spoken version as output. The following piece of code generates speech for a text string (stored in the variable speech_text):

```
import openai
client = openai.OpenAI()

response = client.audio.speech.create(
    model='tts-1', voice='alloy',
    input=speech_text)
```

We're using a new endpoint in this instance (`audio.speech`) and configuring the `create` method using three parameters:

- `model`—The name of the model used to generate spoken output. We use OpenAI's `tts-1` text-to-speech model.
- `input`—We generate spoken output for this text. Submit text in any of the various languages supported by the model (https://github.com/openai/whisper).
- `voice`—We can choose between different voices for speech. Here, we use `alloy`.

That's all we need to generate speech output via OpenAI! We already know how to transcribe speech and how to translate text between different languages, so we now have all we need to code our translator tool.

What about pricing?

At the time of writing, OpenAI charges 1.5 cents per 1,000 tokens for text generation using the TTS model and twice that for the high-quality version (TTS HD). These prices are likely to change over time, so be sure to look at OpenAI's pricing website (https://openai.com/pricing) for updated information.

7.4.3   End-to-end code

Listing 7.3 shows the complete code for our translator tool. Let's start by discussing the libraries it imports (❶). Besides the `openai` and `argparse` libraries included in each project so far, we import `sounddevice` and `scipy` to record and store audio files, along with the `time` library to limit recording time.

Listing 7.3   Translating spoken input into a different language

```
import argparse        ❶ Imports libraries
import openai
import playsound
import requests
import scipy.io.wavfile
import sounddevice
import time

client = openai.OpenAI()

def record(output_path):                    ❷ Records audio
    """ Record audio and store in .wav file.

    Args:
        output_path: store audio recording there.
    """
    sample_rate = 44100
    nr_frames = 5 * sample_rate
    recording = sounddevice.rec(
```

```
            nr_frames, samplerate=sample_rate, channels=1)
    sounddevice.wait()
    scipy.io.wavfile.write(output_path, sample_rate, recording)
```

```
def transcribe(audio_path):                    ❸ Transcribes audio
    """ Transcribe audio file to text.

    Args:
        audio_path: path to audio file.

    Returns:
        transcribed text.
    """
    with open(audio_path, 'rb') as audio_file:
        transcription = client.audio.transcriptions.create(
            file=audio_file, model='whisper-1')
        return transcription.text
```

❹ **Generates a prompt for translation**

```
def create_prompt(to_translate, to_language):
    """ Generate prompt to translate text to target language.

    Args:
        to_translate: translate this text.
        to_language: translate text to this language.

    Returns:
        Translated text.
    """
    parts = []
    parts += [f'Translate this text to {to_language}:']
    parts += [to_translate]
    parts += ['Translated text:']
    return '\n'.join(parts)
```

```
def call_llm(prompt):                          ❺ Uses the language model
    """ Query large language model and return answer.

    Args:
        prompt: input prompt for language model.

    Returns:
        Answer by language model.
    """
    for nr_retries in range(1, 4):
        try:
            response = client.chat.completions.create(
                model='gpt-4o',
                messages=[
                    {'role':'user', 'content':prompt}
                    ]
                )
```

```
            return response.choices[0].message.content
        except:
            time.sleep(nr_retries * 2)
    raise Exception('Cannot query OpenAI model!')


def generate_speech(speech_text):          ❻ Generates speech
    """ Generates speech for given text.

    Args:
        speech_text: generate speech for this text.

    Returns:
        query result.
    """
    response = client.audio.speech.create(
        model='tts-1', voice='alloy',
        input=speech_text)
    return response.content


if __name__ == '__main__':          ❼ Translates speech to speech

    parser = argparse.ArgumentParser()
    parser.add_argument('tolanguage', type=str, help='Target language')
    args = parser.parse_args()

    while True:     ❽ Main loop

        user_input = input('Press enter to record (type quit to quit).')
        if user_input == 'quit':
            break

        audio_path = 'to_translate.wav'     ❾ Transcribes the input
        record(audio_path)
        to_translate = transcribe(audio_path)
        print(f'Original text: {to_translate}')

        ❿ Translates to the target language
        prompt = create_prompt(to_translate, args.tolanguage)
        translated = call_llm(prompt)
        print(f'Translated text: {translated}')

        speech = generate_speech(translated)          ⓫ Generates speech output
        with open('translation.mp3', 'wb') as file:
            file.write(speech)

        playsound.playsound('translation.mp3')     ⓬ Plays the generated speech
```

The `playsound` library is used to play audio files generated by OpenAI's models. Because we generate speech via OpenAI's HTTP interface, we import the `requests` library to create HTTP requests. Next, we will discuss the functions used in listing 7.3.

As in the previous project, we record audio data from the microphone. The `record` function (❷) records 5 seconds of audio input and stores it into a .wav file on disk. The `transcribe` function (❸) transcribes that audio input to text. Both functions have been discussed in more detail in the prior projects in this chapter.

The `create_prompt` function (❹) generates a prompt for translation. As in prior projects, the prompt contains a task description, together with all relevant input data. In this case, we want to translate from the initial language (English) to the target language (French). Note that the target language is specified as an input parameter (`to_language`). This input parameter corresponds to a text snippet describing the desired output language. In the simplest case, this can be the name of a language (e.g., "French"). On the other hand, users can request a specific dialect (e.g., "German with Swabian dialect") or style (e.g., "English in the style of Shakespeare"). The target language is integrated into the task description that appears in the prompt along with the text to translate.

Note that we do not need to specify the input language. We assume that the language model is able to recognize the language of the input text (otherwise, we cannot expect the model to translate either).

After invoking the `call_llm` function (❺) with the prompt, we should obtain translated text. The `generate_speech` function (❻) generates the corresponding speech using the approach we discussed in the previous section.

The translator application (❼) expects as input a text describing the target language. This parameter is a string that can contain arbitrary text. It simply replaces a placeholder in the prompt used for translation. In the main loop (❽), users press Enter to speak or enter `quit` to terminate the application.

When recording user input, we first store 5 seconds of audio recording in a file named to_translate.wav before transcribing the input via the `transcribe` function (❾). After that, we use GPT-4o to translate the input to the target language (❿) and then generate speech from the translation (⓫). We store the generated speech as an .mp3 file on disk (this means we can easily hear the last output again) and, finally, use the `playsound` library to—you guessed it—play the generated sound file.

7.4.4 *Trying it out*

Time to try our translator! You can find the code on the companion website as listing 3 in the chapter 7 section. Download the code, and switch to the containing folder in the terminal. We can choose our target language for translation. Of course, the quality of the translation and sound output may vary, depending on that choice. In particular, the model we use for transcription, as well as the model we use for speech generation, support a set of about 60 common languages. Transcribing audio input or generating audio output in less common languages may fail. Look online to see the current list of supported languages for transcription (https://help.openai.com/en/articles/7031512-whisper-api-faq) as well as speech generation (https://platform.openai.com/docs/guides/text-to-speech). For now, consistent with our scenario at the beginning of this section, we will go with French as the target language. In the terminal, enter the following command to start our translator:

```
python listing3.py "French"
```

Strictly speaking, the quotes around the word "French" are unnecessary. However, as we can enter multiword descriptions of the desired target language, we will need quotes in the following examples to avoid errors if the console misinterprets our input as values for multiple parameters.

As in our previous project, we need to give our application access to the microphone. Click Yes if you are asked for microphone access; if not, be sure the security settings allow it. The following is an extract from a conversation with our translator tool:

```
Press enter to record (type quit to quit).
Original text: Hello my colleagues in Paris.
Translated text: Bonjour mes collègues à Paris.
Press enter to record (type quit to quit).
Original text: Let me teach you something
about language models.
Translated text: Laisse-moi t'apprendre
quelque chose à propos des modèles de langage.
```

You see transcribed input and the generated translation. You should also hear the spoken version of the translation (if not, check your settings for audio output). Not bad for a few lines of Python code!

Translating to French seems like a reasonable use case for our translator tool. However, it may not be the one with the highest "fun factor." Let's try something different to show the flexibility of language models: let's see if we can "translate" our audio input to a highly polished version. In the terminal, enter the following instructions:

```
python listing3.py "English in the style of Shakespeare"
```

This is what we get when translating our simple greeting into a much more refined version (perhaps a nice intro to a course on language models for our U.S. colleagues at Banana):

```
Press enter to record (type quit to quit).
Original text: Hello, my dear colleagues.
Translated text: Hark, my fair allies, I bid thee well met!
Press enter to record (type quit to quit).
Original text: Let me teach you
something about language models.
Translated text: Pray, lend me thine ear
as I shalt educate thee on language models.
```

Try a few more target languages! The possibilities are (almost) unlimited.

Summary

- OpenAI's Whisper model transcribes speech input to text.
- Access transcription via the audio transcriptions endpoint.
- Pricing for transcription is based on the number of minutes.
- OpenAI offers several models for generating speech from text.
- You can choose the voice and quality for generated speech.
- Speech generation pricing depends on the number of tokens.

Part 3

Advanced topics

This part of the book will help you write applications with language models that are more effective and cost-efficient.

Chapter 8 broadens our scope from OpenAI's language models to other providers. Before applying language models to large data sets, it is crucial to compare models offered by different providers. That way, you get the optimal tradeoff between cost and quality for your specific scenario. The chapter discusses some of the most popular providers, their models, and the libraries they offer.

Chapter 9 demonstrates techniques for cost optimization in an example scenario. It covers topics such as prompt engineering, the optimal tuning of model configuration parameters, and fine-tuning, a process by which a language model is specialized for one specific task. As shown in this chapter, using those methods can yield significant improvements in terms of quality and cost.

Chapter 10 discusses two software frameworks that have become very popular for developing complex applications on top of language models: LangChain and LlamaIndex. Both can be useful for data analysis. In particular, the chapter shows how to use those frameworks to build agents, an approach that enables language models to solve complex data analysis tasks using a variety of computational tools.

GPT alternatives 8

Time to meet some of GPT's "friends"! So far, we have been focusing on GPT and other OpenAI models. But OpenAI is not the only game in town. Quite the contrary: we are currently witnessing a "Cambrian explosion" of language models, with new models popping up every week. Before using language models in production, you want to make sure you're using the best model for your task. In this chapter, we'll look at many of the OpenAI alternatives out there and discuss the pros and cons of different models as well as how to use them.

Almost all language models nowadays are based on a similar architecture (the Transformer architecture). However, models from different providers may differ in the way they are trained, the way they represent text, or the way in which they are offered and priced. All those factors can make a difference in terms of processing fees and output quality for your specific task. Models like GPT-4o are powerful and solve almost any task. But this generality comes at a cost: if a small, specialized model is available, trained for just the task you're interested in, using such a model may very well be the optimal choice.

You will notice throughout the following sections that many of the models we discuss can be accessed via interfaces that are similar to OpenAI's interface. That's good news for you: no need to get into a novel and complex framework each time you want to try a different model! And with that, let's start our exploration of GPT alternatives.

Why isn't my favorite model listed?

If your favorite model or model provider is not listed in this chapter, don't panic! With the growing number of providers and models, it has become impossible to give a full overview of available models. If a model is not included here, it does not mean it can't be the best alternative for your task. The interfaces of different providers tend to be similar, so you should still be able to use what you have learned so far to employ other models without much trouble. Also, note that we list model providers in alphabetical order in this chapter. Don't infer any priority from that (we're not discussing the best providers first).

8.1 Anthropic

Many of the stories by Isaac Asimov, one of the most prolific science-fiction authors of all time, center on the "three laws of robotics" and their interpretation:

1 A robot may not injure a human being or, through inaction, allow a human being to come to harm.
2 A robot must obey orders given to it by human beings except where such orders would conflict with the First Law.
3 A robot must protect its own existence as long as such protection does not conflict with the First or Second Law.

The goal here is to have a concise set of guidelines that makes sure robots are helpful and harmless. Whether the previously mentioned laws provided any inspiration, this idea connects to the language models produced by Anthropic, yet another provider of large-scale language models.

Anthropic, founded in 2021 (by several former OpenAI members), has repeatedly touted the idea of "Constitutional AI" [1] as one of the distinguishing factors, compared to other models. In a nutshell, this means that when training models to provide users with accurate and inoffensive answers, we rely on a small set of rules—a "constitution," so to speak—to judge the quality of answers. Instead of relying on human testers to label answers generated by the model during training, we employ a second AI, charged with evaluating the answers of the former according to the constitution.

At the time of writing, Claude 3.5 (a reference to the amazing Claude Shannon) is the latest model released by Anthropic. In this section, we will try Claude via (you guessed it) a web interface and a Python library.

8.1.1   *Chatting with Claude*

We will have a quick chat with Claude (currently in version 3.5) to get a sense of its capabilities. First, go to the Anthropic website at www.anthropic.com, and click the Talk to Claude button.

Unless you have created an Anthropic account before, you will be asked to provide an email address and a phone number. After verifying your data, you should see Claude's chat interface, shown in figure 8.1.

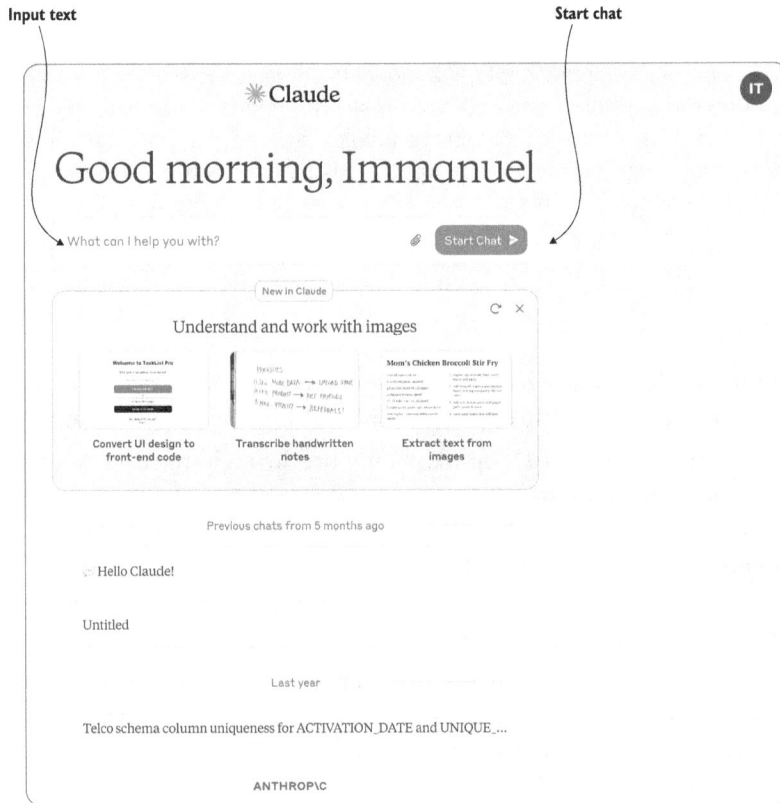

Figure 8.1   Web interface for Anthropic's chatbot Claude

The interface is pretty intuitive: simply enter text in the corresponding field, and click the button on the right to start chatting! Begin with a friendly greeting, chat about the weather, or try using Claude to solve some of the tasks from chapter 2 (e.g., classifying reviews by sentiment or translating questions to SQL queries).

8.1.2   *Python library*

Assuming you have created an account with Anthropic, you can create keys at the following URL: https://console.anthropic.com/settings/keys. Be sure to copy your access key after creating it (as you will not be able to access it again afterward)!

After obtaining your access key, go to the terminal and run the following command:

```
pip install anthropic==0.28
```

This will install the Anthropic Python library. If you are familiar with OpenAI's Python library (and chances are that, after reading the previous chapters, you are), you should get used to the Anthropic library very quickly.

For instance, the following listing shows Python code for answering questions using Claude. Of course, this code does not do anything that you cannot do via the web interface. The purpose is just to show how easy it is to use Claude via the Python interface.

Listing 8.1 Answering questions with Anthropic's Claude model

```
import argparse
from anthropic import Anthropic

if __name__ == '__main__':

    parser = argparse.ArgumentParser()              ❶ Defines parameters
    parser.add_argument('ai_key', type=str, help='Anthropic access key')
    parser.add_argument('question', type=str, help='A question for Claude')
    args = parser.parse_args()

    anthropic = Anthropic(api_key=args.ai_key)      ❷ Configures Anthropic

    completion = anthropic.messages.create(         ❸ Uses Claude for completion
        model='claude-3-5-sonnet-20241022',
        max_tokens=100,
        messages=[
            {
                'role':'user',
                'content':args.question
            }])
    print(completion.content)      ❹ Prints the completion result
```

As input parameters (❶), we use the Anthropic access key and a question we would like answered. Similar to OpenAI's libraries, we configure access using the access key (❷). After that, we can construct prompts for completion by Claude (❸).

Using Anthropic's `anthropic.messages` endpoint, we specify the ID of the model to use (`claude-3-5-sonnet-20241022` is the newest model by Anthropic at the time of writing) and the maximum number of tokens for completion (using the `max_tokens` parameter). Similar to OpenAI's chat models, Claude is designed for chats between users and the model. Therefore, the input to Claude is a list of messages (containing only a single element in this specific scenario). We obtain the result of Claude's prompt completion in the `content` field (which we print (❹)).

You can find this listing as the Anthropic item on the companion website. To execute it, open your terminal, and switch to the containing folder. Then, execute the following command:

```
python anthropic_claude.py ... "What is constitutional AI?"
```

Replace the three dots with your Anthropic access key. When executing the program, you should see an answer to your question, generated by Anthropic's model.

8.2   Cohere

We briefly discussed hallucinations in chapter 2. Essentially, a hallucination occurs when language models make stuff up because they don't have access to data that is relevant to the task at hand. The Canadian startup Cohere puts a particular emphasis on avoiding such hallucinations using a method called *grounding*. Grounding the answer of a language model means linking it to real data, thereby reducing the chances of "creative output" not based in reality.

Cohere supports a wide range of connectors, enabling its models to access external data. For instance, web search is supported, as well access to various databases. Internally, Cohere accesses those data sources and provides the language model with information tailored to the request. But even better, Cohere shows you all the data sources used to generate your answer. If you are the suspicious type (and when it comes to answers from language models, you generally should be), you can follow up on references and validate that they support the generated answer.

Let's see how all that works in practice. Time to chat with Cohere's Command R+ model!

8.2.1   Chatting with Command R+

At the time of writing, Command R+ is one of Cohere's latest models. As usual, you can try it via web interface and use it via Python when processing large amounts of data. First, we'll try the web interface. For that, go to https://cohere.com/, and click Try Now. After signing up for an account, click Playground. You should see the web interface in figure 8.2.

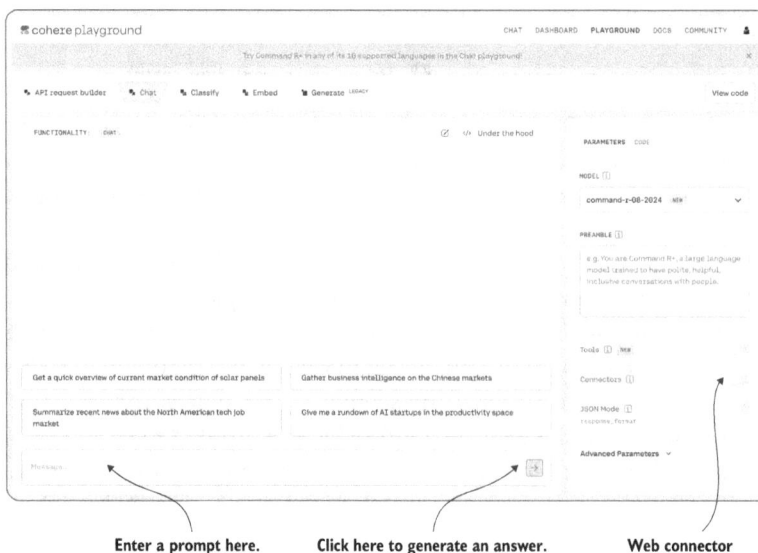

Figure 8.2   Web interface for chatting with Cohere's language model Command R+

Figure 8.2 shows where to enter your prompt and the button to generate an answer. What about the window on the right (containing the Web Connector button)? This is where you specify connectors to use when generating your replies. A connector enables Cohere to access external data sources. We can activate (or deactivate) the web connector by toggling the corresponding button. This connector enables Cohere to query the web, similar to what all of us would do when trying to answer a hard question that involves factual knowledge. Give it a try, and see how the replies to factual questions change if the web connector is activated or deactivated!

What is RAG?

You may have noticed that Cohere's website prominently advertises *RAG*, but what is that? RAG stands for Retrieval Augmented Generation. It means that when generating an answer, we augment the input used by the language model with data we retrieve from an external source.

8.2.2 Python library

Cohere offers a Python library similar to the ones we have seen in previous sections. Enter the following command in the terminal to install the required library:

```
pip install cohere==4.43
```

Listing 8.2 (available as the Cohere item on the website) contains code for a simple question-answering interface. Users enter their access key and a question on the command line. Visit https://dashboard.cohere.com/api-keys to get your access key. In listing 8.2, after configuring the Cohere library with the access key (❶), we generate an answer using the Cohere library (❷). Note the reference to `connectors` in the call to the `chat` function! Here, we specify a list of connectors, enabling Cohere's model to access data from external sources. Connectors are specified as a list (i.e., we can enable access not to just one but to a multitude of connectors). Here we use the connector with ID `web-search` (that's the same web search connector we used over the web interface in the previous section).

Finally (❸), we print the answer generated by the model and a list of the web sources consulted to generate the answer (along with the queries issued to retrieve those documents). That enables us to verify that the generated answer is indeed implied by the source material.

Listing 8.2   Answering questions using Cohere's Python library

```
import argparse
import cohere

if __name__ == '__main__':

    parser = argparse.ArgumentParser()
```

```
parser.add_argument('ai_key', type=str, help='Cohere access key')
parser.add_argument('question', type=str, help='Answer this question')
args = parser.parse_args()

client = cohere.Client(args.ai_key)    ❶ Configures access
```

❷ **Generates an answer using Cohere**
```
prompt = f'Answer this question: {args.question}'
result = client.chat(prompt, connectors=[{'id': 'web-search'}])
```

❸ **Prints answer and citations**
```
print(f'Answer: result.text')
print(f'Web searches: result.search_results')
print(f'Web results: result.documents')
```

Let's try it! Switch to the folder containing the code, and run the following command in the terminal (replace the three dots with your Cohere access key):

```
python cohereqa.py ... "Where was Steve Jobs born?"
```

You will get an answer similar to the following (which is slightly abbreviated):

❶ **Generated answer**
```
Answer: Steven Paul Jobs was born in San Francisco, California, United States.
His birth name was later changed to Steve Jobs after
he was adopted by Paul and Clara Jobs.

Jobs was born to Abdulfattah Jandali and Joanne Schieble on 24th February, 1955.
After being put up for adoption, Jobs was adopted by Paul and Clara Jobs,
a lower-middle-class couple.
```

```
Web searches: [    ❷ Web search queries
    {'search_query':
        {'text': 'Where was Steve Jobs born',
        'generation_id': '...'},
    'document_ids': [
        'web-search_1:0', 'web-search_3:1', 'web-search_4:0',
        'web-search_5:0', 'web-search_9:1'],
    'connector': {'id': 'web-search'}
    }]
```

```
Web results: [    ❸ Web documents used
    {'id': 'web-search_4:0', 'snippet': 'Short Biography of Steve Jobs
    The story of Steve Jobs from cradle to grave - and beyond. Steven
    Paul Jobs was born on February 24, 1955 in San Francisco, California.
    ... ', 'title': 'Short Bio | all about Steve Jobs.com',
    'url': 'https://allaboutstevejobs.com/bio/short_bio'},
    ...]
```

Let's have a closer look. The initial part of the output (❶) is the answer generated by the model. The answer seems reasonable, but can we trust it? This is where the remaining parts of the output come into play. The middle part (❷) provides us with information on the web used by Cohere to inform the generated answer. Those web queries are chosen automatically based on the input question. In this case, web queries correspond precisely to the input question (this is not necessarily the case for longer input text). At the end of the output (❸), we find text snippets and the URLs of the documents retrieved via the prior queries. In this case, text snippets taken from the web documents (e.g., "Steven Paul Jobs was born on February 24, 1955 in San Francisco, California") make a good case supporting the answer from the model.

8.3 Google

Google, a company that needs no introduction, has been deeply involved with language models since the very beginning. In fact, the Transformer architecture [2] used by virtually all language models was invented (primarily) by Google researchers. No wonder Google is developing its own models. At the time of writing, Gemini is one of Google's most recent models, and we'll try it in this section.

8.3.1 Chatting with Gemini

To try Gemini, go to https://gemini.google.com/. After signing up for an account, you should see the interface depicted in figure 8.3.

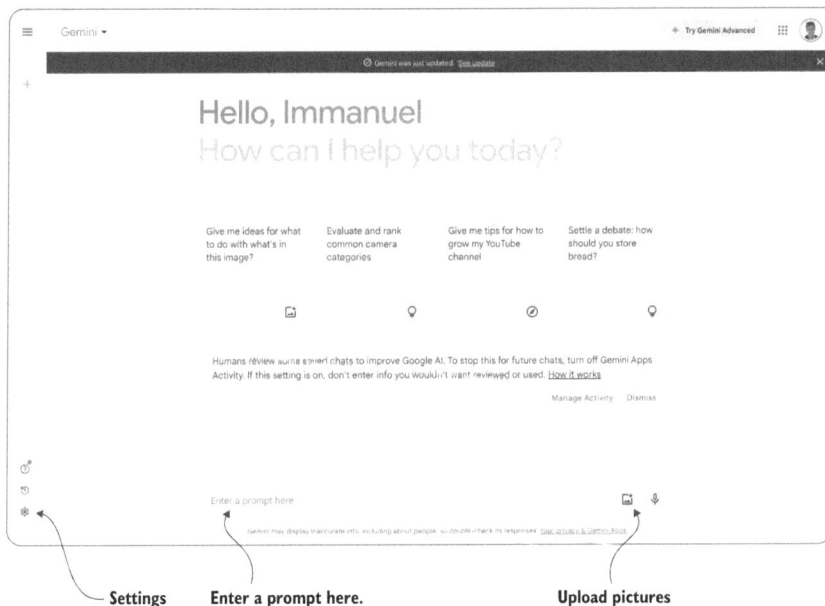

Figure 8.3   Web interface for chatting with Google's Gemini model. Click Settings to activate additional functionality.

Simply enter your text in the corresponding input field (labeled Enter prompt here in figure 8.3), and press Enter to generate an answer. Gemini is not limited to text input. Click the button on the right to upload pictures. In your chats with Gemini, you can reference those pictures and ask questions about them.

One particularity of Gemini, distinguishing it from all the other models we have discussed so far, is its integration with other Google tools. Click the Settings button (marked in figure 8.3) and then the Extensions option. For instance, you can give Gemini access to your emails by clicking the associated button. Ever had the problem of finding information hidden in year-old emails in your inbox? Google's Gemini has the potential to help with that.

8.3.2 The Python library

Like other providers of language models, Google offers a Python library for model access. You can install the library using the following code in the terminal:

```
pip install google-generativeai==0.7
```

Go to https://aistudio.google.com/app/apikey to get your access key for the Google API. Follow the instructions, and copy the key after creating it. Listing 8.3 shows how to use Gemini in Python to answer questions. The steps are similar to the previous libraries. The input parameters (❶) include the access key (alternatively, we can store the key in an environment variable) as well as the question to answer. Next, we configure the Google library with the access key (❷). Now we can generate a model and use it to answer questions via the `generate_content` method (❸). Finally, we print out the generated question (❹).

Listing 8.3   Answering questions using Google's Gemini model

```
import argparse
import google.generativeai as genai

if __name__ == '__main__':
```
❶ Defines the input parameters
```
    parser = argparse.ArgumentParser()
    parser.add_argument('api_key', type=str, help='Google API key')
    parser.add_argument('question', type=str, help='Question to answer')
    args = parser.parse_args()
```
❷ Configures the API with the access key
```
    genai.configure(api_key=args.api_key)
```
❸ Generates an answer with Gemini
```
    model = genai.GenerativeModel('gemini-1.5-flash')
    reply = model.generate_content(args.question)
```
❹ Prints the answer
```
    print(reply.text)
```

You can find the code on the book's website using the Google link. In the terminal, change to the directory containing the code. For instance, run the following command to test Gemini (replace the three dots with your Google access key):

```
python google.py ... "What is the meaning of life?"
```

A full overview of Google's library is beyond the scope of this book. However, knowing the libraries of other providers of large language models, you should be able to familiarize yourself quickly with this API as well.

8.4 Hugging Face

Providers like OpenAI invest millions of dollars to train models like GPT-4o. The result of all that expensive training is values for model parameters that make the model perform best. After investing all that money, you would not necessarily want to share the results of training freely, right? Hence, models like GPT-4o are typically closed, meaning OpenAI does not share the parameter values that result from training (note that OpenAI has shared other models, such as Whisper). Instead, OpenAI processes prompts for you on its own infrastructure while charging you a processing fee (that's how we ultimately pay for all that expensive model training).

More and more, however, language model providers face competition from an extremely lively open source sector. Universities, startup companies, and enthusiasts all train their own models and often release the models (and their parameter values) freely to the public. That enables you to run those models yourself, locally, on your own dedicated infrastructure. For smaller models, a laptop with a GPU will often suffice. For larger models, you may need to use a GPU cluster (or resort to cloud providers that run those open source models for you). Besides potential financial advantages (running models on your own infrastructure may be cheaper), other considerations can make running models locally the only viable choice. For instance, you may not want to trust external providers with particularly sensitive data. If you don't want to send your data, running locally is the only option.

Typically, open source models are significantly smaller than the models offered by cloud providers. That makes sense because after all, who has a few million dollars lying around to train a model? However, due to the sheer number of models available, it is often possible to find an open source model that is specialized in solving just the task you're interested in. For instance, the Hugging Face Transformers platform features over 1,000,000 Transformer models at the time of writing! Whatever task you are facing, chances are that you may find just the right model. In this section, we will look at the Hugging Face platform and see how to use its models locally.

8.4.1 Web platform

Go to https://huggingface.co/. Hugging Face Transformers offers various resources around Transformer models. That includes not only the models but also data sets you can use to train your own models as well as cloud offerings that let you run open source models on Hugging Face's cloud infrastructure.

For the moment, we are interested in models. Click the Models button to see the list of models shown in figure 8.4.

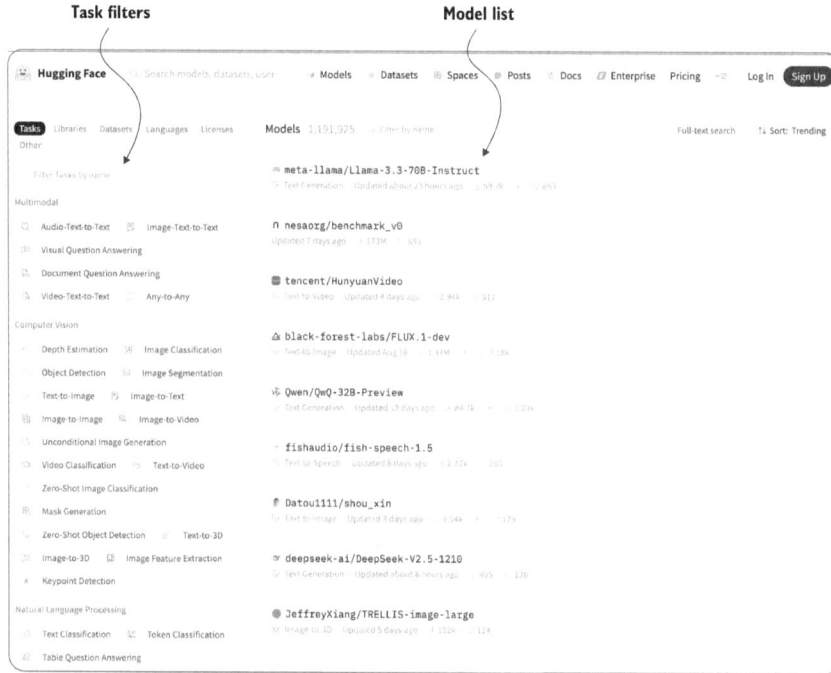

Figure 8.4   Overview of Hugging Face Transformer models. Click the Tasks filters to narrow the selec-tion. Click models in the Models list to see details.

We're seeing a list of over 1 million Transformer models (and, as the number of models is growing daily, you will probably see even more)! Whew. That's a few too many. Let's narrow them down. On the left side of the screen are various filter options to get the list down to the models you really care about. For instance, we can filter by the type of task we need the model to do. This includes text classification (e.g., classifying reviews by sentiment), visual question answering (e.g., does the picture show an apple?), and speech-to-text transcription (e.g., transcribing voice queries to text). For almost all the tasks we have discussed in this book, you may be able to find a specialized model. Click any of the standard tasks to see only the models that solve that task.

When you click one of the remaining models, you will see a detailed model description such as that shown in figure 8.5 for the BLIP model from Salesforce, a model that processes images to generate suitable captions. On the left side is a thorough description of the model along with links to relevant papers and code samples showing you how to use the model on different hardware platforms (i.e., locally). On the right side is an interface that allows you to try the model on a few sample pictures.

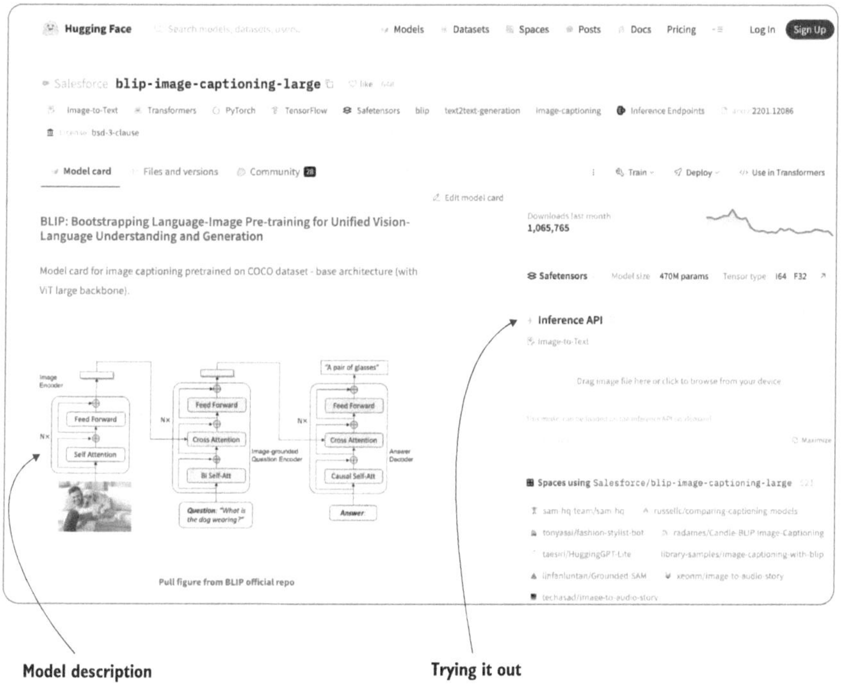

Figure 8.5 Detailed description of Salesforce's BLIP model (https://huggingface.co/Salesforce/blip-image-captioning-large). Read the description on the left, or try the model via the interface on the right.

8.4.2 Python library

We are now about to run Transformer models on our own local infrastructure! The performance you get will, of course, depend on the properties of the hardware you're using. However, even with moderate computation power, you should be able to work with the models we're about to try. But first, we must install the Hugging Face Transformers library. Enter the following commands in your terminal:

```
pip install transformers==4.36
```

The Transformers library is based on PyTorch, a popular machine-learning framework. If you haven't installed PyTorch yet, run the following command in your terminal (otherwise, you will receive an error message when trying to run the following code):

```
pip install torch==2.1.2
```

That's it for the setup! We're ready to use the Hugging Face Transformers library, which we import via `import transformers`. The Transformers library offers a plethora of features and various ways to use the model in its repository (or to train your own models, for that matter). In this section, we'll only cover a small subset of them, but it's enough to get a first impression.

Let's assume that you have found a model in the Hugging Face model repository that you would like to try. To make things more concrete, let's say we're talking about the Roberta model for sentiment classification, offered by Cardiff University (you can find that model at https://mng.bz/rKoX). Compared to GPT-4o and most other models discussed in this section, this is a fairly small model. However, it is specialized for analyzing text to determine the underlying sentiment. Although it is much less generic than GPT-4o and similar models, it does one task and does it fairly well. If you are looking to classify reviews, for instance, you may find this model very suitable.

The easiest way to use a model via the Transformers library is via a `pipeline`. The following command creates a pipeline for sentiment classification based on the Roberta model:

```
sentiment_pipeline = transformers.pipeline(
    model='cardiffnlp/twitter-roberta-base-sentiment-latest')
```

As you see, we specify the model using the last part of its URL: the name of the account providing the model (`cardiffnlp`) followed by the ID of the model itself. When using this code for the first time, the Transformers library will automatically download the model from its public model repository. Note that this code works in part because the model we are referring to is associated with a specific task class. For other models, you may have to specify the types of tasks you want them to solve as a separate input parameter.

We created a pipeline! Now we can use it to classify text—for example, like so (we assume that the variable `text_to_classify` contains, you guessed it, the text to classify):

```
result = sentiment_pipeline(text_to_classify)
```

We have all we need to build a simple application that classifies reviews (based on whether the underlying sentiment is positive, meaning a good review, or negative, meaning the review is bad). The next listing shows the corresponding code (you can find it as the Hugging Face item on the book's website).

Listing 8.4   Sentiment classification using Hugging Face Transformers

```
import argparse
import transformers

if __name__ == '__main__':
    parser = argparse.ArgumentParser()
    parser.add_argument('review', type=str, help='Text of a review')
    args = parser.parse_args()

    sentiment_pipeline = transformers.pipeline(          ❶ Creates a pipeline
```

```
        model='cardiffnlp/twitter-roberta-base-sentiment-latest')

    result = sentiment_pipeline(args.review)          ❷ Applies the pipeline to input

    print(result)                                      ❸ Prints out the classification result
```

You may notice a difference from all the code we have seen previously: we don't need to specify an access key! Because the Hugging Face models are publicly available and we're running them on our own infrastructure, there is no need to provide any kind of credentials. Instead, the only input is a review text that we want to classify.

The code composes the snippets discussed earlier. It creates a pipeline (❶), uses it to classify the input text (❷), and finally prints out the result (❸). You can try it by switching to the containing folder in your terminal and entering, for instance, the following:

```
python huggingface.py "This movie was really awful!"
```

When running the code for the first time, you may have to wait for a few minutes while the Transformers library downloads the model you are referencing. But no worries: the library caches the downloaded model so you won't have to wait when you run the code a second time. After processing finishes, you should see output like this:

```
['label': 'negative', 'score': 0.9412825107574463]
```

That's certainly correct for the sample input: the review is concise and 100% negative. Try it with a few different reviews, and compare the output to what you get with models like GPT-4o. In the majority of cases, the classification result should be fairly similar. Of course, GPT-4o is a much more generic model and can be used to solve a variety of other tasks as well. But as long as you're interested in classifying reviews, this model offers an interesting tradeoff between quality and cost.

Summary

- In addition to OpenAI, several other providers offer large language models. Most providers offer closed-source models via a cloud API. The models differ based on their generality, output quality, and pricing.
- Most providers offer a Python library to access language models.
- Hugging Face Transformers offers various models for free download.

References

[1] Bai, Y., Kadavath, S., Kundu, S., et al. (2022). Constitutional AI: Harmlessness from AI Feedback. *CoRR abs/2212.0*, 1–32.

[2] Vaswani, A., Shazeer, N., Parmar, N., et al. (2017). Attention is All You Need. In *Advances in Neural Information Processing Systems*, pp. 5999–6009.

Optimizing cost and quality

This chapter covers

- Model choice and tuning
- Prompt engineering
- Fine-tuning models

Analyzing data with large language models is a great way to burn money quickly. If you've been using GPT-4 (or a similarly large model) for a while, you've probably noticed how fees pile up quickly, forcing you to recharge your account regularly. But do we always need to use the largest (and most expensive) model? Can't we make smaller models perform almost as well? How can we get the most bang for our buck?

This chapter is about saving money when using language models on large data sets. Fortunately, we have quite a few options for doing so. First, we have lots of choices when it comes to large language models. Selecting a model that is as small (or, rather, as cheap) as possible while still performing well on our analysis task can go a long way toward balancing our budget. Second, models typically have various tuning parameters, allowing us to tune everything from the overall text generation strategy to the way specific tokens are (de-)prioritized. We want to optimize our settings there to turn small models into GPT-4 alternatives for certain tasks. Third, we can use prompt engineering to tweak the way we ask the model our questions, sometimes leading to surprisingly different results!

156

And finally, if none of these methods cut it, we can choose to create our own models, highly customized for only the task we care about. Of course, assuming we don't want to spend millions on pretraining, we won't start training new models from scratch. Instead, we will typically choose to fine-tune existing models with just a few hundred samples. That's often enough to get significantly better performance than when using the base model.

Of course, what works best depends on the task we're trying to solve, as well as on data properties. Fortunately, if we want to analyze large amounts of data, we can afford to spend a little money on trying different tuning options on a data sample. Chances are, this upfront investment will pay off once we analyze the entire data set! Throughout this chapter, we will apply all of these tuning options in an example scenario.

9.1 Example scenario

You're back at Banana and trying to classify user reviews. Users can leave free-form text reviews about their experiences with Banana products on the Banana website. You want to know whether those reviews are positive (i.e., the user was happy with the product) or negative (i.e., reading them will scare away potential customers!). Of course, you can use language models for that task (you saw that in chapter 4). For instance, you can use GPT-4 (at the time of writing, this is OpenAI's largest model for text processing). Provide GPT-4 with a review, together with instructions for how to classify it (including a description of possible class labels, such as "positive" and "negative"), and the output should be correct for most reviews.

However, analyzing data with GPT-4 costs about 6 cents per 1,000 tokens. That (6 cents) may not sound like much, but Banana receives thousands of product reviews every day! Let's assume the average review contains about 100 tokens (about 400 characters). Furthermore, let's assume that Banana receives about 10,000 reviews per day. That means you collect $100 \times 10,000$ tokens per day: about 1 million tokens per day and 365 million tokens per year. How much does it cost to analyze one year's worth of comments? About $365,000,000 \times \frac{0.06}{1000} = 21,900$ dollars.

That may put a bit of a dent in your budget! Can't you get it cheaper? For example, at the time of writing, GPT-3.5 Turbo is priced at only around 0.0005 dollars per thousand tokens (tokens are priced differently depending on whether they are read or generated, but we will neglect that for now to simplify the calculations). That means only $365,000,000 \times \frac{0.0005}{1000} = 182.5$ dollars to analyze one year's worth of comments. Much better! But to get satisfactory output quality, you may have to do a little extra work to ensure that you're using the model in the best possible way.

> **TIP** Instead of GPT-3.5 Turbo, you can also use alternative models such as GPT-4o mini (the model ID is `gpt-4o-mini`) in the following examples.

That's what we will do in this example. Starting from the most naive implementation of our classifier, we will gradually refine our implementation and try all the various tuning options discussed in the introduction to this chapter!

9.2   *Untuned classifier*

Let's begin with the base version of our classifier. Again, the goal is to take a review and decide whether it should be classified as positive (`pos`) or negative (`neg`). We will use the following prompt template to classify reviews:

```
[Review]
Is the sentiment positive or negative?
Answer ("pos"/"neg"):
```

In this prompt template, `[Review]` is a placeholder that gets replaced with the actual review text. For example, after substitution, our prompt may look like this (the first two lines correspond to an abbreviated version of the review to classify, apparently a new movie streaming on Banana TV that doesn't match the reviewer's taste):

```
I am willing to tolerate almost anything in a Sci-Fi movie,
but this was almost intolerable. ...
Is the sentiment positive or negative?
Answer ("pos"/"neg"):
```

Ideally, if we send this prompt to a GPT model, we expect either `pos` or `neg` as the reply (in this specific case, we expect `neg`). Listing 9.1 shows the complete Python code; we won't spend too much time discussing it because it is similar to the classifiers we saw in chapter 4. The `create_prompt` function (❶) instantiates the prompt template for a specific review (stored in the input parameter `text`). The result is a prompt that we can send to our language model using the `call_llm` function (❷). We call GPT-3.5 Turbo here (❸) (saving costs). We also set `temperature` to 0, which means we're minimizing randomness when generating output. This means you should see the same results when running the code repeatedly. You may also notice that `call_llm` is a little longer in listing 9.1 than the versions we have seen in previous listings. That's because we retrieve not only the answer generated by our language model but also the number of tokens used (❹). Counting the number of tokens will allow us to calculate the invocation costs on a data sample.

Listing 9.1   Classifying reviews as positive or negative: base version

```python
import argparse
import openai
import pandas as pd
import time

client = openai.OpenAI()

def create_prompt(text):                          ❶ Generates prompts
    """ Create prompt for sentiment classification.

    Args:
        text: text to classify.

    Returns:
```

```
        Prompt for text classification.
    """
    task = 'Is the sentiment positive or negative?'
    answer_format = 'Answer ("pos"/"neg")'
    return f'{text}\n{task}\n{answer_format}:'


def call_llm(prompt):                                    ❷ Invokes the LLM
    """ Query large language model and return answer.

    Args:
        prompt: input prompt for language model.

    Returns:
        Answer by language model and total number of tokens.
    """
    for nr_retries in range(1, 4):
        try:
                  ❸ Generates an answer
            response = client.chat.completions.create(
                model='gpt-3.5-turbo',
                messages=[
                    {'role':'user', 'content':prompt}
                    ],
                temperature=0
                )
                  ❹ Extracts answer and token usage
            answer = response.choices[0].message.content
            nr_tokens = response.usage.total_tokens
            return answer, nr_tokens

        except Exception as e:
            print(f'Exception: {e}')
            time.sleep(nr_retries * 2)

    raise Exception('Cannot query OpenAI model!')


if __name__ == '__main__':

    parser = argparse.ArgumentParser()                   ❺ Parses arguments
    parser.add_argument('file_path', type=str, help='Path to input file')
    args = parser.parse_args()

    df = pd.read_csv(args.file_path)

    nr_correct = 0
    nr_tokens = 0

    for _, row in df.iterrows():       ❻ Iterates over reviews

        text = row['text']             ❼ Classifies the review
        prompt = create_prompt(text)
        label, current_tokens = call_llm(prompt)

        ground_truth = row['sentiment']            ❽ Updates counters
```

```
        if label == ground_truth:
            nr_correct += 1
        nr_tokens += current_tokens

        print(f'Label: {label}; Ground truth: {ground_truth}')
    print(f'Number of correct labels:\t{nr_correct}')
    print(f'Number of tokens used   :\t{nr_tokens}')
```

We will assume that reviews to classify are stored in a .csv file. We expect users to specify the path of that .csv file as a command-line argument (❺). After reading the .csv file, we iterate over the reviews (❻) in the order in which they appear in the input file. For each review, we extract the associated text (❼) (we assume it's stored in the text column), create a prompt for classification, and call the language model. The result is the answer text generated by the language model (hopefully it's one of the two class labels, pos or neg), as well as the number of tokens used.

Our goal is to try different methods of querying a language model and compare the output quality and costs. To judge the output quality, we assume that the input .csv file contains not only the review text but also a ground-truth label. This means we assume that each review has already been associated with the correct class label, stored in the sentiment column (because our two class labels describe the sentiment of the review). After receiving the language model's output, we compare the output to the ground truth (❽) and update the number of correctly classified reviews (variable nr_correct). At the same time, we sum up the total number of tokens used (because processing fees are proportional to that) and store them in the counter called nr_tokens. After iterating over all reviews, listing 9.1 prints out the final number of correct classifications and the number of tokens used.

9.3   *Model tuning*

Let's try it! You can find listing 9.1 under Untuned Classifier on the book's website. We reuse the movie reviews from chapter 4; search for the Reviews.csv link in the chapter 4 section. The file contains 10 reviews, along with the corresponding ground truth. Let's assume that the code for listing 9.1 and the reviews are stored in the same folder on disk. Open your terminal, switch to that folder, and run the following command:

```
python basic_classifier.py reviews.csv
```

You should see the following output:

```
Label: neg; Ground truth: neg
Label: neg; Ground truth: neg
Label: neg; Ground truth: neg
Label: neg; Ground truth: neg
Label: pos; Ground truth: pos
Label: pos; Ground truth: neg      ❶ Incorrect label
Label: pos; Ground truth: neg
```

```
Label: negative; Ground truth: neg        ❷ Nonexistent label
Label: negative; Ground truth: pos
Label: neg; Ground truth: neg
Number of correct labels:    6
Number of tokens used   :    2228
```

The first 10 lines describe the results for each review. We have the label generated by the language model and then the ground-truth label (taken from the input file). At the end, we have the number of correctly classified reviews and the number of tokens used.

Out of 10 reviews, we classified 6 correctly. Well, at least that's better than 50%, but it's still not a great result. What went wrong? Looking at output gives us some ideas. There are cases (❶) where the language model simply picks the wrong class label. That's not unexpected. However, there are also cases (❷) where the language model picks a class label that doesn't even exist! Granted, it's not too far off (`negative` instead of `neg`), and that seems easy to fix.

We focus on the (probably) low-hanging fruit of making the language model generate only one of our two possible class labels. How do we do that? Enter the `logit_bias` parameter. The `logit_bias` parameter enables users to change the likelihood that certain tokens are selected (we briefly discussed this and other GPT parameters in chapter 3). In this specific case, we would like to significantly increase the probability of the tokens associated with our two class labels (`neg` and `pos`). The `logit_bias` parameter is specified as a Python dictionary, mapping token IDs to a bias. A positive bias means we want to increase the probability that the language model generates the corresponding token. A negative bias means we decrease the probability of generating the associated token.

In this case, we want to increase the chances that GPT-3.5 selects one of the two tokens representing class labels. So we want to select a high bias for those two token IDs. Bias scores range from –100 to +100. We will go with the maximum and assign a bias of +100 to the tokens representing class labels. First we need to find their token IDs. Language models represent text as a sequence of token IDs. To change token bias, we need to reference the IDs of the tokens we care about.

A *tokenizer* is the component that transforms text into token IDs. You can find tokenizers for all GPT models at https://platform.openai.com/tokenizer. We're using GPT-3.5, so select the one labeled GPT 3.5 & GPT-4. Figure 9.1 shows the tokenizer web interface.

We can enter text in the text box and click the Token IDs button to see the token IDs for our input text. Using the tokenizer, we learn that the token `pos` has ID 981 and the token `neg` has token ID 29875. Now we're ready to add a bias to our model invocation as follows:

```
import openai
client = openai.OpenAI()

response = client.chat.completions.create(
```

```
model='gpt-3.5-turbo',
messages=[
    {'role':'user', 'content':prompt}
    ],
logit_bias = {981:100, 29875:100},     ❶ Defines the bias
temperature=0
)
```

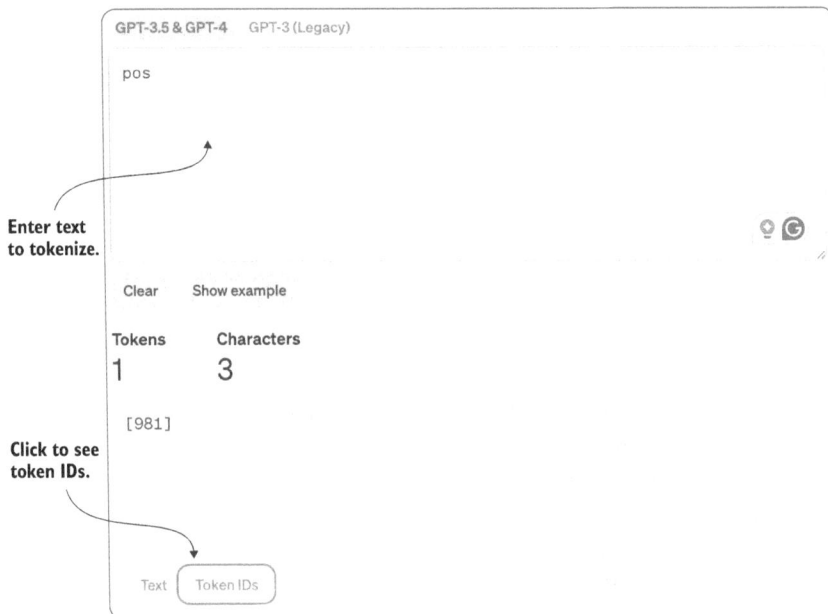

Figure 9.1   GPT tokenizer at https://platform.openai.com/tokenizer: enter text to learn the associated token IDs.

Compared to the previous call (in listing 9.1), we add the logit bias (❶) by mapping the IDs of the two tokens we're interested in (pos with token ID 981 and neg with token ID 29875) to the highest possible bias value of 100. That should fix the problem of generating tokens that do not correspond to class labels, right?

> **WARNING**   The code described next causes problems and results in long running times and significant monetary fees. Do not try it without integrating the fix presented at the end of this section!

Let's try it to be sure. You can add the logit bias to the code from listing 9.1. Alternatively, later in this chapter, we will present a tunable version of the classifier that will allow you to try different combinations of tuning parameters (including the logit bias). If you execute the classifier with biases added, you will likely see output similar to the following (actually, as executing the code takes a long time and incurs non-negligible costs, you may just want to trust me on this):

❶ Nonexistent labels for each input:

```
Label: negnegnegnegnegnegnegnegnegneg ...; Ground truth: neg
Label: negposnegnegnegnegnegnegnegneg ...; Ground truth: neg
Label: negposnegnegnegnegnegnegnegneg ...; Ground truth: neg
Label: negposnegposnegnegnegnegnegneg ...; Ground truth: neg
Label: posnegposnegposnegposnegposneg ...; Ground truth: pos
Label: posnegpospospospospospospospos ...; Ground truth: neg
Label: posnegpospospospospospospospos ...; Ground truth: neg
Label: negposnegposnegposnegposnegpos ...; Ground truth: neg
Label: negposnegposnegposnegposnegpos ...; Ground truth: pos
Label: negposnegposnegnegnegnegnegneg ...; Ground truth: neg
Number of correct labels:      0
Number of tokens used    :   2318   ❷ Increased token usage
```

Oh, no—not a single correct classification! What happened? Comparing generated "labels" to the ground truth reveals the problem (**❶**): we're only generating the two possible tokens (which is great!) but just way too many of them (which is not so great!). That increases token consumption (**❷**) (note that the output length was limited for generating the example output; otherwise, token consumption would be much higher), but more importantly, it means our output does not correspond to any class label.

Why does the model generate so many tokens?

We essentially restrict the model to generate text using only two tokens. Those are the two tokens we want to see in our output. However, we forgot to enable the model to generate any tokens that indicate the end of output! That is why the model cannot stop generating.

There are multiple ways to fix this. We could, of course, add postprocessing to extract only the first token from the output generated by the language model. That would (mostly) fix our problem with the class labels. Look at the output, and you'll see that using the first token leads to correct output in 7 of 10 cases. However, there is (another) problem with this approach: we're paying to generate tokens that we don't ultimately use! That's clearly not what we want. So let's tune our model even more by restricting the output length as well. All we need is a single token (this works only because our two possible class labels can be represented by a single token). That's what the max_tokens parameter does. Let's use it when calling our language model:

```
response = client.chat.completions.create(
    model='gpt-3.5-turbo',
    messages=[
        {'role':'user', 'content':prompt}
        ],
    logit_bias = {981:100, 29875:100},   ◄── Defines the bias
    temperature=0, max_tokens=1
```

```
)
```

When you try it (which should be fast and not costly), you should see this output:

```
Label: neg; Ground truth: neg
Label: neg; Ground truth: neg
Label: neg; Ground truth: neg
Label: neg; Ground truth: neg
Label: pos; Ground truth: pos
Label: pos; Ground truth: neg
Label: pos; Ground truth: neg
Label: neg; Ground truth: neg
Label: neg; Ground truth: pos
Label: neg; Ground truth: neg
Number of correct labels:    7    ❶ Improves on the untuned classifier
Number of tokens used    :    2228  ❷ Reduces token usage
```

Much better! We have improved the number of correctly handled cases from six (for the unturned version) to seven (❶). That may not sound like much. However, thinking about the entire data set, it essentially means we have improved precision from 60% to 70%: that is, thousands more reviews will now be classified correctly! There is a caveat, of course. In reality, you should probably use a much larger sample. Due to random variations, the accuracy you observe on a sample may not be representative of the accuracy for the entire data set. To keep things simple (and your cost relatively low when trying it), we restrict ourselves to 10 samples here. As an additional bonus, our token consumption has again been reduced (❷) (actually, the gap in token consumption, compared to a version without any output size bound, is likely to be much, much larger). Note that the two parameters discussed here are only a small subset of the available tuning options. You will find more details on relevant parameters in chapter 3. Whenever you tune a model for a new task, be sure to consider all parameters that may be potentially relevant. Then try a few reasonable settings on a data sample to see which option performs best.

9.4   *Model selection*

Let's assume that we have maxed out our ability to get better performance by tuning our current model. What else can we do? We can, of course, select a different model. We saw a few GPT alternatives in the last chapter. If you can select a model specifically trained for the task you're interested in (e.g., text classification), that's often worth a look. Other factors that can influence your model choices are whether the data you plan to apply the model to is sensitive and whether sending that data to specific providers of language models is acceptable.

If you want to learn about the relative performance of different models, have a look at https://crfm.stanford.edu/helm/lite/latest/. This website contains the results of HELM, Stanford's Holistic Evaluation of Language Models benchmark. The benchmark compares language models on various scenarios and contains results for specific tasks, as well as average performance, aggregated over various scenarios. You may want to check this out to get a sense of which models may be interesting to you. However, as various factors can influence a language model's performance, it still pays to evaluate different models on the specific task you're interested in.

To keep things simple, let's only consider GPT-4 as an alternative to GPT-3.5 Turbo (which we used up to this point). Replace the name of the model in the language model invocation:

```
response = client.chat.completions.create(
    model='gpt-4',
    messages=[
        {'role':'user', 'content':prompt}
        ],
    logit_bias = {981:100, 29875:100},   ⟵ Defines the bias
    temperature=0, max_tokens=1
    )
```

Running the resulting code should lead to the following output:

```
Label: neg; Ground truth: neg
Label: neg; Ground truth: neg
Label: neg; Ground truth: neg
Label: neg; Ground truth: neg
Label: pos; Ground truth: pos
Label: pos; Ground truth: neg
Label: pos; Ground truth: neg
Label: neg; Ground truth: neg
Label: pos; Ground truth: pos      ❶ Correct classification result
Label: neg; Ground truth: neg
Number of correct labels:    8     ❷ Best result so far
Number of tokens used    :  2228   ❸ Same number of tokens
```

Compared to the prior version, GPT-4 manages to solve one more test case accurately (❶)! That brings our accuracy to 80% (❷), while our token consumption remains constant (❸). That, by the way, is not guaranteed to be the case if we change the model. As different models may use different tokenizers, representing the same text may require a different number of tokens for different models. In this specific case, because GPT-4 and GPT-3.5 use the same tokenizer, the number of tokens does not change.

Does that mean we're paying the same amount of money? Not quite. Because GPT-4 incurs much higher fees per token, we're paying roughly 120 times more than before (the relative difference between the per-token prices of GPT-4 and GPT-3.5 Turbo). That's why we're trying to make GPT-3.5 perform as well as possible without resorting to GPT-4.

Occasionally, during model selection and model tuning, it makes sense to look at the test data yourself. That gives you a better impression of the sweet spots and limitations of various models and enables you to judge whether the test cases on which your model performs badly are representative. For instance, the following review is solved correctly by GPT-4 but not by GPT-3.5:

```
If you want to see a film starring Stan Laurel from the Laurel & Hardy
comedies, this is not the film for you. Stan would not begin to find the
character and rhythms of those films for another two years. If, however,
you want a good travesty of the Rudolph Valentino BLOOD AND SAND, which
had been made the previous year, this is the movie for you. All the
stops are pulled out, both in physical comedy and on the title cards
and if the movie is not held together by character, the plot of
Valentino's movie is used - well sort of.
```

This review contains positive (toward the end) as well as negative (the beginning) aspects. Although the final verdict is positive, we may conclude that spending more money to properly analyze borderline cases like that review is not worth it.

9.5   *Prompt engineering*

Setting aside options to swap models, what else can we do to improve performance with our model? One area we haven't looked at yet is the definition of the prompt we use for classification. Changing the prompt template can have a significant effect on result quality. The fact that prompt tuning is often crucial has even led to the introduction of a dedicated term, *prompt engineering*, describing the process of searching for optimal prompt templates. What's more, the challenges of prompt engineering have led to the creation of multiple platforms offering prompt templates for a plethora of different tasks. If you're out of ideas for prompt variants, have a look at https://promptbase.com/, https://prompthero.com/, and similar platforms. The business model of such platforms is to enable users to buy and sell prompt templates that optimize the performance of specific models for specific tasks.

Figuring out what prompt works best typically requires some experimentation. Next, we will focus on the basics and explore a classical technique to increase output quality by changing the prompt. We're talking about few-shot learning here, which means we're helping the model by giving it a few examples. That's something we know from everyday life: it is often hard to understand a new task or approach based on a pure description alone. It is much better to see some examples to get the hang of it. For instance, in the previous sections, we could have just discussed the semantics of a few relevant model-tuning parameters. But isn't it much better to see how they can be tuned in a concrete example scenario?

Of course it is. Language models "feel" the same way, and adding a few helpful examples can often improve their performance. So how do we show them examples? Easy: we specify those examples as part of the prompt. For instance, in our classification scenario, we want the language models to classify reviews. An example would be a review together with the reference class label.

We will use the following prompt template to integrate a single sample into the prompt:

```
[Sample Review]
Is the sentiment positive or negative?
Answer ("pos"/"neg"):[Sample Solution]
[Review to Classify]
Is the sentiment positive or negative?
Answer ("pos"/"neg"):
```

If we replace the placeholders with the sample review, the sample review solution, and the review we're interested in classifying, we get, for instance, the following prompt:

```
Now, I won't deny that when I purchased    ❶ Sample review
this off eBay, I had high expectations. ...
Is the sentiment positive or negative?     ❷ Instructions
Answer ("pos"/"neg"):neg                    ❸ Sample solution
I am willing to tolerate almost anything          ❹ Review to classify
in a Sci-Fi movie, but this was almost intolerable. ...
Is the sentiment positive or negative?           ❺ Instructions
Answer ("pos"/"neg"):
```

You see a sample review (❶), instructions (❷), and the reference class for the sample review (❸). After that, you find the review we want to classify (❹) and the classification instructions (again) (❺), but no solution yet (of course not—that's what we want the language model to generate). In this prompt, we provide exactly one example of a correctly solved task to the model. Doing so may help the model better understand what we're asking it to do.

Of course, there are many options to provide samples in the prompt. We have chosen what is arguably the most straightforward solution: we use the same prompt structure twice for the two reviews. Because we're using exactly the same structure, our prompt is slightly redundant: we repeat the task instructions (❷ and ❺), including the specification of the two possible class labels. Although we won't do so here, it might be interesting to experiment and see whether you can integrate examples into the prompt in a different way, removing redundancies and reducing the prompt length (thereby reducing the number of tokens processed and, ultimately, processing fees).

Up to now, we have only considered adding a single example. But sometimes, seeing one example is not enough. That's why it may make sense to add more than one example for the language model as well. Let's assume that we have a few samples: reviews with associated class labels, stored in a data frame called samples. We can use the following code to generate prompts that integrate those samples:

```
def create_single_text_prompt(text, label):      ❶ Creates a prompt for one review
    """ Create prompt for classifying a single text.

    Args:
        text: text to classify.
        label: correct class label (empty if unavailable).

    Returns:
        Prompt for text classification.
```

```
    """
    task = 'Is the sentiment positive or negative?'
    answer_format = 'Answer ("pos"/"neg")'
    return f'{text}\n{task}\n{answer_format}:{label}'

def create_prompt(text, samples):                    ❷ Generates a prompt for all reviews
    """ Generates prompt for sentiment classification.

    Args:
        text: classify this text.
        samples: integrate these samples into prompt.

    Returns:
        Input for LLM.
    """
    parts = []
    for _, row in samples.iterrows():          ❸ Integrates the  samples
        sample_text = row['text']
        sample_label = row['sentiment']
        prompt = create_single_text_prompt(sample_text, sample_label)
        parts += [prompt]

    prompt = create_single_text_prompt(text, '')    ❹ Adds the review to classify
    parts += [prompt]
    return '\n'.join(parts)
```

The `create_single_text_prompt` function (❶) instantiates the following template for a single review:

```
[Review]
Is the sentiment positive or negative?
Answer ("pos"/"neg"):[Label]
```

We use the same function to specify sample reviews, as well as to specify the review, along with the classification task that we want the language model to solve for us. If we specify a sample review, the [Label] placeholder will be replaced with the reference class label for the corresponding review. If we specify the task the language model should solve, we do not know the correct class label yet. In that case, we replace the [Label] placeholder with the empty string. It will be up to the language model to complete the prompt with the actual class label.

The `create_prompt` function (❷) generates the complete prompt, considering all sample reviews, as well as the review we want to classify. First (❸), it iterates over the sample reviews. We assume that our `samples` data frame stores review text in the `text` column and the associated class labels in the `sentiment` column. We add a prompt part (❹) for the sample review using the `create_single_text_prompt` function (discussed earlier). Finally, we add instructions to classify the review we're interested in.

Let's switch back to using GPT-3.5 Turbo. However, this time, we will use our new prompt-generation function. For the moment, we will restrict ourselves to a single example review in the prompt. On the book's companion website, you can find training reviews with the correct class labels under Reviews Training, leading to the file train_reviews.csv. The reviews in this file do not overlap with those in the reviews.csv file (which we use to test our approach). Adding just the first review from train_reviews.csv as a sample to the prompts, you should now see the following output:

```
Label: neg; Ground truth: neg
Label: neg; Ground truth: neg
Label: neg; Ground truth: neg
Label: neg; Ground truth: neg
Label: pos; Ground truth: pos
Label: pos; Ground truth: neg
Label: pos; Ground truth: neg
Label: neg; Ground truth: neg
Label: pos; Ground truth: pos
Label: neg; Ground truth: neg
Number of correct labels:    8       ❶ Equivalent to GPT-4 result
Number of tokens used   :    4078    ❷ Token usage roughly doubles
```

Hooray! We have increased precision to 80% (❶). That's the same accuracy we got when using GPT-4 on the original prompts (without sample reviews). At the same time, our token usage has increased (❷). More precisely, because we're adding a second review to each prompt (i.e., we have one sample review and the review to classify), our token consumption has roughly doubled compared to the last version. However, compared to using GPT-4 on shorter prompts, our current approach is still about 60 times cheaper (because using GPT-4 is about 120 times more expensive than using GPT-3.5 Turbo).

9.6 Tunable classifier

Now that we have seen quite a few tuning options, you may be tempted to try new variations. For instance, do we still need to add bias (essentially restricting the output to the two possible class labels) if we're adding samples? Can we get even better precision when using a larger model together with multiple samples in the prompt? Changing your code to try a new combination quickly becomes tedious. But no worries, we've got you covered! On the book's website, you can find listing 9.2 under Tunable Classifier. This implementation lets you try all the tuning variants by setting the right command-line parameters. We will quickly discuss the code, which integrates all the code variants discussed previously.

Generating prompts (❶) works as described in the last section. The `create_prompt` function takes the review text to classify and sample reviews as input. The sample reviews are added to the prompt, potentially supporting the language models in classifying the review we're interested in. Note that we can still see how the language model performs without any samples (by not specifying any samples). Classification without any samples corresponds to a special case.

Listing 9.2   Tunable version of sentiment classifier

```python
import argparse
import openai
import pandas as pd
import time

client = openai.OpenAI()

def create_single_text_prompt(text, label):
    """ Create prompt for classifying a single text.

    Args:
        text: text to classify.
        label: correct class label (empty if unavailable).

    Returns:
        Prompt for text classification.
    """
    task = 'Is the sentiment positive or negative?'
    answer_format = 'Answer ("pos"/"neg")'
    return f'{text}\n{task}\n{answer_format}:{label}'

def create_prompt(text, samples):                    ❶ Generates prompts with samples
    """ Generates prompt for sentiment classification.

    Args:
        text: classify this text.
        samples: integrate these samples into prompt.

    Returns:
        Input for LLM.
    """
    parts = []
    for _, row in samples.iterrows():
        sample_text = row['text']
        sample_label = row['sentiment']
        prompt = create_single_text_prompt(sample_text, sample_label)
        parts += [prompt]

    prompt = create_single_text_prompt(text, '')
    parts += [prompt]
    return '\n'.join(parts)
```

❷ **Calls language models with parameters**

```python
def call_llm(prompt, model, max_tokens, out_tokens):
    """ Query large language model and return answer.

    Args:
        prompt: input prompt for language model.
        model: name of OpenAI model to choose.
        max_tokens: maximum output length in tokens.
        out_tokens: prioritize these token IDs in output.
```

```
    Returns:
        Answer by language model and total number of tokens.
    """
    optional_parameters = {}
    if max_tokens:
        optional_parameters['max_tokens'] = max_tokens
    if out_tokens:
        logit_bias = {int(tid):100 for tid in out_tokens.split(',')}
        optional_parameters['logit_bias'] = logit_bias

    for nr_retries in range(1, 4):
        try:
            response = client.chat.completions.create(
                model=model,
                messages=[
                    {'role':'user', 'content':prompt}
                    ],
                **optional_parameters, temperature=0
                )

            answer = response.choices[0].message.content
            nr_tokens = response.usage.total_tokens
            return answer, nr_tokens

        except Exception as e:
            print(f'Exception: {e}')
            time.sleep(nr_retries * 2)

    raise Exception('Cannot query OpenAI model!')


if __name__ == '__main__':

    parser = argparse.ArgumentParser()             ❸ Parses command-line parameters
    parser.add_argument('file_path', type=str, help='Path to input file')
    parser.add_argument('model', type=str, help='Name of OpenAI model')
    parser.add_argument('max_tokens', type=int, help='Maximum output size')
    parser.add_argument('out_tokens', type=str, help='Tokens to prioritize')
    parser.add_argument('nr_samples', type=int, help='Number of samples')
    parser.add_argument('sample_path', type=str, help='Path to samples')
    args = parser.parse_args()

    df = pd.read_csv(args.file_path)

    samples = pd.DataFrame()      ❹ Reads samples from disk
    if args.nr_samples:
        samples = pd.read_csv(args.sample_path)
        samples = samples[:args.nr_samples]

    nr_correct = 0
    nr_tokens = 0

    for _, row in df.iterrows():

        text = row['text']        ❺ Classifies the review
```

```
prompt = create_prompt(text, samples)
label, current_tokens = call_llm(
    prompt, args.model,
    args.max_tokens,
    args.out_tokens)

ground_truth = row['sentiment']      ❻ Updates the counters
if label == ground_truth:
    nr_correct += 1
nr_tokens += current_tokens

print(f'Label: {label}; Ground truth: {ground_truth}')
```

❼ **Prints out the counters**
```
print(f'Number of correct labels:\t{nr_correct}')
print(f'Number of tokens used   :\t{nr_tokens}')
```

Our `call_llm` function (❷) integrates all the tuning parameters mentioned earlier. First is the name of the model to call (the `model` parameter). Second, we can specify the maximum number of output tokens (`max_tokens`). Finally, we can specify bias: tokens that should be prioritized when generating output. The `out_tokens` parameter allows users to specify a comma-separated list of token IDs to which we assign a high priority (essentially limiting output to one of these tokens). Although the model name is required, setting a value of 0 for the `max_tokens` parameter and the empty string for the `out_tokens` parameter allows us to avoid changing OpenAI's default settings.

The tunable classifier uses quite a few command-line parameters (❸). Let's discuss them in the order in which you need to specify them:

- `file_path`—Path to the .csv file containing reviews used to evaluate our language model
- `model`—Name of the language model we want to use (e.g., `gpt-3.5-turbo`)
- `max_tokens`—Maximum number of output tokens to generate per input review
- `out_tokens`—A comma-separated list of tokens to prioritize when generating output
- `nr_samples`—Number of review samples with solutions to integrate into each prompt
- `sample_path`—Path to the .csv file containing reviews with correct class labels to use as samples (this can be empty if the `nr_samples` parameter is set to 0)

WARNING   Limiting the number of output tokens is almost always a good idea. In particular, you should do it whenever biasing output toward specific tokens without including any of the "stop" tokens (indicating the end of output).

After parsing input parameters, the classifier reads samples from disk (❹) and classifies reviews (❺) while updating counters (❻) that are ultimately printed (❼).

Let's see how we can simulate all the different versions of our classifier that we have discussed so far. Using the following invocation should give us the untuned version of our classifier, assuming that the file reviews.csv is located in the same directory as the code itself:

```
python tunable_classifier.py reviews.csv
    gpt-3.5-turbo 0 "" 0 ""
```

Note that we don't specify any tokens to prioritize (we specify the empty string), don't restrict the output length (setting it to 0 means no restrictions), and set the number of samples in the prompt to 0 (which means we can set the path to the file containing samples to the empty string as well).

The following command, on the other hand, will give us the version that restricts the output length while prioritizing the tokens that correspond to our class labels:

```
python tunable_classifier.py reviews.csv
    gpt-3.5-turbo 1 "981,29875" 0 ""
```

Finally, we can get the last version we discussed, using one sample per prompt while tuning the model as before, via the following command (assuming the file train_reviews.csv is located in the same repository as the code):

```
python tunable_classifier.py reviews.csv
    gpt-3.5-turbo 1 "981,29875" 1 "train_reviews.csv"
```

Feel free to try new combinations that we haven't discussed!

9.7 Fine-tuning

So far, we have done everything in our power to squeeze the best performance out of existing models. Those models have been trained for tasks that are, perhaps, similar but not *exactly* like the one we're interested in. Wouldn't it be nice to get a model customized specifically for our task? That is possible when using fine-tuning. Let's see how to implement fine-tuning with OpenAI's models in practice.

Fine-tuning means we take an existing model, such as OpenAI's GPT-3.5 Turbo model, and specialize it for a task we're interested in. Of course, in principle, we could train our model from scratch. But that is typically prohibitively expensive, and in addition, we usually don't find enough task-specific training data to sustain a large model during training. That's why it is much better to rely on fine-tuning.

Fine-tuning is typically the last thing we try when maximizing performance for a specific task. The reason is that fine-tuning requires a certain upfront investment in terms of time and money. During fine-tuning, we pay OpenAI to create a customized version of one of its base models just for our task. The price is based on the size of the training data and the number of times that training data is read (i.e., the number of *epochs*). For example, at the time of writing, fine-tuning GPT-3.5 Turbo costs about 0.8 cents per 1,000 tokens of training data and epoch. Also, after fine-tuning, we pay to use the fine-tuned model. The price per token is higher for the fine-tuned model than for the base version. That makes sense as, at least in theory, the fine-tuned model should perform better for our specific task.

One possible advantage of fine-tuning is that we improve the accuracy of the model output. Another possible advantage is that we may be able to shorten our prompts. When using a generic model, the prompt needs to contain a description of the task to perform (along with all relevant data). On the other hand, our fine-tuned model should be specialized to perform a single task and perform well on it. If the model only needs to do one task, in principle it should be possible to leave the task description out of the prompt because it is implicit. Besides the task description, we can leave out other information that is helpful for a generic model but not required for a specialized one. For instance, it may be necessary to integrate samples into the prompt for the generic model to obtain reasonable output quality, whereas that is unnecessary for the fine-tuned version.

In our specific scenario, we want to map reviews to a class label (based on the underlying sentiment of the review author). Previously, we specified the classification task as part of the prompt (and even provided some helpful examples). Now, perhaps, when fine-tuning a model, we can leave out those instructions. More precisely, we may no longer need to use prompts like the following (a prompt containing sample reviews (❶) with instructions (❷) and sample solutions (❸), along with the review to classify (❹) and corresponding instructions (❺)):

```
Now, I won't deny that when I purchased    ❶ Sample review
this off eBay, I had high expectations. ...
Is the sentiment positive or negative?   ❷ Instructions
Answer ("pos"/"neg"):neg              ❸ Sample solution
I am willing to tolerate almost anything           ❹ Review to classify
in a Sci-Fi movie, but this was almost intolerable. ...
Is the sentiment positive or negative?      ❺ Instructions
Answer ("pos"/"neg"):
```

Instead, we can assume that the model implicitly knows that it should classify reviews and which class labels are available. Under that assumption, we can simplify the prompt to this:

```
I am willing to tolerate almost anything
in a Sci-Fi movie, but this was almost intolerable. ...
```

This prompt merely states the review that we want to classify. We assume that all other task-specific information (such as instructions and samples) is already implicitly known to the model. As you certainly noticed, this prompt is much shorter than the previous version. That means we *may* save money when using the fine-tuned model instead of the base version. On the other hand, keep in mind that using the fine-tuned model is more expensive per token than using the base version. We postpone the corresponding calculations to later. But first, let's see whether we can even make such concise prompts work in practice via fine-tuning.

9.8   *Generating training data*

First we have to generate our training data for fine-tuning. We will use the reviews with associated class labels contained in the file train_reviews.csv, available on the companion website under Review Training. OpenAI expects training data for fine-tuning in a very specific format. Before we can fine-tune, we need to transform our .csv data into the required format.

Training data for fine-tuning OpenAI's chat models generally takes the form of successful interactions with the model (i.e., examples where the model produces the output we ideally want it to produce). In the case of OpenAI's chat models, such interactions are described via message histories. Each message is described by a Python dictionary object. For instance, the following describes a successful completion, given the earlier example review as input:

```
{'messages':[
    {'role':'user', 'content':'I am willing to tolerate almost anything
     ...'},
    {'role':'assistant', 'content':'neg'}
]}
```

This is a negative review (i.e., the review author does not want to recommend the movie), and therefore, we ideally want the model to generate a message that contains the single token neg. That's the interaction depicted here.

To make fine-tuning worth it, you typically want to use at least 50 samples and up to a few thousand samples. Using more samples for fine-tuning can improve performance but is also more expensive. On the other hand, this is a one-time fee because you can reuse the same fine-tuned model for a potentially large data set (and the usage fees for the fine-tuned model do not depend on the amount of training data used for fine-tuning). The example file (reviews_train.csv) contains 100 samples and is therefore within the range of data sizes where fine-tuning may become useful.

OpenAI expects data for fine-tuning in JSON-lines format (such files typically have the suffix .jsonl). Files that comply with this format essentially contain one Python dictionary in each line. In this case, each line describes one successful interaction with the model (using the same format as in the previous example). To handle JSON-lines files more easily from Python, we will use the jsonlines library. As a first step, go to the terminal and install the library using the following command:

```
pip install jsonlines==4.0
```

Now we can use the library to transform our .csv data into the format required by OpenAI. Listing 9.3 uses the get_samples function (❶) to prepare samples in the required format. The input is a pandas DataFrame (df parameter) containing the training samples in the usual format (we assume that the text column contains the reviews and the sentiment column contains the associated class labels). We turn each sample into a successful message exchange with the model. First, we create the message sent by the user (❷), which only includes the review text. Second, we create the desired answer message to generate by the model (associated with the "assistant" role) (❸). The full set of training samples is a list of message exchanges, each prepared in the previously mentioned format.

> **Listing 9.3   Generating training data for fine-tuning**

```python
import argparse
import jsonlines
import pandas

def get_samples(df):                              ❶ Generates training data
    """ Generate samples from a data frame.

    Args:
        df: data frame containing samples.

    Returns:
        List of samples in OpenAI format for fine-tuning.
    """
    samples = []
    for _, row in df.iterrows():

        ❷ Creates a user message
        text = row['text']
        user_message = {'role':'user', 'content':text}

        ❸ Creates an assistant message
        label = row['sentiment']
        assistant_message = {'role':'assistant', 'content':label}

        sample = {'messages':[user_message, assistant_message]}
        samples += [sample]

    return samples


if __name__ == '__main__':

    ❹ Parses the command-line arguments
    parser = argparse.ArgumentParser()
    parser.add_argument('in_path', type=str, help='Path to input')
    parser.add_argument('out_path', type=str, help='Path to output')
    args = parser.parse_args()

    df = pandas.read_csv(args.in_path)
    samples = get_samples(df)

    ❺ Stores the training data in new format
    with jsonlines.open(args.out_path, 'w') as file:
        for sample in samples:
            file.write(sample)
```

Listing 9.3 expects as input a path to the .csv file with training samples, as well as the path to the output file (❹). The output file follows the JSON-lines format, so we ideally assign an output path ending with .jsonl. After transforming the input .csv file into the fine-tuning format, we use the `jsonlines` library to write the transformed samples into the JSON-lines file (❺).

As usual, you don't need to enter the code for this listing. You can find it on the website under Prepare Fine-Tuning. Run it from the terminal using the following command (we assume that the file train_reviews.csv is located in the same repository as the code):

```
python prep_fine_tuning.py    train_reviews.csv train_reviews.jsonl
```

You may want to manually inspect the train_reviews.jsonl file that was (hopefully) generated by running this command. You should see one training sample on each line, represented as a Python dictionary.

9.9   Starting a fine-tuning job

Now that we have our training data in the right format, we can create a fine-tuning job on OpenAI's platform. Of course, because the model is stored only on OpenAI's platform, we cannot do the fine-tuning ourselves. Instead, we send our training data to OpenAI and request to use that data to create a customized model. To create a customized model, we must first choose a base model. In this case, we will start from the GPT-3.5 Turbo model (which makes it easier to compare with the results we have obtained so far).

We can create a fine-tuning job using the following code snippet (assuming that `in_path` is the path to the file containing training data):

```
import openai
client = openai.OpenAI()

reply = client.files.create(
    file=open(in_path, 'rb'), purpose='fine-tune')
```

The `reply` object will contain a Python object with metadata about our fine-tuning job (assuming the job creation succeeds). Most importantly, we get the ID of the job we just created in the `reply.id` field. Fine-tuning jobs typically take a while (around 15 minutes is typical for the fine-tuning job we describe here). That means we have to wait until our fine-tuned model has been created. The job ID allows us to verify the status of our fine-tuning job and retrieve the ID of the freshly created model once it is available. We can retrieve status information about our fine-tuning job using the following piece of Python code:

```
reply = client.fine_tuning.jobs.retrieve(job_id)
```

The `reply.status` field reports the status of the fine-tuning job, which will eventually reach the value `succeeded`. After that has happened, we can retrieve the ID of the fine-tuned model in `reply.fine_tuned_model`.

Listing 9.4 starts the fine-tuning process, waits until the corresponding job finishes, and finally prints out the ID of the generated model. Given a path to a file containing training data, the code first uploads the file containing training data (❶). It retrieves the file ID assigned by OpenAI and uses it to create a fine-tuning job (❷). Then, we iterate until the fine-tuning job completes successfully (❸). In each iteration, we print out a timer (measuring seconds since the start of the fine-tuning job) and check for status updates with regard to the job (❹). Finally, we retrieve the model ID and print it (❺).

Listing 9.4   Fine-tuning a GPT model using training data

```
import argparse
import openai
import time

client = openai.OpenAI()

if __name__ == '__main__':

    parser = argparse.ArgumentParser()
    parser.add_argument('in_path', type=str, help='Path to input file')
    args = parser.parse_args()

    reply = client.files.create(              ❶ Uploads training data to OpenAI
        file=open(args.in_path, 'rb'), purpose='fine-tune')
    file_id = reply.id

    reply = client.fine_tuning.jobs.create(   ❷ Creates a fine-tuning job
        training_file=file_id, model='gpt-3.5-turbo')
    job_id = reply.id
    print(f'Job ID: job_id')

    status = None
    start_s = time.time()

    while not (status == 'succeeded'):   ❸ Iterates until the job completes

        time.sleep(5)
        total_s = time.time() - start_s
        print(f'Fine-tuning since total_s seconds.')

        ❹ Gets the job status
        reply = client.fine_tuning.jobs.retrieve(job_id)
        status = reply.status
        print(f'Status: {status}')

    ❺ Retrieves the ID of the fine-tuned model
    print(f'Fine-tuning is finished!')
    model_id = reply.fine_tuned_model
    print(f'Model ID: {model_id}')
```

You can find the code on the website under Start Fine-Tuning. Run it using the following command (where train_reviews.jsonl is the previously generated file):

```
python fine_tune.py train_reviews.jsonl
```

If you run the script to completion, you will see output such as the following (this is, of course, just part of the output; dots represent missing lines):

```
Job ID: ...
Fine-tuning since 5.00495171546936 seconds.
Status: validating_files
...
Fine-tuning since 46.79299879074097 seconds.
Status: running
...
Fine-tuning since 834.6565797328949 seconds.
Status: succeeded
Fine-tuning is finished!
Model ID: ft:gpt-3.5-turbo-0613...
```

After printing out the job ID, we receive regular updates on the job status, typically proceeding from `validating_files` to `running` to (hopefully) `succeeded`. The problem is that the job may take a while to finish (for the previous example, about 14 minutes). If you don't want to run the script continuously (e.g., to switch off your computer), you can interrupt the script after the fine-tuning job has started (you will know because the script prints out the job ID at that point). The fine-tuning job will proceed as planned on OpenAI's servers. Depending on your setup, you may even receive an email notifying you once the job has finished. Otherwise, you can periodically run this script.

Listing 9.5 Checking for the status of fine-tuning jobs

```
import argparse
import openai

client = openai.OpenAI()


if __name__ == '__main__':
    parser = argparse.ArgumentParser()
    parser.add_argument('job_id', type=str, help='ID of fine-tuning job')
    args = parser.parse_args()
```
❶ **Retrieves and prints the job metadata**
```
    job_info = client.fine_tuning.jobs.retrieve(args.job_id)
    print(job_info)
```

Given the job ID (retrieved from the output of listing 9.4), the script retrieves and prints the job metadata (❶), including the job status and the ID of the resulting model (after the job has finished successfully).

9.10 *Using the fine-tuned model*

Congratulations! You have created a specialized model, fine-tuned to the task (review classification) you care about. How can you use it? Fortunately, doing so is straightforward using the OpenAI library. Instead of specifying the name of one of the standard models (e.g., `gpt-3.5-turbo`), we now specify the ID of our fine-tuned model, like so (replace the placeholder `[Fine-tuned model ID]` with the actual model ID):

```
import openai
client = openai.OpenAI()

response = client.chat.completions.create(
    model='[Fine-tuned model ID]',
    messages=[
        {'role':'user', 'content':prompt}
        ]
    )
```

As before, we assume that the `prompt` variable contains the prompt text. The prompts, however, differ for our fine-tuned model. Previously, we described the classification task, along with the review text. Now we have trained our custom model to map the review text alone to an appropriate class. That means our prompt-generation function simplifies to the following (in fact, you might argue that creating a dedicated function is no longer required):

```
def create_prompt(text):
    """ Create prompt for sentiment classification.

    Args:
        text: text to classify.

    Returns:
        Prompt for text classification.
    """
    return text
```

Instead of generating multipart prompts, we return the review text to classify. You may want to find out what happens when using the simplified prompt with the original model (`gpt-3.5-turbo`). You will see output like this:

```
Label: I understand your concern about smoking in movies,
especially those intended for children and adolescents.
Smoking in films can have an influence on young viewers
and potentially normalize the behavior. However, it is
important to note that not all instances of smoking in
movies are the result of intentional product placement
or sponsorship by tobacco companies.
...
```

Clearly, the model gets confused about our intentions—that is, what we expect it to do with the input reviews. Instead of generating correct class labels, it writes elaborate analyses commenting on the primary points raised in the reviews. This is not unexpected. Imagine if someone handed you a review without any further instructions. How would you know that the person wanted you to classify the review, let alone the correct labels of the possible classes? It would be almost impossible to do so, and the same applies to language models.

However, if we switch to our fine-tuned model and provide the same prompts as input, we will get the following output instead:

```
Label: neg; Ground truth: neg
Label: neg; Ground truth: neg
Label: neg; Ground truth: neg
Label: neg; Ground truth: neg
Label: pos; Ground truth: pos
Label: pos; Ground truth: neg
Label: pos; Ground truth: neg
Label: neg; Ground truth: neg
Label: neg; Ground truth: pos
Label: neg; Ground truth: neg
Number of correct labels:     7     ❶ Improved accuracy
Number of tokens used    :    2085   ❷ Lower token consumption
```

Note that even without setting any tuning parameters (or providing any samples in the prompt), we now get an accuracy of 70% (❶), rather than the 60% in our original version! Also, the number of tokens used is reduced by about 200 compared to the initial version (❷). This is because we omit the instructions (and class labels) in each prompt.

Okay! We have seen that we can fine-tune a model to classify reviews accurately while reducing the prompt size. But the question remains: Was it worth it? Let's do some calculations to find that out. We set aside the cost of generating the fine-tuned model because we only have to do that once (and in our example scenario, we assume that we want to analyze one year's worth of reviews). Without fine-tuning, we can achieve the same accuracy (70%) with the generic model when exploiting tuning parameters (setting bias and a limit on the number of output tokens). In that case, we use 2,228 tokens for our 10 sample reviews. After fine-tuning, we only use 2,085 tokens for our sample reviews. However, with the generic model, we pay 0.05 cents per 1,000 input tokens. On the other hand, for the fine-tuned model, we pay 0.3 cents per 1,000 tokens. That means our cost per token is six times higher after fine-tuning! The moderate decrease in the number of tokens processed does not amortize the higher fees per token in this specific scenario.

In general, fine-tuning can be very helpful in increasing quality and possibly reducing costs. However, be aware that it comes with various overheads. Before using a fine-tuned model in production, evaluate it experimentally, do your calculations, and make sure it is worth it!

Summary

- Tuning parameter settings can influence model performance and cost.
- Consider limiting output length and introducing token logit bias.
- Do not always use the largest available model, as doing so increases cost.
- Identify the best model for your task by evaluating it on samples.

- The design of the prompt can have a significant effect on performance.
- Include samples of correctly solved tasks in the prompt for few-shot learning.
- Fine-tuning allows you to specialize base models to the tasks you care about. It may allow you to reduce prompt size due to specialization.
- Fine-tuning incurs overhead proportional to the amount of data trained on. It also increases the cost per token when you use the resulting model.

Software frameworks 10

This chapter covers

- Building applications with LangChain
- Solving complex tasks with agents
- Querying data with LlamaIndex

Up to now, we've mostly been using OpenAI's Python library to interact with language models. This library offers basic functionality for sending prompts and retrieving answers from GPT and other OpenAI models (as well as options for tuning and fine-tuning). The libraries from other providers, such as Anthropic and Cohere, offer similar functionality. As long as your data-analysis tasks are simple, this is probably all you need. However, what if your data analysis requires a complex multistep pipeline, possibly integrating many different data formats?

At that point, you may want to switch to a more powerful software framework. Several higher-level frameworks for building complex applications on top of language models are currently emerging. In this chapter, we'll discuss two of the most popular contenders: LangChain and LlamaIndex. The former is a general framework for building applications using large language models. What's more, it comes with various useful built-in components that implement popular use cases for language models. LlamaIndex, on the other hand, specifically supports use cases where language models need to interact with large data sets.

To get the hang of it, we'll first write a simple text-classification pipeline using LangChain. Then we'll explore some of the advanced features of LangChain. More precisely, we'll see how LangChain supports *agents* on top of language models. Creating an agent means putting the language model itself into the driver's seat, giving it lots of freedom on how to accomplish a given task while using a collection of tools provided by the user. We will use such agents to solve complex data-analysis tasks independently, using a mix of tools to access different data sources. Next, we'll see how LlamaIndex easily ingests large amounts of data in diverse data formats and makes them usable for language models. Internally, it uses cheap language models to map data snippets and analysis tasks to vector representations, after which it maps tasks to data based on the similarity between those vectors. Finally, we'll compare the two frameworks and discuss tradeoffs between those frameworks and the libraries offered by OpenAI and other language model providers.

10.1 LangChain

If you want to create a complex application based on language models, you should probably check out LangChain. The framework launched in October 2022 and has been gaining popularity quickly (leading to the creation of a corresponding startup in April 2023). At the time of writing, LangChain is still developing rapidly. Be sure to run the code in this section with the right LangChain version (because future versions may change the interfaces).

As the name suggests, LangChain relates to language models (Lang) and chains. In LangChain terminology, a *chain* is simply a sequence of steps. Each step may correspond to the invocation of a language model, a data-processing step, or the invocation of an arbitrary tool. The important point here is that we no longer assume that a single call to a language model will solve our problem (which was the case for most of the scenarios we have discussed in this book). Instead, we assume that we need a complex network of connected components. That's the scenario where LangChain shines!

To use LangChain, you first need to install it. Go to a terminal, and run the following command:

```
pip install langchain==0.1.13
```

As we mentioned, you need to install the right LangChain version if you want to run the following code samples! LangChain is currently changing so quickly that the code may not work with a different version.

Beyond the LangChain core, you may want to install libraries that support language models from specific providers. In the following sections, we'll be using OpenAI's models. Run the following command in the terminal (and, again, make sure to use the version specified):

```
pip install langchain-openai==0.1.1
```

Support for other providers, such as Anthropic and Cohere, is equally available.

Okay, that's it! After running these commands, you're ready to run the sample projects discussed next.

10.2 Classifying reviews with LangChain

One of the first projects we did was text analysis with language models. Remember chapter 4? We used language models to classify reviews based on the underlying sentiment (is this a recommendation or a warning?). We'll do the same here; we will just use LangChain in our code. Comparing the LangChain code with the original should give you a first impression of how LangChain can help simplify building applications with language models.

10.2.1 Overview

We will create a chain to classify text documents. A LangChain chain may involve many steps, each implemented by invoking a language model or a generic Python function (e.g., to parse the results of language model invocations into a standardized format). The term *chain* is actually slightly misleading. Although you may imagine a chain as a sequence of consecutive steps, the chains in LangChain are much more powerful. For instance, they may involve parallel steps as well as conditional execution. However, for the simple text-classification application, we won't need such advanced features. Instead, we will restrict ourselves to a simple chain with just a few steps.

Our chain will integrate several standard components offered by LangChain. The first component in our chain is a prompt template. As in chapter 4, this template describes the classification task and the expected output format. You may wonder what has changed compared to the previous code version. After all, we have been discussing prompt templates all along. The difference is that LangChain introduces a dedicated class to represent prompt templates. This class offers various convenience functions for prompt templates: for example, for creating and instantiating them. At the same time, LangChain offers a hub allowing users to upload and download prompt templates (as well as many other components). In our simple scenario, we won't need any of these advanced features. Instead, we just need to instantiate our prompt template by passing a single parameter (the text to classify) as input.

The second step in our chain is a language model. Again, we have been using language models throughout this book, but LangChain adds several helpful functions on top of the language model object. For instance, it is easy to automatically log all language model invocations, and LangChain offers convenience functions for different invocation scenarios (e.g., batch and stream processing). Again, we won't use those advanced features here. Instead, we will pass the prompt (the first step in our chain) to the language model to generate a reply.

The third step in our chain is a parser, extracting the answer string from the reply generated by the language model. You may remember from chapter 3 that OpenAI's language models generate detailed replies, integrating one or multiple answers as well as various types of metadata (e.g., information about token usage). The parser automatically extracts the answer string we're looking for from the result object (which works for OpenAI models as well as for all other providers). The result of the pipeline is a single token indicating whether the input review is a recommendation. Figure 10.1 illustrates the three steps of this pipeline.

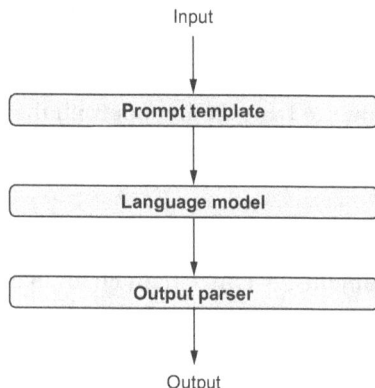

Figure 10.1   Components in our LangChain classification chain

10.2.2 *Creating a classification chain*

Time to implement our chain in Python! First we need a prompt template. We use the same template as in chapter 4, but this time, we use LangChain's `ChatPromptTemplate` class:

```
from langchain_core.prompts.chat import ChatPromptTemplate
prompt = ChatPromptTemplate.from_template(
    '{text}\n'                          ❶ Text placeholder
    'Is the sentiment positive or negative?\n'
    'Answer ("Positive"/"Negative")\n')
```

You may notice the reference to chat models (after all, the class we're instantiating is called `ChatPromptTemplate`). As discussed in chapter 3, chat models process a history of prior messages rather than a single input message. Many of the most recently released models are chat models. In LangChain, chat models require a specialized prompt template (which instantiates into a sequence of messages rather than a single text). This is the type of template we're creating here. The template is the same as we used in chapter 4. It contains a placeholder (❶) for the input text to classify. We generally use curly braces ({}) to mark placeholders in prompt templates; they are replaced with concrete values when instantiating the prompt.

Second, we need a language model to process prompts. The following code instantiates the GPT-4o model from OpenAI:

```
from langchain_openai import ChatOpenAI
llm = ChatOpenAI(
    model='gpt-4o', temperature=0,
    max_tokens=1)
```

The ChatOpenAI class covers all chat models by OpenAI. It is imported from the langchain_openai package, featuring functionality to support the use of OpenAI models in LangChain. Other providers, such as Anthropic and Cohere, have their own associated packages offering comparable functionality for their models (note that you need to install those packages separately via pip). The parameters in the constructor of ChatOpenAI may seem familiar: we choose the model (gpt-4o), set temperature to 0 (to reduce the degree of randomness in the output), and limit the maximum number of output tokens to one (because both possible class labels, Positive and Negative, consist of a single token).

Third, we need to extract the answer string from the (more detailed) reply of our language model. That's easy to do with StrOutputParser. LangChain output parsers implement a wide range of transformations on the output of a model invocation. In this case, we only need a very simple transformation, extracting the desired answer string. The following piece of code creates a corresponding parser:

```
from langchain_core.output_parsers.string import StrOutputParser
parser = StrOutputParser()
```

Finally, we'll put all the components together in a chain. To do so, we can use the LangChain Expression Language (LCEL). If you're a Linux user, the following syntax should look familiar to you:

```
from langchain_core.runnables.passthrough import RunnablePassthrough
chain = ({'text':RunnablePassthrough()} | prompt | llm | parser)
```

To use the output of an operation as input for the following step, we connect them with the pipe symbol (|). The command creates a chain that connects the previously mentioned components. In addition, it specifies the input that the chain expects. In our case, the prompt template has a placeholder for the text to classify.

At the start of the chain, we mark this parameter as RunnablePassthrough. This gives us a lot of flexibility in terms of how we pass inputs to the chain. For instance, the following code illustrates how to process a list of inputs using the previously created chain:

```
inputs = ['This movie is great!', 'This movie is bad!']
outputs = chain.batch(inputs)
```

10.2.3 Putting it together

Time to finalize our code for text classification! The code in listing 10.1 takes as input a path to a .csv file containing a text column. Executing the code generates a result file containing an additional column called class with the classification result. In other words, the code does exactly the same thing as that from chapter 4, but this time using LangChain.

> **Listing 10.1 Sentiment classification using LangChain**

```
from langchain_openai import ChatOpenAI
from langchain_core.prompts.chat import ChatPromptTemplate
```

```
from langchain_core.output_parsers.string import StrOutputParser
from langchain_core.runnables.passthrough import RunnablePassthrough

import argparse
import pandas as pd

def create_chain():                                  ❶ Creates a chain
    """ Creates chain for text classification.

    Returns:
        a chain for text classification.
    """
    prompt = ChatPromptTemplate.from_template(    ❷ Creates a prompt template
        '{text}\n'
        'Is the sentiment positive or negative?\n'
        'Answer ("Positive"/"Negative")\n')
    llm = ChatOpenAI(                       ❸ Creates an LLM object
        model='gpt-4o', temperature=0,
        max_tokens=1)
    parser = StrOutputParser()        ❹ Creates an output parser

    ❺ Creates a chain
    chain = ({'text':RunnablePassthrough()} | prompt | llm | parser)
    return chain


if __name__ == '__main__':

    parser = argparse.ArgumentParser()
    parser.add_argument('file_path', type=str, help='Path to input file')
    args = parser.parse_args()

    df = pd.read_csv(args.file_path)     ❻ Reads the data

    chain = create_chain()                   ❼ Creates a chain
    results = chain.batch(list(df['text']))      ❽ Uses it

    df['class'] = results          ❾ Stores the output
    df.to_csv('result.csv')
```

The create_chain function (❶) implements the steps discussed in the last section. It generates a prompt template for classification (❷), then a chat model (❸), and finally an output parser (❹). The result is a chain connecting all those components (❺).

After reading the command-line parameters, the code reads the input data (❻), creates a corresponding chain (❼), and finally applies the chain to the list of input texts (❽). The classification results are added to the input data and stored on disk (❾).

10.2.4 *Trying it out*

Time to try it! As usual, you will find the code for listing 10.1 on the book's companion website in the chapter 10 section. Download the code (the listing1.py file) and, optionally, a file containing reviews to classify (such as reviews.csv from chapter 4). Open the terminal, and switch to the folder containing the code. Assuming that reviews.csv is located in the same folder, run the following command:

```
python listing1.py reviews.csv
```

Check the folder containing the code. You should see a new file, result.csv, with the desired classification results. So far, we have only verified that we can do the same things using LangChain that we can do with OpenAI's libraries directly (even though, arguably, the LangChain code is cleaner). In the next section, we'll see that LangChain enables us to do much more than that.

10.3 Agents: Putting the large language model into the driver's seat

So far, you may have considered language models as (highly sophisticated) tools. Based on your input, the language model produces output. If data processing requires more than the language model can accomplish, it is up to you, the developer, to add the necessary infrastructure. For instance, assume that you're building a question-answering system for math questions. Realizing that language models are bad at calculating things (which, ironically for a computer program, they are), you may consider the following approach: based on the user question, the language model translates the input into a mathematical formula. Then that formula is parsed and evaluated by a simple calculator tool. The output of that tool is sent to the user.

So far, so good. It gets more complicated in situations where you have not one but multiple math tools. Perhaps one tool solves differential equations, and another evaluates simple arithmetic equations. In such cases, you can expand your approach with a classification stage, mapping the user input to the most suitable tool. However, this approach breaks down in situations where answering the user question may require not applying a single tool but multiple invocations of different tools, possibly using the output of one tool as input for the next invocations. In such cases, manually covering each possible sequence of required tool invocations is simply not feasible.

This is the type of use case where *agents* become useful. Agents ? are a fairly novel way of using large language models. At the core of this approach is a change in perspective. Instead of considering the language model a tool used as a step within a pipeline designed by the developer, we make the language model an independent agent. Rather than trying to orchestrate the order in which the language model and other processing steps are applied (which we did in the last section), we leave it up to the language model to decide which processing steps are applied in which order. The advantage of this approach is that it is much more flexible, freeing us as developers from having to foresee each possible development in advance to create an associated branch in our processing logic.

Agents can be useful for complex data-analysis tasks where it is unclear, a priori, which data sources or processing methods may be required to satisfy a user's request.

Two terms are central to the agent approach, and we will look at them next: the *agent* and its *tools*.

Let's start by discussing tools. A tool can encapsulate arbitrary functionality. It is a function that the language model can use if it deems it necessary. When we use LangChain or similar frameworks to implement agents, a tool is typically implemented as a Python function. Each tool must be associated with a description in natural language. This description is shown to the language model as part of the prompts. Based on this description, the language model can decide whether a tool seems helpful in a given context. To use a tool, the language model requires a description of the input parameters and the output semantics. Similar to human programmers, choosing meaningful parameter names and writing precise documentation helps language models use tools effectively. Because agents are implemented via language models, a full description of all available tools is typically provided as part of the input prompt.

Agents use tools whenever they are required to solve a complex task specified by the user. Agents are implemented via language models. Although fine-tuning can improve the performance of language models as agents, generic models should work in principle. The secret behind turning language models into agents lies less within the model itself but rather in the way it is prompted. At a minimum, corresponding prompts integrate the following components:

- A description of a high-level task the agent should solve. This description is provided by the user.
- A list of available tools, together with a description of their functionality and their input and output parameters.
- A description of the expected output format. This enables mapping the output of the language model to tool invocations.

Given such a prompt, the language model can produce output requesting specific tool invocations. The infrastructure implementing the agent approach parses the output, maps it to corresponding tools and input parameter values, and obtains the invocation result. In the next iteration, the result of the tool invocation is added to the input prompt. In this way, the language model can essentially *access* the results of tool invocations. Based on that, the language model can choose to apply more tools (possibly using the results of prior tool invocations as inputs) or terminate if a final answer is available.

Figure 10.2 summarizes this process. The user-specified task, together with a detailed description of all tools, forms the input to the language model. The output of the language model is parsed and mapped to an action. Either this action represents the invocation of a tool (in that case, the invocation command contains values for all input parameters of the tool), or it represents termination (in this case, the termination command contains what the language model believes is an answer to the input task). If the action is a tool invocation, the corresponding call is executed. The result is added to the prompt used in the next iteration. Iterations continue until the language model decides to terminate (or until a user-specified limit on the number of iterations is reached).

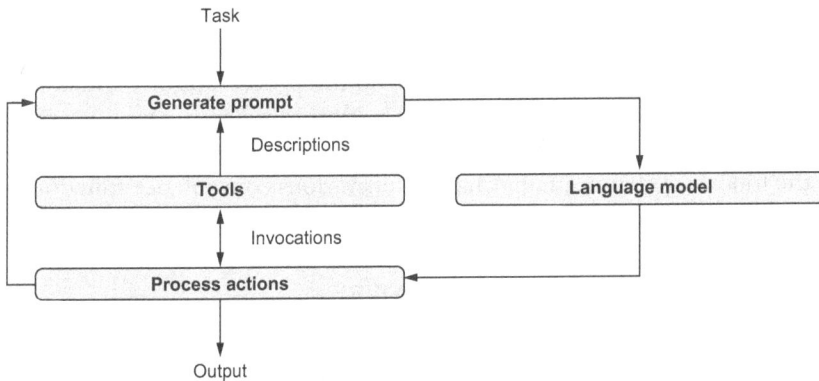

Figure 10.2 Using language models as agents. Given a prompt describing the task and available tools, the language model decides on termination and tool invocations. Results of tool invocations are added to the prompt used for the next iteration.

At this point, you may be curious what the corresponding prompts look like. Let's examine the standard prompt template used for agents in LangChain. You can download the prompt template from LangChain's hub. If you want to do so, install the hub first using the following command in the terminal:

```
pip install langchainhub==0.1.15
```

Then run the following code in Python to print out the standard template for one of the most popular agent types:

```
from langchain import hub
prompt = hub.pull('hwchase17/react')
print(prompt.template)
```

You should see the following output:

❶ General scenario

```
Answer the following questions as best you can.
You have access to the following tools:
```

{tools}   **❷ Tool descriptions**

```
Use the following format:
```
❸ Format description

```
Question: the input question you must answer
Thought: you should always think about what to do
Action: the action to take, should be one of [{tool_names}]
Action Input: the input to the action
Observation: the result of the action
... (this Thought/Action/Action Input/Observation can repeat N times)
Thought: I now know the final answer
Final Answer: the final answer to the original input question
```

```
Begin!
```

Question: {input}   ❹ **User input**
Thought:{agent_scratchpad}   ❺ **Prior results**

This prompt template describes the general scenario (❶) (there is a question that needs answering), available tools (❷), and the process to solve the task (❸). The prompt template contains multiple placeholders representing tool descriptions (❷), the input from the user (❹), and the results of prior iterations (❺). As we will see in the following sections, LangChain offers various convenience functions to create and execute agents based on this and similar prompt templates.

10.4 *Building an agent for data analysis*

In this section, we will use LangChain to build an agent for data analysis. This agent will be able to access different data sources with structured and unstructured data. What's more, the agent will decide which of those sources to access and in which order. It may even use information obtained from one source to query a second source (e.g., to access a structured database about video game sales to identify the most sold game in a specific year and then use the game title to query the web for further information).

10.4.1 *Overview*

Our data-analysis agent implements the approach we discussed in the previous section. It uses a language model to decide which tools to invoke in which order and with what input parameters. In our example scenario, we will provide the agent with tools to access a relational database (as well as obtain information about its structure, such as the names of available tables). We also provide the agent with a tool that enables web search (exploiting existing search engines in the background). Taken together, we get an agent that can query a relational database and use the web to obtain information that relates to the database content.

Let's start our discussion with a more detailed description of the tools we will provide to the agent. In total, the agent will have access to the following five tools:

- `sql_db_list_tables` lists all tables in the relational database.
- `sql_db_schema` returns the SQL schema of a table, given the table name.
- `sql_db_query_checker` enables the agent to validate an SQL query.
- `sql_db_query` evaluates an SQL query and returns the query result.
- `search` enables the agent to search the web via keywords, returning web text.

The first four tools help the agent access a relational database. The last tool enables the agent to retrieve information from the web. Given a user-specified task, the agent decides (using the underlying language model) which of these tools to invoke and in which order. Figure 10.3 illustrates this scenario.

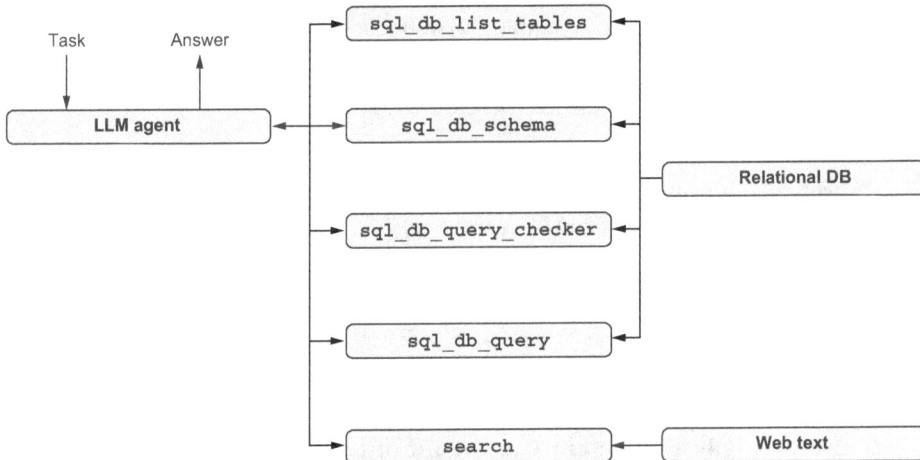

Figure 10.3   The data agent uses multiple tools to explore the structure and query a relational database. In addition, the agent can retrieve web text via the web search tool.

10.4.2 Creating an agent with LangChain

Creating an agent with LangChain is fast! LangChain even offers specialized constructors for agents that access a structured database. We will use those features in the following code.

Agents are implemented via language models. To create an agent, we first have to create a language model object:

```
from langchain_openai import ChatOpenAI
llm = ChatOpenAI(
    temperature=0, model='gpt-4o')
```

We're creating an OpenAI language model of type chat. More precisely, we refer to the GPT-4o model again.

Next, we create an object representing our relational database. We will query an SQLite database stored on disk. Assume that dbpath stores the path of the corresponding database file (typically, such files have the .db suffix). We can create a database object using the following code:

```
from langchain_community.utilities.sql_database import SQLDatabase
db = SQLDatabase.from_uri(f'sqlite:///{dbpath}')
```

We mentioned four tools for accessing the relational database. Fortunately, all of these tools will be automatically created from the database object. However, we still need to create a tool for web search.

We will use a built-in component of LangChain, the SerpAPI tool. To use this tool, you first need to register for an account on the SerpAPI website. Open your browser, go to https://serpapi.com/, click the Register button, and create a corresponding account. To execute the code presented next, you will need to retrieve your API access key (available at https://serpapi.com/dashboard). You also need to install a

LangChain extension to enable the web search tool. Go to the terminal, and run the following command:

```
pip install google-search-results==2.4.2
```

After that, all it takes is the following snippet of Python code to generate a tool for web search (assuming that `llm` contains the previously created language model object and `serpaikey` the SerpAPI access key):

```
from langchain.agents.load_tools import load_tools
extra_tools = load_tools(
    ['serpapi'], serpapi_api_key=serpaikey, llm=llm)
```

The `load_tools` function is used for standard tools by passing the names of the desired tools as parameters. In this case, we only need the web search tool, and we pass only a single entry in the list of tool names (`serpapi`). After the call to `load_tools`, we store the result in `extra_tools`: a list of tools with a single entry (the web search tool). We now have all the components we need to create an agent using LangChain.

Assume that `db` contains the database object, created previously, and `llm` the language model generated before. We initialize an agent for SQL-based data access using the following code:

```
from langchain_community.agent_toolkits.sql.base import create_sql_agent
agent = create_sql_agent(
    llm=llm, db=db, verbose=True,
    agent_type='openai-tools',
    extra_tools=extra_tools)
```

The `create_sql_agent` command is a convenience function offered by LangChain to create agents for SQL-based data access. The four previously mentioned tools for relational database access (useful for retrieving table names, showing table schemata, validating SQL queries, and, ultimately, issuing them) are added automatically without us having to add them explicitly. There is only one more tool we want in addition to the SQL-focused tools: the web search capability. Such tools are specified in a list via the `extra_tools` input parameter. Setting the `verbose` flag to `True` enables us to follow the "thought process" leading the agent to call specific tools (we will see some example output later). The agent type, `openai-tools` in this case, determines the precise prompt to use as well as which parsers to use to map the output of the language model to tool invocations.

After creating the agent, we use the following code to apply the agent to a specific task (we assume that the variable `task` stores a natural language description of the task we want to solve):

```
agent.invoke({'input':task})
```

10.4.3 *Complete code for data-analysis agent*

Listing 10.2 brings all of this together: after reading the SerpAPI API access key, as well as the path to the database file and a question from the command line, it creates a language model object (❶), then a database (❷), the web search tool (❸), and, finally, the agent (❹). It invokes the agent (❺) on the input question. The output produced by the agent terminates with an answer to that question (or with a failure message if the agent is unable to find an answer).

Listing 10.2   Agent for data analysis with web search capability

```
import argparse

from langchain.agents.load_tools import load_tools
from langchain_community.utilities.sql_database import SQLDatabase
from langchain_community.agent_toolkits.sql.base import create_sql_agent
from langchain_openai import ChatOpenAI

if __name__ == '__main__':

    parser = argparse.ArgumentParser()
    parser.add_argument('serpaikey', type=str, help='SERP API access key')
    parser.add_argument('dbpath', type=str, help='Path to SQLite database')
    parser.add_argument('question', type=str, help='A question to answer')
    args = parser.parse_args()

    llm = ChatOpenAI(                    ❶ Creates an LLM client
        temperature=0, model='gpt-4o')

    ❷ Creates a database object
    db = SQLDatabase.from_uri(f'sqlite:///{args.dbpath}')
    extra_tools = load_tools(            ❸ Adds a web search tool
        ['serpapi'], serpapi_api_key=args.serpaikey, llm=llm)
    agent = create_sql_agent(       ❹ Creates the agent
        llm=llm, db=db, verbose=True,
        agent_type='openai-tools',
        extra_tools=extra_tools)
    agent.invoke({'input':args.question})     ❺ Invokes the agent with input
```

10.4.4 Trying it out

Let's see how that works in practice! Download the code for listing 10.2 from the book's companion website. Besides the code, you will need an SQLite database to try the data agent. We will use the SQLite database from chapter 5, storing information about video games (you can find the corresponding file on the book's companion website under the Games SQLite link).

Open the terminal, and switch to the directory containing the code. We will assume that the database file, games.db, is located in the same directory. Run the following code (replace [SerpAPI key] with your search key, available at https://serpapi.com/dashboard):

```
python listing2.py [SerpAPI key] games.db
```
➥ 'What was the most sold game in 2016, and how is it played?'

You should see output like the following (the output you see may differ slightly due to changing web content, small changes to the GPT-4o model, and a few other factors):

```
[1m> Entering new SQL Agent Executor chain...[0m
[32;1m[1;3m
```

❶ The agent retrieves the list of tables.

```
Invoking: `sql_db_list_tables` with `{'tool_input': ''}`
```

```
[0m[38;5;200m[1;3mgames[0m[32;1m[1;3m
```

❷ The agent retrieves the table schema.

```
Invoking: `sql_db_schema` with `{'table_names': 'games'}`
```

```
[0m[33;1m[1;3m
CREATE TABLE games (
    rank INTEGER,
    name TEXT,
    platform TEXT,
    year INTEGER,
    genre TEXT,
    publisher TEXT,
    americasales NUMERIC,
    eusales NUMERIC,
    japansales NUMERIC,
    othersales NUMERIC,
    globalsales NUMERIC
)

/*
3 rows from the games table:
rank    name    platform    year    genre    publisher
americasales    eusales    japansales    othersales    globalsales
1    Wii Sports    Wii    2006    Sports    Nintendo    41.4900000000
29.0200000000    3.7700000000    8.4600000000    82.7400000000
2    Super Mario Bros.    NES    1985    Platform    Nintendo    29.0800000000
3.5800000000    6.8100000000    0.7700000000    40.2400000000
3    Mario Kart Wii    Wii    2008    Racing    Nintendo    15.8500000000
12.8800000000    3.7900000000    3.3100000000    35.8200000000
*/[0m[32;1m[1;3m
```

❸ The agent verifies the SQL query.

```
Invoking: `sql_db_query_checker` with `{'query': 'SELECT name
FROM games WHERE year = 2016 ORDER BY globalsales DESC LIMIT 1'}`
responded: The games table contains the information we need.
I will query for the game with the highest global sales in 2016.
```

```
[0m[36;1m[1;3mSELECT name FROM games WHERE year = 2016
ORDER BY globalsales DESC LIMIT 1[0m[32;1m[1;3m
```

❹ The agent queries for the top game.

```
Invoking: `sql_db_query` with `{'query': 'SELECT name
FROM games WHERE year = 2016 ORDER BY globalsales DESC LIMIT 1'}`
```

```
[0m[36;1m[1;3m[('FIFA 17',)][0m[32;1m[1;3m
```

❺ The agent searches the web for FIFA 17.

```
Invoking: `Search` with `How to play FIFA 17`
```

```
[0m[33;1m[1;3m["A Beginner's Guide To Complete FIFA 17 Domination ... The
main steps you should take are to jump right in with a quick play game. ...
EA Sports FIFA ...", 'Play FIFA 17 up to 5 days before launch for a full
10 hours when you join EA Access on Xbox One and Origin Access on PC.',
"1. Shield the ball in 360 degrees · 2. Use Driven Shots and Driven Headers
·
3. Use set piece upgrades to score with style · 4. Make Fifa 17's ...",
'Play FIFA 17 as much as you want with EA Access or Origin Access
for only $4.99 per month. Now available in The Vault.',
'Cautiously Start An Online Match. Score Early After Some Self-Proclaimed
Beautiful Build Up Play. Concede 4 Goals In A Row And Convince ...',
'FIFA 17 TUTORIALS & ULTIMATE TEAM
Twitter: https://twitter.com/KrasiFIFA
Instagram: http://instagram.com/KrasiFIFA How I record my ...',
"Draft mode is another way to play FIFA Ultimate Team,
giving you the ability to play with Players you don't own.
You'll have the opportunity to draft a random ..."]
```

❻ The agent formulates the final answer.

```
[0m[32;1m[1;3mThe most sold game in 2016 was FIFA 17.
```

```
To play FIFA 17, you can follow these steps:
```

```
1. Jump right in with a quick play game.
2. Shield the ball in 360 degrees.
3. Use Driven Shots and Driven Headers.
4. Use set piece upgrades to score with style.
5. Start an online match cautiously.
6. Score early after some self-proclaimed beautiful build-up play.
7. Draft mode is another way to play FIFA Ultimate Team,
giving you the ability to play with players you don't own.
You'll have the opportunity to draft a random team.
```

```
Remember, practice makes perfect![0m
```

```
[1m> Finished chain.[0m
```

Remember that we switched the agent's output to verbose mode. That means the output contains a full log of tools invoked by the agent, as well as the agent's reasoning process. Let's take a closer look at the output to see what happened.

First, the agent retrieves a list of the tables available in the relational database (using `sql_db_list_tables`) (❶). Clearly, that's a reasonable step when confronted with a new database. The result of the tool invocation reveals that the database contains only a single table (called `games`). The agent becomes "curious" about the table contents. It invokes the `sql_db_schema` tool to get further information about the `games` table (❷). Note that this tool consumes input parameters, specifically the name of the table to investigate. The log shows the values of all input parameters for each tool invocation.

The invocation of the `sql_db_schema` tool returns the SQL command that was used to create the `games` table, together with a small sample of the table's content. Next, the agent considers an SQL query to retrieve relevant information about the input question ("What was the most sold game in 2016 and how is it played?"). In the first step, it validates that the following query is syntactically correct by invoking the `sql_db_query_checker` tool (❸):

```
SELECT name FROM games WHERE year = 2016 ORDER BY globalsales DESC LIMIT 1
```

At the same time, the agent uses the opportunity to "reflect" on the usefulness of the query under consideration, as evidenced by the output "The games table contains the information we need. I will query for the game with the highest global sales in 2016." It may seem strange that a language model can benefit from this type of monologue instead of writing out tool invocations directly. Yet it has been shown that enabling agents to explicitly reason about the problem at hand and the steps they are taking to solve it can improve their performance [1]. That's what's happening here as well.

Finally, the agent decides to use the previously validated query to retrieve information from the database, using the `sql_db_query` tool (❹). The SQL query returns the game that generated the most revenue in 2016: FIFA 17, a soccer simulation produced by Electronic Arts. But the input question asks for more than that: "What was the most sold game in 2016 and *how is it played?*" The second part of the question cannot be answered from database content. To its credit, the agent realizes that and tries to access the web instead: it issues a web search request using the `Search` tool for the search string "How to play FIFA 17" (❺). Note that the agent was able to automatically formulate a suitable search string from the result of the SQL query and the input question. The result of the web search is a collection of text snippets (shown in the output) that contain information about how to play FIFA 2017.

Finally, the agent uses the information returned by the web search (in combination with information from the SQL database) to formulate a final answer (❻). The final answer identifies FIFA 17 as the most popular game in 2016 and contains detailed instructions for how to play it well. We have seen that the agent can perform a complex sequence of tool invocations to find the desired answer without having to specify the process to follow by hand. If you're interested, try querying the agent with a few more, possibly more complicated, questions and see whether it can answer them as well.

10.5 *Adding custom tools*

So far, we have used standard tools offered by LangChain for the most common use cases. What happens if we have specialized requirements? For example, say you want to make a data source accessible via a custom API, or you have specialized analysis functions that an agent can apply to your data. In those cases, you can define your own custom tools and make them accessible to a LangChain agent.

10.5.1 *The currency converter*

In the last section, we analyzed a data set about video game sales. The original data reports sales values in US dollars. What about other currencies? To enable agents to reason about game sales using multiple currencies, we will add a currency-converter tool. Given an amount in US dollars as input, together with the name of a target currency, this tool returns the equivalent value in the target currency.

Listing 10.3 shows how to add the currency-converter tool to our data agent. At its core, a tool is nothing but a Python function. Our currency converter is implemented by the `convert_currency` function (❷). How does LangChain know that we want to turn the function into a tool? That's done by the `@tool` decorator (❶), which needs to directly precede the function name. Typically, we do not have to specify types for parameters and return values of Python functions (even though it does improve the readability of your code). If you plan to turn a function into a tool, however, you should specify all these types. The reason is as follows: to use your function properly as a tool, the agent needs to invoke it with parameters of the right type. All types you specify in the function header will be made accessible to the agent as part of the description of your tool. Hence, associating parameters with types helps your agent avoid unnecessary invocation errors.

Besides parameter types, the agent should know a little about what your tool can accomplish. The first important piece of information is the name of your function. By default, your tool will be named after your function. Don't call your function XYZ, because that will make it very hard to understand what's going on! The name of the function in listing 10.3, `convert_currency`, should make it pretty clear what the function does. Similarly, the names of the input parameters, `USD_amount` (of type `float`) and `currency` (of type `str`), are pretty self-explanatory (which is good!). The function output is a converted amount in the target currency or an error message if the requested target currency is not supported (that's why the output type is a `Union` of string and float values). As a rule of thumb, if you plan to use a Python function as a tool, write it the same way you would to enable human coders to understand your function without reading its code in detail.

In addition to the names of the function and its parameters, the agent "sees" the function documentation (❸). Again, make sure your documentation is well structured, and explain the semantics of your tool and associated parameters. In this case, the documentation describes the function of the tool, the semantics of the input parameters (even with an example of an admissible value for the second parameter), and the output semantics.

The `convert_currency` function uses a small database of currencies with associated conversion factors. For instance, it contains conversion factors for euros and yen but not many other currencies. If you're creating a tool for your agent, take into account cases in which the agent does not use the tool properly. This may happen if the tool description is incomplete or if the language model makes a mistake (which happens even to state-of-the-art language models). In this case, we're adding specialized handling for the case that the target currency is not supported (i.e., a corresponding conversion factor is missing) (❹). If the target currency is not supported, the function returns a helpful error message that contains the full set of supported currencies. This helps the agent to restrict the parameter to the set of admissible options for the following invocations. If the target currency is supported, the function returns the converted amount (❺).

Listing 10.3 Data-analysis agent with currency-converter tool

```
import argparse

from langchain.agents.load_tools import load_tools
from langchain.tools import tool
from langchain_community.utilities.sql_database import SQLDatabase
from langchain_community.agent_toolkits.sql.base import create_sql_agent
from langchain_openai import ChatOpenAI
from typing import Union
```

`@tool`   ❶ **Turns the function into a tool**

❷ **Function signature with types**

```
def convert_currency(USD_amount: float, currency: str) -> Union[float, str]:
```

    ❸ **Function documentation**

```
    """ Converts an amount in US dollars to another currency.

    Args:
        USD_amount: amount in US dollars.
        currency: name of target currency (e.g., "Yen").

    Returns:
        input amount in target currency.
    """
    conversion_factors = {
        'Euro':0.93, 'Yen':151.28, 'Yun':0.14,
        'Pound':1.26, 'Won':0.00074, 'Rupee':0.012}

    if currency not in conversion_factors:
```

    ❹ **Helpful error message for the agent**

```
        error_message = (
            f'Unknown currency: {currency}!'
            f'Use one of {conversion_factors.keys()}')
        return error_message
```

❺ **Converts and returns the result**

```
    conversion_factor = conversion_factors[currency]
    converted_amount = USD_amount * conversion_factor
    return converted_amount


if __name__ == '__main__':

    parser = argparse.ArgumentParser()
```

```
parser.add_argument('serpaikey', type=str, help='SERP API access key')
parser.add_argument('dbpath', type=str, help='Path to SQLite database')
parser.add_argument('question', type=str, help='A question to answer')
args = parser.parse_args()

llm = ChatOpenAI(
    temperature=0, model='gpt-4o')
db = SQLDatabase.from_uri(f'sqlite:///{args.dbpath}')
extra_tools = load_tools(
    ['serpapi'], serpapi_api_key=args.serpaikey, llm=llm)
```

❻ Adds the currency-converter tool

```
extra_tools.append(convert_currency)

agent = create_sql_agent(
    llm=llm, db=db, verbose=True,
    agent_type='openai-tools',
    extra_tools=extra_tools)
agent.invoke({'input':args.question})
```

After creating a tool based on a Python function, we just need to make the tool available to our agent. Listing 10.3 creates almost the same agent as listing 10.2, with the only difference being that we add the currency-converter tool (**❻**). Because we're using the SQL agent again, the converter tool and the web search tool are inserted into the list of extra tools (added on top of the standard tools for SQL access that are automatically provided to the agent). By default, the tool name equals the name of the function it is based on. Hence, we're simply adding `convert_currency` to the list of extra tools (**❻**) to enhance the agent with currency conversion abilities.

10.5.2 *Trying it out*

Let's see whether our agent is able to use our newly added tool! Download the code for listing 10.3 from the book's companion website. You can use the same database file as before (and assume that the games.db file is located in the same folder as the code). Then, open the terminal and execute the following code (substituting your SerpAPI access key for [SerpAPI key]):

```
python listing3.py [SerpAPI key] games.db    'What revenue was generated by
computer games in 2015?    How much is it in Yen?'
```

Clearly, answering that question requires the currency-converter tool. When running the code, you will see output like the following:

```
[1m> Entering new SQL Agent Executor chain...[0m
[32;1m[1;3m
```

❶ The agent retrieves the database tables.

```
Invoking: `sql_db_list_tables` with ''tool_input': '''

[0m[38;5;200m[1;3mgames [0m[32;1m[1;3m
```

❷ The agent queries for the table schema.

```
Invoking: `sql_db_schema` with ''table_names': 'games''
```

```
[0m[33;1m[1;3m
CREATE TABLE games (
    rank INTEGER,
    name TEXT,
    platform TEXT,
    year INTEGER,
    genre TEXT,
    publisher TEXT,
    americasales NUMERIC,
    eusales NUMERIC,
    japansales NUMERIC,
    othersales NUMERIC,
    globalsales NUMERIC
)

/*
3 rows from the games table:
rank    name    platform    year    genre    publisher    americasales
eusales    japansales    othersales    globalsales
1    Wii Sports    Wii    2006    Sports    Nintendo    41.4900000000
29.0200000000    3.7700000000    8.4600000000    82.7400000000
2    Super Mario Bros.    NES    1985    Platform    Nintendo    29.0800000000
3.5800000000    6.8100000000    0.7700000000    40.2400000000
3    Mario Kart Wii    Wii    2008    Racing    Nintendo    15.8500000000
12.8800000000    3.7900000000    3.3100000000    35.8200000000
*/[0m[32;1m[1;3m
```

❸ The agent verifies the SQL query.

Invoking: `sql_db_query_checker` with `{'query': 'SELECT SUM(globalsales) as total_revenue FROM games WHERE year = 2015'}`
responded: The "games" table contains the information we need.
The "globalsales" column represents the global revenue generated by
each game. We can sum this column for the games released in 2015 to
get the total revenue. Let's write and check the SQL query.

```
[0m[36;1m[1;3mSELECT SUM(globalsales) as total_revenue
FROM games WHERE year = 2015[0m[32;1m[1;3m
```

❹ The agent queries for sales in 2015.

Invoking: `sql_db_query` with `{'query': 'SELECT SUM(globalsales) as total_revenue FROM games WHERE year = 2015'}`

```
[0m[36;1m[1;3m[(264.43999999999795,)][0m[32;1m[1;3m
```

❺ The agent converts the currencies.

Invoking: `convert_currency` with `{'USD_amount': 264.43999999999795, 'currency': 'Yen'}`

```
[0m[38;5;200m[1;3m40004.48319999969[0m[32;1m[1;3m
```

❻ The agent formulates the final answer.

The total revenue generated by computer games in 2015

```
was approximately $264.44 million.
In Japanese Yen, this is approximately ¥40,004,483,200.[0m

[1m> Finished chain.[0m
```

Similarly to before, the agent first explores the database by retrieving the set of tables (❶) and then, after finding out that the database only contains a single table, retrieving the schema for that table (❷). Correctly, the agent infers that the database contains useful information about the input question and first validates (❸) and then executes (❹) a corresponding SQL query. The SQL query returns the total value of computer game sales in 2015, expressed in US dollars. To answer the final part of the question ("How much is it in Yen?"), the agent then applies the currency-converter tool (❺). Note that the agent chooses appropriate values for the two input parameters based on the function description and types. Finally, the agent formulates the answer to the input question (❻).

10.6 Indexing multimodal data with LlamaIndex

LangChain is by no means the only framework that makes it easier to use language models for data analysis. In this section, we discuss another framework that has recently appeared and is quickly gaining popularity: LlamaIndex.

10.6.1 Overview

LlamaIndex shines for use cases where language models need to access large collections of data, possibly integrating various data types. In such cases, it is generally not advisable (or even possible) to directly feed all the data into the language model. Instead, we need a mechanism that quickly identifies relevant data for a given task, passing only relevant data to the language model. As the name suggests, LlamaIndex indexes data to quickly identify relevant subsets. More precisely, LlamaIndex associates pieces of data (e.g., chunks of text) with embedding vectors. We briefly discussed embedding vectors in chapter 4. In short, an embedding vector represents the semantics of text as a vector calculated by a language model. If two documents have similar embedding vectors (the distance between the vectors is small), we assume that they discuss similar topics.

A typical LlamaIndex data-processing pipeline entails the following steps. First, it loads data, possibly in various formats, and performs preprocessing. For example, preprocessing may entail dividing long text documents into smaller chunks that are more convenient to handle. Next, LlamaIndex indexes the data. As discussed before, this means associating data chunks with embedding vectors. By default, LlamaIndex uses fairly small language models (e.g., OpenAI's ada models) to calculate embedding vectors. This makes the indexing step cheap. Furthermore, LlamaIndex can store the generated index (the embedding vectors) on disk to avoid having to regenerate them for each new task.

LlamaIndex offers support for various use cases based on the generated index. For instance, it can use indexed data to answer natural language questions. Given a question as input, it first calculates an embedding vector for the question text. Then it compares the vector representing the question to precalculated vectors representing data chunks. It identifies the data items with the most similar vectors. The associated data is included in the prompt, together with the input question. The goal is to generate an answer to the question, exploiting relevant data as context. Whereas small models are used for indexing, we typically use larger models to generate the final reply. Figure 10.4 illustrates this data-processing pipeline.

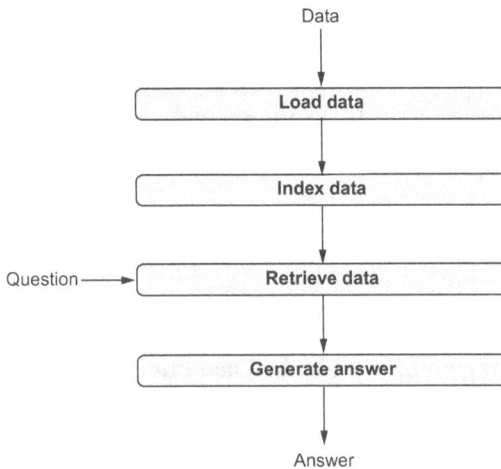

Figure 10.4   Primary steps of a typical LlamaIndex data-processing pipeline. LlamaIndex loads and indexes data to enable fast retrieval. Given a question, LlamaIndex identifies relevant data items and submits them, together with the input question, to a language model to generate an answer.

10.6.2 Installing LlamaIndex

Let's implement the pipeline from the last section in Python. To use LlamaIndex, we first have to install a few packages. Go to your terminal, and run the following command:

```
pip install llama-index==0.10.25
```

That will set you up with LlamaIndex's core packages. However, you will use LlamaIndex to analyze a diverse collection of data formats. To enable LlamaIndex to properly access and parse all of them, you need to install a few additional packages. Run the following commands in your terminal:

```
pip install torch==2.1.2
pip install transformers==4.36.0
pip install python-pptx==0.6.23
pip install Pillow==10.2.0
```

These libraries are necessary to analyze .pdf documents and PowerPoint presentations, all of which we will need for the following project.

10.6.3 *Implementing a simple question-answering system*

You're back at Banana and confronted with a challenging problem: being a global company, Banana has many different units. Your boss wants you to analyze data from different units, for example, to compare their performance. However, different units have widely varying preferences in terms of data formats. Some units publish their results as simple text documents, whereas others regularly turn out elaborate PowerPoint presentations. How do you integrate all those different data formats? Fortunately, LlamaIndex makes that easy.

Look at listing 10.4: in just a few lines of Python code, it handles the task. The code accepts the following input parameters:

- A link to a data repository. This repository may contain files of various types.
- A question to answer. LlamaIndex will use the data in the repository to answer it.

After parsing those parameters from the command line (❶), we load data from the input repository (❷). Fortunately, LlamaIndex makes this step very straightforward: no need to add handling for different file types and so on. Instead, passing the directory path is sufficient. Next, we index the data we just loaded (❸). By default, LlamaIndex uses OpenAI's ada models to calculate embedding vectors. Data conversions and chunking (e.g., splitting large text documents into pieces small enough to be processed by OpenAI's ada models) are all handled automatically. Now we create a query engine on top of the index (❹). This engine will automatically retrieve data related to an input question using the index. Finally, we use the previously generated engine to answer the input question (❺) and print the result.

> **Listing 10.4 A simple question-answering system with LlamaIndex**

```
import argparse
import openai

from llama_index.core import VectorStoreIndex, SimpleDirectoryReader


if __name__ == '__main__':
```
❶ **Parses the command-line parameters**
```
    parser = argparse.ArgumentParser()
    parser.add_argument('datadir', type=str, help='Path to data directory')
    parser.add_argument('question', type=str, help='A question to answer')
    args = parser.parse_args()
```
❷ **Loads data from the directory**
```
    documents = SimpleDirectoryReader(args.datadir).load_data()
```
❸ **Indexes the data**
```
    index = VectorStoreIndex.from_documents(documents)
```
❹ **Enables querying on the index**
```
    engine = index.as_query_engine()
```

❺ Generates the answer

```
answer = engine.query(args.question)
print(answer)
```

Although LlamaIndex offers various ways to configure and specialize each step of this pipeline (and to create other pipelines), using the default settings in each step leads to particularly concise code.

10.6.4 *Trying it out*

Let's try our pipeline using some example data. You can download listing 10.4 from the book's companion website. Also download the bananareports.zip file from the website, and unzip it in the same folder as the code (use the Banana Reports link). Look inside the folder: you will find (short) business reports in text, .pdf documents, and PowerPoint presentations. Time to answer a few questions! Open your terminal, and change to the directory containing the code and the bananareports folder (after unzipping). Now run the following command:

```
python listing4.py bananareports  'How much did the Plantain unit make
➥ in 2023?'
```

You should see output like the following:

```
The Plantain unit made 30 million USD in 2023.
```

Have a look at the corresponding file. You will find that the Plantain unit did indeed make 30 million USD. Try asking for the other units (Pisang Raja and Cavendish); you should see the correct results. You can even try more complex questions—such as "Which unit made the most in 2023?"—requiring a comparison of different files. Again, the system should be able to find an accurate answer.

10.7 Concluding remarks

LangChain and LlamaIndex are two popular frameworks for using language models. You have seen that implementing even complex applications, like those based on agents, is fairly quick when using those frameworks. LangChain and LlamaIndex have overlapping functionality: for example, both frameworks provide support for implementing agents based on language models. LlamaIndex particularly shines in scenarios that follow the high-level template we saw in the previous section (providing functionality on top of data indexes). LangChain has a more general focus on supporting developers in building complex applications using language models.

Both frameworks are relatively young at the time of writing, so the previous characterizations may not hold for future versions. In addition, their interfaces are evolving quickly, and running with the newest framework versions may require code changes. If your application does not require complex logic, you may consider using lower-level libraries such as the one by OpenAI.

Of course, this chapter does not cover these two frameworks in much detail. The intent is to give you an impression of what the frameworks can do for you, enabling you to make informed choices about which frameworks to study in more depth.

Summary

- LangChain and LlamaIndex enable complex applications on top of language models.
- LangChain and LlamaIndex make it easy to create agents. Agents use language models to control invocations of various tools (standard tools as well as custom tools). They can solve complex tasks if given access to suitable tools.
- In LangChain, use the `@tool` decorator to turn functions into tools.
- LlamaIndex indexes various data types by creating embedding vectors.
- LlamaIndex makes it easy to explore and query indexed data.

References

[1] Wei, J., Wang, X., Schuurmans, D., et al. (2022). Chain-of-Thought Prompting Elicits Reasoning in Large Language Models. *Advances in Neural Information Processing Systems 35*, 24824–24837.

index